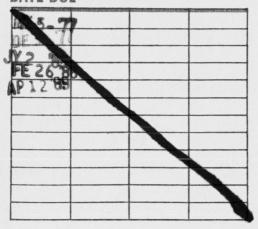

*trans*action/**Society** Book Series

TA/S-1   *Campus Power Struggle* / Howard S. Becker
TA/S-2   *Cuban Communism* / Irving Louis Horowitz
TA/S-3   *The Changing South* / Raymond W. Mack
TA/S-4   *Where Medicine Fails* / Anselm L. Strauss
TA/S-5   *The Sexual Scene* / John H. Gagnon and William Simon
TA/S-6   *Black Experience: Soul* / Lee Rainwater
TA/S-7   *Black Experience: The Transformation of Activism* / August Meier
TA/S-8   *Law and Order: Modern Criminals* / James F. Short, Jr.
TA/S-9   *Law and Order: The Scales of Justice* / Abraham S. Blumberg
TA/S-10 *Social Science and National Policy* / Fred R. Harris
TA/S-11 *Peace and the War Industry* / Kenneth E. Boulding
TA/S-12 *America and the Asian Revolutions* / Robert Jay Lifton
TA/S-13 *Law and Order: Police Encounters* / Michael Lipsky
TA/S-14 *American Bureaucracy* / Warren G. Bennis
TA/S-15 *The Values of Social Science* / Norman K. Denzin
TA/S-16 *Ghetto Revolts* / Peter H. Rossi
TA/S-17 *The Future Society* / Donald N. Michael
TA/S-18 *Awakening Minorities: American Indians, Mexican Americans, Puerto Ricans* / John R. Howard
TA/S-19 *The American Military* / Martin Oppenheimer
TA/S-20 *Total Institutions* / Samuel E. Wallace
TA/S-21 *The Anti-American Generation* / Edgar Z. Friedenberg
TA/S-22 *Religion in Radical Transition* / Jeffrey K. Hadden
TA/S-23 *Culture and Civility in San Francisco* / Howard S. Becker
TA/S-24 *Poor Americans: How the White Poor Live* / Marc Pilisuk and Phyllis Pilisuk
TA/S-25 *Games, Sport and Power* / Gregory P. Stone
TA/S-26 *Beyond Conflict and Containment: Critical Studies of Military and Foreign Policy* / Milton J. Rosenberg
TA/S-27 *Muckraking Sociology: Research as Social Criticism* / Gary T. Marx
TA/S-28 *Children and Their Caretakers* / Norman K. Denzin
TA/S-29 *How We Lost the War on Poverty* / Marc Pilisuk and Phyllis Pilisuk
TA/S-30 *Human Intelligence* / J. McVicker Hunt

The Scales of Justice

Second Edition

Edited by
ABRAHAM S. BLUMBERG

Transaction Books
New Brunswick, New Jersey
Distributed by E.P. Dutton & Co., Inc.

Contents

I. Introduction

Law and Order: The Counterfeit Crusade   1
Abraham S. Blumberg

II. In the Bargain Basement

The Tipped Scales of American Justice   47
Stuart S. Nagel

Lawyers With Convictions   67
Abraham S. Blumberg

Winners and Losers: Garnishment and
    Bankruptcy in Wisconsin   85
Herbert Jacobs

III. The Sting of Justice

Double Standard of American Justice   107
Stuart Nagel and Lenore J. Weitzman

The Moral Career of a Bum 131
James P. Spradley

IV. The Lawyer as Champion

Lawyers for the Poor 159
Dallin H. Oaks and Warren Lehman

Store Front Lawyers in San Francisco 173
Jerome E. Carlin

V. Big Daddy Will Take Care of You

Justice Stumbles Over Science 201
David L. Bazelon

Juvenile Justice—Quest and Realities 219
Edwin M. Lemert

Delinquents Without Crimes 241
Paul Lerman

VI. Pornography—Litmus Test of Liberty

Pornography—Raging Menace or Paper Tiger? 271
John H. Gagnon and William Simon

VII. Epilogue

"Viva La Policia" 285
David Durk

Selected Bibliography 293

Notes on Contributors 313

Preface

For the past decade, *trans*action, and now **Society**, has dedicated itself to the task of reporting the strains and conflicts within the American system. But the magazine has done more than this. It has pioneered in social programs for changing the social order, offered the kind of analysis that has permanently restructured the terms of the "dialogue" between peoples and publics, and offered the sort of prognosis that makes for real alterations in economic and political policies directly affecting our lives.

The work done in the magazine has crossed disciplinary boundaries. This represents much more than simple cross-disciplinary "team efforts." It embodies rather a recognition that the social world cannot be easily carved into neat academic disciplines; that, indeed, the study of the experience of blacks in American ghettos, or the manifold uses and abuses of agencies of law enforcement, or the sorts of overseas policies that lead to the celebration of some dictatorships and the condemnation of others, can best be examined from many viewpoints and from the vantage points of many disciplines.

The editors of **Society** magazine are now making available in permanent form the most important work done in the magazine, supplemented in some cases by additional materials edited to reflect the tone and style developed over the years by *trans*action. Like the magazine, this series of books demonstrates the superiority of starting with real world problems and searching out practical solutions, over the zealous guardianship of professional boundaries. Indeed, it is precisely this approach that has elicited enthusiastic support from leading American social scientists, many of whom are represented among the editors of these volumes.

The subject matter of these books concerns social changes and social policies that have aroused the long-standing needs and present-day anxieties of us all. These changes are in organizational lifestyles, concepts of human ability and intelligence, changing patterns of norms and morals, the relationship of social conditions to physical and biological environments, and in the status of social science with respect to national policy making. The editors feel that many of these articles have withstood the test of time, and match in durable interest the best of available social science literature. This collection of essays, then, attempts to address itself to immediate issues without violating the basic insights derived from the classical literature in the various fields of social science.

As the political crises of the sixties have given way to the economic crunch of the seventies, the social scientists involved as editors and authors of this series have gone beyond observation of critical areas, and have entered into the vital and difficult tasks of explanation and interpretation. They have defined issues in a way that makes solutions possible. They have provided answers as well as asked the right questions. These books, based as they are upon the best materials from *tran*saction / **Society** magazine, are dedicated to highlighting social problems alone, and beyond that, to establishing guidelines for social solutions based on the social sciences.

The remarkable success of the book series to date is indicative of the need for such "fastbacks" in college course work and, no less, in the everyday needs of busy people who have not surrendered the need to know, nor the lively sense required to satisfy such knowledge needs. It is also plain that what superficially appeared as a random selection of articles on the basis of subject alone, in fact, represented a careful concern for materials that are addressed to issues at the shank and marrow of society. It is the distillation of the best of these, systematically arranged, that appears in these volumes.

THE EDITORS
*tran*saction / Society

History is little else than a picture of human crimes and misfortunes.

Voltaire
L'Ingenu (1767)

The law, in all its majestic equality, forbids the rich as well as the poor to sleep under bridges on rainy nights, to beg on the streets and to steal bread.

Anatole France
Le Lys Rouge

No man is so exquisitely honest or upright in living, but brings all his actions and thoughts within compasse and danger of the lawes, and that ten times in his life might not lawfully be hanged.

Michael Montaigne
Of Vanitie, 1588

It is the majority which decides what is mad and what isn't.

Louis Ferdinand Celine

Law and Order: The Counterfeit Crusade

ABRAHAM S. BLUMBERG

The task of the poet and the sociologist is ultimately the same: to search out and uncover the secret meaning of things. Yet no combination of rhyme and meter or elaborate research methodology captures and objectively expresses the essence of the American mood as eloquently as the automobile bumper sticker. "When Guns Are Outlawed—Only Outlaws Will Have Guns," "Support Your Local Police," "I Fight Poverty—I Work," "Honor America," "I Am Proud To Be An American," "America: Love It Or Leave It," "New York State—Land of High Taxes," "Abortion Is Murder," "If You Don't Like Police—Next Time You Need Help—Call a Hippie," "Register Communists—Not Guns!" are exclamations of the anger, thwarted hopes and righteous indignation of an ordinarily taciturn middle mass of Americans, for whom the American Dream has turned to ashes. Mountains of heavily mortgaged goods have not brought them the comfort, security and joy

1

promised by the mass media. On the contrary, the typical American, *white or black,* expresses intense anxiety about and preoccupation with "crime and lawlessness," according to Gallup and Harris surveys. These polls consistently indicate that respondents feel the criminal justice system is "too soft" toward criminals. Indeed "crime and lawlessness" topped the list when people were asked about problems facing their communities, ahead of such local problems as crowded schools, transportation and high taxes.

According to a *Life* magazine survey of 43,000 readers (January 14, 1972) approximating the national population distribution, 61 percent of the respondents feel unsafe on the streets of their community. In cities of over 500,000 the percentage of respondents who feel unsafe rises to 80 percent. Ominously, 30 percent indicate that they keep a gun for "self-defense." Small wonder, then, that the "law and order" and "crime in the streets" themes have such incredible appeal as knee-jerk exclamations of patriotic fervor, supplanting the slogans of "anti-communism" in political campaigns at the national and local level. Crime has simply replaced communism as a major domestic issue in the social climate of a waning Cold War.

The relationship of the current themes of "law and order" and "crime in the streets" to the growing resentments and belligerence of the middle mass of Americans will dominate the politics and social life of the United States in the decade ahead. There will undoubtedly be shifts in alliances, new targets, new slogans to match new grievances, and new violence and disorder. And the legal system, the enforcement apparatus and the courts as political instruments will certainly be at the center of the social upheavals that are bound to occur. Rather than the traditionally passive role ascribed to it by Marx and Mills, the middle mass is going to determine the directions we are likely to travel in shaping our legal institutions, either preserving or destroying the remnants of democracy in America.

The usual sociological categories of lower middle class, blue collar-white collar class, working class, *salariat* and *lumpenbourgeoisie* are meaningless and often inadequate in helping us assess the sources of their anguish and distress. Who are the members of the middle mass? The stereotype of the middle-mass man is characterized by a series of rather well-defined social psychological traits. Possessed of unsophisticated views of the world, he tends to see the society he lives in through the lens of very limited experience, meager education, and in terms of his knowledge of people very much like himself. His simplistic attitudes are the source of his intolerance for anything "un-American." Having very little real knowledge or experience of contrasting life styles, he is likely to mistrust the new, the strange, the different, the intellectual, the "arty." He reveres authority, masculinity, physical prowess and is profoundly patriotic. His tolerance, if any, for sexual misconduct, the homosexual, the atheist, extreme styles in clothing or hair, or deviant behavior of any kind is rather low. He tends to dichotomize between "we-they" and "friends-strangers." In a world organized along impersonal, bureaucratic lines he feels powerless, not only because of his earlier deprivations and insecurity, but because his sense of marginality is intensified by a lack of academic and technical credentials. He sees the world as a Hobbesian jungle where only the powerful, the lucky or those with "pull" and "connections" prevail. Because he feels he has so little bargaining power, he tends to be pessimistic about his future, and in this way provides himself with insulation against disappointment and failure.

The conventional sociological conception is that the "working class"—read middle mass—has become the backbone of support for "law and order." But more to the point is that as an economic group they fall somewhere between the welfare-poor and the educated professional and white-collar technicians. They earn anywhere from $6,000 to $11,000 per year in a nation where, in 1971, the median family income before taxes was reported by the U.S. Department of Commerce as $9,700 per year. A modest but barely adequate income for a family of four in most urban areas of America is about $10,750 per year. Many middle-mass families are therefore caught in a disastrous bind of wage rates which never seem to match inflationary costs of everything they must buy simply to survive. For example, the median price of a house is now $25,000, and in the densely populated Northeast it is more than $30,000. Between 1960 and 1970 hospital costs tripled and doctor's fees doubled. By 1970 a single day in most hospitals cost over $80, a complete physical examination over $100.

The myth of American "affluence" is punctured by the fact that the middle mass consists of almost 82,000,000 persons in some 23,500,000 families who are waist deep in debt. Almost half of the breadwinners of the group have never gone beyond the eighth grade. Many depend on more than one income and "moonlight" to maintain their precarious, marginal incomes which have been depleted by inflation. For many the mindless fare of the television tube, the synthetic excitements of gambling, the race track, professional football and the circus escapism of the space program serve to relieve the endless tedium of a life that is at best a series of traps.

It would be easy to dismiss the "law and order" slogan as a code phrase for repression of an increasingly black urban proletariat by a predominantly white, flag-waving lower-middle-class group of troglodytes who are locked into a struggle for jobs, housing, union membership, apprenticeships, higher education and political rewards. Such a simplistic racial explanation only conceals the subtleties of class conflict which have been part of the American landscape since Shays' Rebellion (an armed insurrection by debtor farmers against the merchants, politicians and lawyers of the Massachusetts seaboard towns who were using the legislature and courts to levy high taxes, foreclose mortgages and imprison them for debt).

Another variation of class conflict and violence in American history is the recurring phenomenon of an "in-between" class which is oppressed and exploited by a more privileged group from above and threatened by an emerging group from below. Examples of this situation are the Whiskey Rebellion of 1791-1794, wherein the Scotch-Irish of Pennsylvania were "in-between" the Indians and the wealthy Quakers; the Know-Nothing riots, wherein an urban, Protestant proletariat was "in-between" newly arrived Catholics and rich industrialists; and the Draft Riots of 1863, wherein the Irish Catholic workers were "in-between" blacks who had recently won their freedom and a Protestant aristocracy.

As in the past, little has been done to reduce the tension and sources of conflict that result from the pressure of the poor black, Puerto Rican, Mexican underclass on the "in-between" middle mass. On the contrary, at virtually every economic, social and political friction point, existing conflicts have been exacerbated. In the areas of voting rights, education, skilled jobs, unions and housing, "law and order" is invariably invoked to delay, obstruct, deflect or vitiate—to keep the "outs" out and the "ins" in. In this context "law and order" is a "we-they" dichotomy, a double standard for sanctifying existing social and legal arrangements. An even more appalling aspect of the situation is the extent to which America's upper and upper-middle classes require the middle mass to bear a good deal of the economic and social freight in their meager subsidy of the bottom poor. The upper 20 percent of American families receive 46 percent of the nation's total income. The top 5 percent of the families in the nation receive 19 percent of the national income. The 1 percent at the apex of the income pyramid receives 6.8 percent—more than *twice* the percentage of the national income received by the 20 percent of the families at the bottom! In addition, the income gap between the rich and the poor has grown remarkably. In 1949 there was a $10,600 difference in average income between the top fifth of families and the bottom fifth. By 1969 the gap had increased to $19,000.

Invariably, whether the issues in conflict are jobs, housing or schools, the middle mass and the bottom poor are locked in competition, while the social strata above them are nesting safely away from the fray. In like manner, the white craft union member sees his union card as the only article of value that he can bestow upon his heirs.

At the economic level the middle mass pays much more than its share of income taxes. While the income tax rates are supposed to range progressively from 0.1 percent to 69.2 percent for those with incomes of over $1 million per year, deductions, income exemptions, tax write-offs and discriminatory allowances for privileged individuals, industries and groups have created an actual tax situation in which in 1970 it is estimated that families earning under $10,000 per year paid 28.6 percent of their income in taxes; those of incomes of $1 million or more paid only 28.4 percent! A factory or office worker earning $10,000 per year pays about $1,000 in income taxes. An individual who earns the same income from state and local bonds pays nothing in taxes. According to 1969 tax returns, 21,317 people earning more than $20,000 paid no federal taxes. In that group were 56 persons who earned more than $1 million for the taxable year. Every dollar earned by the wage worker is "ordinary income" and taxable as such, whereas income or profits earned as a result of stock transfers and similar property transactions subjects the income earned to a "capital gains" tax—and exempts half such profits or income from taxation. In the case of corporate income taxes, special depreciation deductions, investment tax credits and depletion allowances have the overall effect of converting corporate earnings and profits from the taxable to the untaxable category. As a consequence, the corporate tax rate over the past 20 years has been cut in half. This has led to some bizarre situations. In 1970 Texaco, with an income of $1.1 billion, paid 6.4 percent in taxes, and Standard Oil of Ohio paid nothing on an income of $66 million.

Tax avoidance loopholes simply mean that the middle mass must pay the taxes not paid by an H.L. Hunt or a J. Paul Getty. The great bulk of social security taxes are paid by the middle mass since that tax is levied on almost everything they earn. Public education, hospitals and welfare are largely funded through local property taxes, sales taxes and excise taxes. The proposed value added tax, although ostensibly designed for the middle mass, will, because of its basic regressive character, hit hardest at those groups least able to pay, and semantic obfuscation will not alter the fact that it is nothing more than a national sales tax.

The American system of estate and gift taxation is another device which tends to preserve the power and privilege of the rich and well-born from one generation to the next, and indirectly serves to impose a continued excessive burden of taxation on the middle mass and bottom poor. A mere 9 percent of all families owns 50 percent of all the private assets in America; some of this is earned wealth, but in the main it is inherited wealth. Through a maze of carefully contrived loopholes the actual rate of taxation on a large estate can be almost negligible, assuring the heirs that the wealth and economic power of their ancestors will pass to them—especially in the area of stock ownership and the power to influence corporate decision-making. In summary, our present tax structure does more than simply preserve and promote inherited wealth; it nurtures the process in which life chances are further curtailed for the middle mass and the poor.

Although the middle mass largely funds lavish military and space programs as well as much more limited poverty programs, they resent the latter. Their attitude is best summed up in the unlikely acronym of a racist group called SPONGE—Society for the Prevention of Negroes Getting Everything. Middle-mass housing is rapidly deteriorating, its refuse collection is erratic, its parks are in shambles, its water and sewer facilities are of dubious quality. Nevertheless, the middle-mass man seldom establishes any sort of connection between his shoddy existence and the fact that during the fiscal year of 1969-1970, for example, the federal government spent 60 cents of every tax dollar for the military, space and Vietnam, but spent only one cent for housing and community development. Instead, he attributes the deteriorating quality of his life, his helplessness, his disappointments and frustrations, to a breakdown in law and order, the "nigger," "spic," "Indian" or whatever group is threatening him. He perceives the existing poverty programs as a free handout to those who will not work, and from which he derives no benefit. His sense of alienation and mistrust of government has led to the stockpiling of handguns and rifles and a growing vigilantism.

Law and order has become an ideology which serves to distort and disrupt relations between the middle mass and the bottom, separating them into hostile enclaves which are in continuous confrontation. Although there are many areas of their lives which are of common interest and concern (housing, health, transportation, education, employment, environmental problems, etc.), they are polarized by the ideology of law and order. But there is an even more basic problem in connection with this concept. Central to the notion of law and order is the promise that it will provide the machinery for orderly change in the allocation of rewards, opportunity structures and access to the means of life in our social system—in a word, justice. Therefore, it is said, there is no need to resort to guns or bayonets to redress grievances or to effect social change. The ballot box, the legislature, the court, the administrative tribunal, will right wrongs before irremediable harm is inflicted and inequities reach explosive proportions.

What is at once vexing and embarrassing about the pledges that are embodied in the law and order concept is that they are simultaneously unredeemed, if not denied outright, by our society's institutional arrangements for their effectuation. Our law enforcement, public welfare and court systems have become the very agencies which blunt the possibilities of orderly change and equitable allocation of life chances. In the various relationships of state versus individual, landord-tenant, creditor-debtor, manufacturer-consumer, the former is heavily favored at the expense of the latter. Most of the conventional law school curriculum is still designed to turn out lawyers whose professional and economic existence is in large measure tied to the former rather than to the latter. *Pro bono publico* law practice may have been an interesting fad in the previous decade, but it is now almost dead except for a few foundation- and government-supported activities. As a consequence, creditors, landlords, corporations, the wealthy and political machines tend to receive more favorable treatment in the courts, legislatures and regulatory agencies because of particularism, private contractual agreements and favorable political arrangements which have the sanction of long usage. These groups receive the *substance,* less powerful groups, the *form* of justice. This aspect of the ideological nature of the law and order slogan can best be examined within the context of the handling of the criminal, the debtor, the delinquent and the mentally ill in our legal system.

We owe an everlasting intellectual debt to Emile Durkheim for his insightful notion that crime is an inevitable feature of social structure: "Crime is normal because a society exempt from it is utterly impossible." Durkheim's classic formulation provides us with a timeless perspective in contemplating the meaning and pervasiveness of crime and deviance in the human situation. Criminologists with an interest in history are quick to recognize that ours is not the best of times nor the worst of times, in comparison to other epochs, in producing criminals, riots, assorted villains, social deviants, grim deeds of violence, genocide, murder and vigilantism. While the technology available for inflicting harm upon others has undergone a radical maximization, it is probably safer to walk the streets of an American city today than those of medieval Italy, Elizabethan England or even Manhattan 50 years ago. Historians would be quick to remind us that Shakespeare's London was characterized by violence in the streets, drunkenness, poverty, unemployment, inflation, prostitution, armed robbery and civic corruption. Durkheim's analysis is confirmed by compelling historical evidence, and it should therefore not surprise us that most (if not all) of us have violated legal norms on more than one occasion without being labeled or officially adjudicated as delinquents and criminals.

No matter which version of the official crime statistics one accepts, it is evident that very few of us are brought to book, i.e., apprehended, processed in the official enforcement and court machinery, and adjudicated as criminals and delinquents. Any society that committed the energy, resources and personnel necessary to root out and punish all "wrong doers" would create enough mass paranoia, violent conflict and savage repression so as to pass into oblivion. On the other hand, every society tends to produce its quotient of crime and deviance and an accompanying apparatus to sort out those persons and kinds of behavior deemed most suitable for processing— usually those readily vulnerable to successful labeling and adjudication.

Modern crime may be said to exist at seven broadly distinct levels. The most profitable, involving the least amount of risk is *upperworld* crime; it is the least susceptible to the official enforcement machinery, and is only rarely represented in the Uniform Crime Reports of the FBI. Upperworld crime is planned like a military campaign in the walnut panelled executive suites of corporations with billions of dollars in assets, in state houses and country clubs. Quite often the criminal venture is simply thought of by the participants as being shrewd business strategy calculated to produce a profit or to perform a "service" for the consumer, the voter or some other constituency, often at the latter's expense. The "Great Electrical Conspiracy" involving General Electric and Westinghouse among others; the speculations of Billie Sol Estes and the activities of the corporate and federal officials without whose help he could not have succeeded in stealing millions; the activities of Bobby Baker; the frauds and larceny connected with the federal highway program; corruption of public officials to avoid prosecution; cost overruns in military procurement; the marketing of harmful drugs—these are but a few of the exorbitantly profitable criminal activities that take place at the upperworld level.

An important component of upperworld activity is "consumer crime." It includes the social and physical harm inflicted upon the consumers of such products as automobiles, overpriced or dangerous drugs, food additives that are carcinogenic, unfair credit, harmful pesticides, auto warranties that do not warrant, damage to property and injuries to the person caused by industrial and vehicle pollution, color television radiation, the built-in larceny of appliances designed to fail after the final installment has probably been paid, household improvement rackets, and the many injuries and deaths caused by faulty heating devices, stoves, power mowers and washing machines—said to cause injury to 300,000 people annually.

The federal government is itself one of the chief polluters of our waterways and the oceans. In addition, the Food and Drug Agency's standards of tolerance for filth in food are incredible, permitting "filth allowances" in canned and processed foods for such items as rodent excreta, insect fragments, larvae and rodent hairs—as long as these are present in allowable quantities. For example, in every eight ounces of chocolate, 150 insect fragments and four rodent hairs are permitted; tomato juice is permitted no more than ten fruit fly eggs or two larvae per 100 grams. The common frankfurter has become a national scandal as a food characterized by high fat, water and bacteria content under permissible U.S. Department of Agriculture standards, which also allow the inclusion of esophagi, lips, snouts, ears and other edible offal in sausage products. In addition, the use of sodium nitrite poses many health problems conveniently ignored by federal and local enforcement agencies which have always been considerate of the meat industry.

The *Wall Street Journal* and *Consumer Reports* are often a better source of record of upperworld criminal activity than the official enforcement agencies such as the FBI, the Food and Drug Administration or the Anti-Trust Division of the Department of Justice. These agencies are ineffectual in dealing with the social harm ultimately inflicted by upperworld activities. Prosecution of violators at this level is relatively unusual.

Related to upperworld crime, especially at the level of the political machine, is *organized* crime. Local political machines which ordinarily control local police and court officials afford the protection organized crime requires. Its activities cut across state lines and national boundaries and range from legitimate enterprises such as labor unions to activities which cater to appetites and pursuits forbidden by penal codes—gambling, usury, drugs, pornography and prostitution. Quite frankly, very little is known about organized crime and organized criminals except that they are seldom grist for the mill of the conventional police, prosecution and court process. The FBI and local enforcement agencies probably have more resources and undercover agents operating in student organizations, black organizations, peace organizations, on campuses and in pursuit of drug users than they have invested in studying the area of organized crime.

One of the major objectives of organized criminals is

similar to that of their counterpart in upperworld crime—monopoly control of a particular activity. The Mafia or Cosa Nostra have become convenient symbols which do not represent the real nature of organized crime in America. Rather than being the almost exclusive domain of Italians, it is in reality much more varied, cutting across racial and ethnic lines. Indeed, one might more advantageously research organized crime in terms of an ethnic succession theory—organized crime as a ladder of mobility of disprivileged working class and underclass individuals. When organized crime is not trafficking in forbidden goods and services, it seeks out hazardous investment in legitimate ventures of low profit potential, unless the enterprises involved can be subjected to monopoly distribution and price control. Thus one can better understand the social and economic implications of the propensity of organized criminals to become involved in labor racketeering and to infiltrate meat processing and distribution, detergents, baking, fuel oil delivery, garbage collection, window washing, garment trucking and contracting, vending machines, linen supplies, and similar goods and services. There is great difficulty, however, in distinguishing the behavior of a significant number of conventional businessmen and their trade practices and those we ordinarily attribute to organized crime, which admittedly sometimes uses extreme methods to resolve conflicts. As a practical matter it is difficult to distinguish between the ethics of usury and the legal "small loan" business. Indeed, what are the differences, if any, between some of the major aspects of legal commercial factoring and illegal loansharking? The nexus of organized crime to upperworld crime and its relationships to local political machines and the political process need a good deal of further study—and action—beginning at the precinct level.

The third, fourth and fifth levels of crime are *violent personal* crime, *public order* crime and *commonplace* crime. There is some degree of overlap in these levels since there are points of congruence in the severity of societal reaction to an offense, the degree of susceptibility of an offense to the official enforcement machinery, and the nature of the social harm that results from the behavior.

Violent personal crime refers most often to those occasional, and sometimes situational, offenses of homicide, assault and rape that are committed by persons who may not have a criminal history and who do not think of themselves as "criminals."

Public order crime covers those categories of offense which are thought to impede the smooth functioning of a society. Included here are the so-called "victimless crimes" of drug addiction, gambling, prostitution, drunkenness, abortion and homosexuality, as well as such offenses as disorderly conduct and vagrancy. Victimless crimes are so designated because there is technically no "victim"; the principals have voluntarily and often eagerly exchanged forbidden goods and services. Because of the consensual nature and secrecy of these transactions, seldom will any of the participants come forward as a complainant. As a consequence, police may act illegally in their zeal to enforce the unenforceable.

Public order offenders commit secondary crimes in order to obtain funds to purchase the goods or services made scarce by the enforcement process. Thus, in the case of drugs, especially heroin, the FBI estimates that about one-third of the robberies, burglaries and larcenies committed during 1970 were drug related. In addition, harsh treatment of heroin users and relentless police action in attempting to deal with heroin use simply drive users to other, more available addictives, such as barbiturates, which are legally manufactured at the rate of billions of pills per year. It is also noteworthy that of the 8,117,700 arrests in 1970, almost one-third were alcohol related (1,825,000 for drunkenness; 555,000 driving while under the influence). Nevertheless, the law and order advocates tend to soft-pedal alcohol as the *real* addiction problem in America—perhaps because it is a multibillion dollar industry.

In the area of public order crime the enforcement agents make a considerable number of arrests but appear to accomplish little by way of solutions to problems. In terms of a cost-benefit ratio, the rigid law and order approach is counterproductive. For example, in 1971 the New York City police estimated gambling to be a $236 million industry in that city; the department spent $60 million worth of manpower and resources to put it down; the city spent an additional $2.5 million in court costs to process the cases; but the penalty fines added up to only $67,000!

The fifth and least honorific level of crime is often the least remunerative, least protected, and of the sort most readily committed by persons of the middle mass and bottom poor because of their limited range of skills and circumscribed options for action; it may be called "commonplace" crime. Except for the activities of some confidence men and other professional-career criminals whose offenses may bring them into the world of organized and upperworld crime, crime at this level ranges from shoplifting to gang thefts. It is usually the most visible sort of criminal activity and therefore the most vulnerable to the official instruments of law enforcement. Included in this category are vandalism, auto theft, burglary, check forgery, and petty thefts and acts of fraud which range from "ripping-off" through attempts to cheat or steal from public utilities, banks, large corporations, the government, universities and other agencies of the establishment.

The rip-off is not to be considered the sole province of vandalizing gang youths of the lower strata; it is also an upper-middle-class activity involving such behavior as students using recycled term papers and cheating on examinations, as well as university professors using their relatives and friends as "consultants" on publicly funded projects. The various occupational crimes that may occur in the practice of law, medicine or dentistry, or in the military or academia have become endemic and quite properly belong in the category of commonplace crime, although the higher one's social and occupational status, the less vulnerable one is to possible discovery or processing by official enforcement agencies. Many industrial cost accounting systems allow for a percentage of theft by their own employees, middlemen, handlers, shippers and customers as simply another cost that must be taken into account in pricing their product or services. Many employees see various forms of embezzlement, such as padding expense accounts and inventory thefts, kickbacks and commercial bribes, as the only way in which they can redress grievances, such as adjusting the balance of what they perceive to be inequities in their compensation. Thus, the rip-off, in its various forms has become institutionalized as part of the American way of life.

A sixth level of criminal vulnerability, *political* crime, is one that we do not recognize overtly, except in connection with our treason or sedition laws. Political crime is best understood in terms of Albert Camus' novel *The Stranger,* in which the author makes the point that criminals are often punished for the qualities they possess, rather than the deeds for which they have been condemned. Eugene V. Debs, Alger Hiss and the Berrigan brothers are notable political criminals, and Dr. Benjamin Spock was almost added to the list. In many instances the political criminal is not actually convicted for the substance of the real grievance we harbor against him, but for a legalistic substitute; in the case of Alger Hiss, for perjury. In a narrow sense all crimes may be seen as political, in that the police, courts and prisons are but administrative arms of a polity, its apparatus and its ideologies as embodied in its criminal laws. But a true political crime is generally recognized by at least three characteristics:

1. It is committed by an individual or group which opposes some aspect of the policies of the regime in power. The party in power attempts to snuff out the opposition.

2. The ruling party uses the arrest or trial of a particular person or group of persons as an example or warning to others not to engage in political opposition.

3. Under the guise of prosecuting an individual or group of individuals for some substantive crime, the regime uses the criminal trial as a forum to discredit and stigmatize the holders of opposing political views and seeks thereby to label them and their views as socially opprobrious.

There has been little systematic research into the seventh category of criminal activity—*professional* crime. The traditional definition of a professional criminal is one who derives a substantial portion of his income from illegal activities. He is a professional in the sense that he develops a set of skills and has a major commitment to criminal activity as a way of life—as a career. His offenses are not casual but are carefully planned to the point of appropriate business arrangements or a "fix" with enforcement authorities. The professional is in a sense a businessman, exchanging information, techniques and economic opportunities with a circle of associates who are engaged in similar activities.

In the last decade the professional criminal has apparently become a generalist rather than a specialist in one sort of crime. Further, certain types of professional crime, such as safecracking, have become almost obsolete. Technology and the computer have threatened other types, such as check forgery. But because of his organizational ties, technical knowledge and planning, the professional criminal remains relatively immune from the enforcement process when he commits such crimes as arson, hijacking, burglary, theft of securities, homicide, hustling, confidence games, credit card thefts, car thefts, stripping of autos, fencing stolen merchandise and selling drugs.

Public order and commonplace offenses constitute the great bulk of crimes which are duly reported in the Uniform Crime Reports of the FBI in any given year, and thereby render the official data meaningless. The history of those crimes which tend to distort our official statistics and to jam our courts is quite clear. Moral entrepreneurs are outraged by behavior they perceive as odious, and invoke the righteous indignation of legislators who enact penal statutes calculated to inhibit, deter and/or punish the behavior complained of (fornication, vagrancy, gambling, disorderly conduct, sodomy, lewdness, lascivious carriage, drunkenness, prostitution, possession of marijuana, abortion, homosexuality, etc., *ad nauseam*). Penal codes are attempting to regulate areas of human conduct which would involve the installation of a telescreen in every bedroom for their proper enforcement. The sweep of the criminal sanction has become so great that administrative enforcement of some of our laws has become a joke; for example, our vehicle and traffic laws. During 1971 there were 53,665 deaths resulting from automobile accidents. How many of these deaths were homicides, not accidents at all?

Each year there are over 4 million auto injuries. How

many of these deaths and injuries are the consequence of the negligence, shoddy workmanship and greed which are incident to a production process calculated to stimulate consumption rather than a concern for the consumer?

Consumer frauds involving shady credit practices as well as outright larceny involve an annual take far in excess of all robberies and burglaries combined. In 1967, the F.B.I. reported to the President's Crime Commission that property valued at $1.4 billion was stolen as a result of *all* the robberies, burglaries, larcenies and auto thefts. By way of contrast, the amount stolen annually in the field of "home improvement" alone, is in excess of $1 billion. The gross revenue from loansharking, which is but a single activity of organized crime, is thought to produce profits in the multibillion dollar range. The take from illegal gambling is said to be $20 billion each year. Alcoholism and its ensuing drunkenness is said to affect the lives of 9 million persons and to cost $10 billion in lost work time and an additional $5 billion in health and welfare expenses.

Nevertheless, a good deal of the administrative time and resources of our criminal process are devoted to areas which are not appropriately suited to the criminal process, and instead simply clog the channels of enforcement, relegating more serious conduct to a secondary priority. Surely the removal of abortion, vagrancy, drunkenness, disorderly conduct, prostitution, drug usage and most so-called "sex offenses" as grist for the criminal process mill would free the system for more urgent crime control, and would help speed the development of more humane alternatives to many of these problems.

In summary, our penal sanctions and the law enforcement and court bureaucracies which administer them are in large measure organized and geared to detecting, sorting out and adjudicating the kinds of crimes and delinquencies most often and most visibly engaged in by the marginal strata of society. The selection of suitable candidates for the adjudication process (criminals, delinquents or the mentally ill) is not some version of a roulette game, but has fairly well-defined limits which have been imposed by the stratification system. The clients served by our enforcement, criminal court, public mental hospital, prison, parole and other "rehabilitation" systems are overwhelmingly drawn from segments of the middle mass and bottom poor.

The harsh fact is that our criminal process, especially at the initial stages of enforcement, is primarily oriented to bureaucratic goals of "efficiency" and "production" rather than any humanistic goals of the rule of law. Those modes of conduct which are most visible, most opprobrious (because they offend the values of dominant social groups) and readily susceptible to labelling (because of their social vulnerability) are called deviant and criminal by the very nature of our lavish criminal sanctions. As a consequence, the annual edition of the Uniform Crime Reports of the FBI consistently indicates that the American crime problem is caused by a group which is very young, black, urban, poor and largely male. We know this to be an absurdity, but we go on appropriating vast sums in support of an enforcement apparatus that produces the same result for our money year after year.

The enforcement and adjudication process boils down to this: intolerably large caseloads of defendants in our criminal justice system, which must be disposed of in an organizational context of limited resources, encourages police, prosecution and court personnel to be concerned largely with strategies that lead to a guilty plea. In this connection rather frank and revealing statements about the criminal courts were made in the *New York Times* by a federal judge and a New York City judge.

The life of a Criminal Court judge has been described as "generally degrading" and the system of justice has been condemned as "dehumanizing" by one of the city's newest judges, former License Commissioner, Joel L. Tyler. "You sit on that bench," Judge Tyler said, "and you get this terrible sense that you can't help anyone who could be helped. Sometimes you look at a young man or woman and you feel that if someone could really get hold of them maybe something good could come of their lives. . . ." "But the system is just too big, the individual is nothing, the lawyers are ciphers and the judge turns out to be a virtual mechanic more often than not. . . .

In the course of a two hour interview, Judge Tyler criticized the handling of narcotics addicts ("It's fantastic, crazy—we march them into the sea like lemmings"); the lawyers for the Legal Aid Society, who handle most arraignments ("They don't fight hard enough"); and the facilities of some of the parts of the Criminal Court ("The traffic courts are a disgrace; the Brooklyn Criminal Court is a rat hole").

But Judge Tyler said that the frustrations of his job went far deeper than the lack of proper physical facilities.

"First," he said, "you get so many cases stacked up you don't have time to really consider the individual. . . ." "At arraignment you may have a minute with each person. Most of them are narcotics addicts, and if you let them go, you know they will be right back on the stuff. If you hold them on bail—most don't make it—they are thrown eventually into a program that is of doubtful value."

The judge was referring to the city's narcotics rehabilitation program, which is based mainly on confronting addicts with their problems through group therapy. It is the leading program in use at Rikers Island prison.

"I think it is crazy, plain stupid, to treat addicts as criminals," he said. "And the theory on which the rehabilitation program is based, that addiction is curable, well, I'd like to see their experience, their statistics. I believe it's damn low, their rate of cure."

Does he have any hope for the administration of criminal justice here? "Not much, but enough to kick about it," he said. "The older judges, some of them, tell me that they started like I did, mad as hell, wanting to reform things, but finally they realized you can't beat the system. When I get to that point I'll hand in my papers."

J. Skelly Wright, a noted federal judge writes:

Despite the presumption of innocence, the defendant in these police and magistrate courts is, prima facie, guilty. The burden is placed upon him to give a satisfactory answer to the question, "What have you got to say for yourself?" He is almost always uncounselled and sometimes he is not even informed of the charges against him until after the so-called trial. Often no records are kept of the proceedings, and in the overwhelming majority of cases these courts are, in practice, courts of last resort. The careful provisions for appeal, certiorari and habeas corpus, which look so fair in the statute books, are almost a dead letter as far as indigent misdemeanor defendants are concerned.

The police and their supporters in the legislatures and the mass media have perpetuated the myth that the U.S. Supreme Court through its rulings has promoted a crime wave. But a close examination of our history reveals that we were in the midst of a "crime wave" long before the Supreme Court ever ruled on the very issues that the law and order ideology insists have caused crime. For example, the *Mapp* decision excluding illegally obtained evidence did not come until 1961, after a long history of abuses at the local level of police authorities who searched people, their homes and personal effects almost at will, and generally mistreated them in the process. The requirement that indigent defendants in felony cases be provided with counsel did not come until 1963 in the *Gideon* case. The *Miranda* ruling in 1966 aroused the special fury of police buffs and the supporters of the law and order ideology generally. All *Miranda* did was require that, regardless of a person's intelligence, social class, race or legal sophistication, he be advised that what he said could be used against him, that he had a right to remain silent and a right to a lawyer. What was good enough for the educated, the socially privileged, the counseled, the knowledgeable, and the professional or organized criminal in the face of a coercive atmosphere of police interrogation was certainly good enough for the poor, the naive, the ignorant, the uneducated, the insecure and the frightened. *Miranda* and other decisions simply spelled out rights declared in our Constitution over 180 years ago and finally delivered on the pledges that were contained in the Bill of Rights. Prior to these decisions it was not uncommon for police and enforcement officials to kick doors down, to search in a fishing expedition fashion or to physically injure a suspect in order to encourage him to "confess." Indeed, the Supreme Court sought to establish a sense of order and decency to an area which had become a quagmire of police lawlessness in the various states. It is perhaps noteworthy that the British have operated under the Judges Rules for over 50 years, guaranteeing the sort of rights covered by *Miranda*. Germany, France and Sweden have similar rules, without the sort of querulous footdragging our own police have manifested.

The irony of the attacks on the Supreme Court over *Miranda* is that research returns indicate that it has not hampered the police at all. It is estimated that only about 20 percent of all crime is ever reported and that only about 25 percent of this total is cleared by an arrest being made. But confessions have never been an important element in this rather low overall clearance rate, which has generally depended on independent evidence and the testimony of witnesses. In spite of *Miranda,* people continue to confess even after warnings have been given, and the endless crush of cases in our courts and overcrowding of our prisons continues. In some communities the police have virtually ignored *Miranda.* Some lawyers and judges had hoped that one of the byproducts of the court's rulings would be the overhaul of the American police system, an upgrading of the personnel and administrative procedures affecting almost 500,000 police and over 40,000 departments. To a very limited extent there have been reforms of major abuses, but not without some ominous developments of police politicization which are potentially destructive of the democratic process.

The law and order mystique of America possesses a rather fascinating internal inconsistency. At the international level, for example, the U.S. government was the prime mover of a resolution which was unanimously adopted by the United Nations General Assembly on December 11, 1946, establishing the proposition that genocide is a crime under international law. Although it has been ratified by 75 nations, we have not done so for fear of the questions that might be raised in connection with our internal racial strife. At the national level, the law and order ideology conveniently ignores the kind of lawlessness inherent in the numerous ploys and strategies which have been designed to blunt the impact of the 1954 Supreme Court decision in *Brown v. The Board of Education.*

The most vehement law and order adherents heap calumny on the Supreme Court, but also oppose gun control legislation as a step toward crime prevention. In 1970 there were 15,810 homicides; 52 percent of them were committed with a handgun, and most of these were perpetrated by persons other than the last recorded owner of the gun. (In 1968, 60 percent of the homicides involving handguns were committed with illegal weapons; similar percentages apply to aggrevated assaults and robberies, according to a staff report of the National Commission on the Causes and Prevention of Violence.) There are approximately 25 million handguns in America, and over two million are being manufactured or imported each year. Over one-third of all robberies and one out of five aggravated assaults are committed with a gun, usually a handgun. A federal study of the years 1960 through 1967 indicates that during that period a total of 411 police officers were killed; 96 percent were killed by firearms, most of them handguns. Of the eight attempted or successful assassinations of presidents of the United States, all but one, the murder of John F. Kennedy, were carried out with handguns. In 1969, 83 of the 86 police officers killed were slain by firearms; handguns accounted for 67 of the deaths.

The counterparts of the law and order crusaders who oppose gun control are found in the various enforcement and domestic intelligence agencies such as the Bureau of Narcotics and Dangerous Drugs and the FBI. Federal and local narcotics enforcement agents in their cruel harassment of drug users and physicians have deliberately chosen to ignore the legal doctrine established in *Lindner v. United States*, 268 U.S. 5 (1925) which would treat addiction as a disease, and the addict as a sick person for whom the medical profession could legally prescribe and treat in the course of private practice. In spite of the enactment of ever more punitive measures in dealing with addiction, the number of addicts grows, setting off a further chain reaction of criminality by those who must use illegal means to get their drugs. It is an obsession of the law and order ideologist that the "junkie" is a criminal, conveniently ignoring that it is their own lawless sangfroid that has achieved the very criminal results that they seemingly seek to avoid. The law and order crusade has also encouraged the use of our draft laws and drug laws to intimidate, silence, restrain or even imprison our young people.

Illicit wiretapping and bugging are endemic, and the FBI has been employed on more than one occasion as a not-too-subtle vehicle to stifle criticism, as in the case of the "investigation" of Daniel Schorr, a television newscaster who had been critical of the federal administration. It is noteworthy that during 1970, out of 148,000 conversations which federal agents overheard *with court approval,* only 48 convictions resulted, mostly for gambling. Gambling and the drug traffic are being employed as a pretext to arouse support for and justify wiretapping. During 1971 the volume of court-approved eavesdropping by local police rose by 37 percent across the country, the heaviest activity being concentrated in New York and New Jersey.

But far more ominous is the development of a proliferating network of domestic surveillance agencies and related activities involving the creation of files and dossiers on almost any person or group that may seize their fancy. Of the total of about 19,000 employees of the FBI, approximately 8,500 are special agents actually involved in the investigation of violations of federal law. However, agent manpower is largely deployed in connection with those offenses, such as the interstate theft of automobiles, petty thefts, robberies and the like, calculated to produce a robust set of figures to legitimate budget requests (which are now in excess of $350 million). Upperworld corporate crime and organized crime have received slight attention, while a significant amount of manpower has been employed in building often useless files and dossiers on persons who have not and are not about to commit a crime. Indeed, in the field of domestic intelligence there are, in addition to the FBI, 26 independent, noncooperating intelligence agencies, who overlap, duplicate and frequently trip over each other: Internal Revenue Service, Secret Service, Alcohol and Tobacco Tax Division, Narcotics Bureau (Treasury), General Accounting Office, Federal Power Commission, Department of the Army, Department of the Navy, Department of the Air Force, Veterans Administration, Central Intelligence Agency, Civil Service Commission and Securities and Exchange Commission. The list also includes Federal Communications Commission, Civil Aeronautics Board, Atomic Energy Commission, Health, Education and Welfare, Department of Labor, Post Office Department, National Security Agency, Coast Guard, Customs Bureau, State Department, Federal Aviation Agency, Immigration and Naturalization Service. It is impossible to estimate the amount of resources and personnel invested in the business of building, maintaining, and disseminating files and dossiers, many of which contain dated, useless, irrelevant and often unverified material. Much of this activity is busy work, performed simply because the funds are available and have to be expended in some fashion.

Although our bail laws are in effect an insidious form of preventive detention, there are well-organized efforts at the federal and local level to formalize those procedures which are ostensibly designed only for dangerous offenders who are likely to commit crimes while on bail or parole. The crucial feature of the preventive detention proposals is: How does one predict who will commit a crime which threatens life and limb? The most serious constitutional shortcoming of the concept of preventive detention is that it seriously compromises any notion of a presumption of innocence. Once we go down this road, we might as well start building concentration camps, because even now our local short-term detention jails are too crowded. Of course we have ample precedents for the practice of preventive detention. In 1942 we removed and "relocated" to "internment camps" 112,000 persons of Japanese ancestry, although not a single one of them was ever found guilty of any act of sabotage or espionage. One of the most common forms of preventive detention occurs in the case of the over 500,000 mentally ill persons who are at any given time detained in prison-like mental hospitals without ever having been convicted of a crime, but who are held on the basis of psychiatric predictions about their *possible* behavior.

The role of the middle mass in influencing the direction which the law and order crusade will take is best demonstrated by the "stop and frisk" decision of the Supreme Court. In response to pressures generated by the drug traffic and violent street crime, state legislatures, taking cognizance of the fact that police were not observing the standard of probable cause anyway, passed the stop and frisk legislation. This legislation wrote into law the much lower standard of "reasonable suspicion" as a basis for police stopping and interrogating persons in the street and frisking them for a possible weapon when an officer reasonably believes that he is in danger. Thus, the police were given statutory comfort and support for what they already were doing when they were fabricating "probable cause." It is noteworthy, however, that the President's Commission on Law Enforcement and Administration of Justice (popularly known as the Crime Commission) indicated in its report that the stop and frisk power is employed by the police against the inhabitants of our urban slums, against racial minorities and the underprivileged. Police will make "field interrogations" of persons simply because their clothing, hair, gait or other mannerisms square with preconceived police notions of who is suspicious—most often Puerto Ricans, blacks, Mexican-Americans or Indians. Police practices of illegal arrests on suspicion or for investigation rather than probable cause were fairly widespread prior to the passage of stop and frisk legislation, especially in neighborhoods inhabited by the poor and racial minorities. Most of the 300,000 annual arrests are made as part of an "aggressive patrol" tactic to demonstrate police "rep" and "muscle," as well as being fishing expeditions. Most of these arrests are terminated without any formal charge being brought.

In June 1968 the United States Supreme Court, after considerable agonizing, upheld the stop and frisk practices of the police on the grounds that the intrusion upon the person occasioned by the "stop" is justified if a policeman "reasonably" suspects a crime is afoot; if the policeman feels there is danger to himself or others the "frisk" for a possible weapon is justified. The lone dissent of Justice Douglas is of interest: "To give the police greater power than a magistrate is to take a long step down the totalitarian path . . . if the individual is no longer to be sovereign, if the police can pick him up whenever they do not like the cut of his gib, if they can seize and search him in their discretion, we enter a new regime."

A police manual's instructions on the methods to be employed for a frisk are worth recording. Keep in mind that the subject of the search, which usually takes place in public, is standing facing a wall with his hands raised.

"The officer must feel with sensitive fingers every portion of the prisoner's body. A thorough search must be made of the prisoner's arms and armpits, waistline and back, the groin and area about the testicles, the entire surface of the legs down to the feet." This is more than a petty indignity or minor intrusion by a policeman who has "reasonable" suspicion—and of course, a policeman may always feel that he is in danger. Having been given this authority, the police now have virtually unlimited power over the lives of all of us. The Supreme Court will not be there to supervise the propriety of the hundreds of thousands of stops and frisks which will take place.

The grave danger incurred by the extreme sensitivity of office holders and office seekers to the middle-mass concern with crime in the streets is that there will be increasing pressure by the law and order ideologues to neutralize the Bill of Rights, in effect establishing a "friendly fascism." Despite the rather elaborate instruments of control now available to the law and order crusade, an 80 percent to 90 percent conviction rate, electronic eavesdropping and other more elaborate technologies, stop and frisk, a bail system which amounts to preventive detention, maximum security prisons and mental hospitals which are filled to capacity, the middle mass remains sold on the notion that more of the same is the answer to the crime problem. They have bought the illusion of a crime-free society and are almost ready to accept some version of a blue-coated garrison state to achieve it. In pursuit of "order," they seek a more sophisticated crime control technology and more elaborate controls over the lives of all. The middle mass is deceived by the law and order ideology in that it promises that we can achieve peace of mind and the good life without addressing ourselves to the underlying issues of poverty, race, housing, education, health and employment.

In still another way the law and order ideology has served to conceal one of the real problems of the middle mass. In its concern with crime and order, the middle mass has not saved any of its righteous indignation for the shameless manner in which our civil courts act as collection agencies for the merchants and finance companies which all too often beguile them into buying goods they cannot afford at outrageous prices bloated by interest, service and insurance charges.

As of 1972, our national consumer debt amounted to almost $125 billion. Most people are in debt in some fashion. The average annual rate of interest charged on many installment loans ranges from 18 percent to 42 percent. In virtually every state in the union these are "seller's contracts," in that they are lawfully designed to give every possible legal advantage to the seller in advance of the sale, with very limited recourse by the buyer should the goods be defective and the performance or services incomplete. There are four major weapons that are written into the laws in the various states that are used by the seller against the buyer: (1) a "confession of judgment" in which the purchaser signs away any rights to a court defense in advance; (2) garnishment laws which permit the seller to exact a portion of the purchaser's wages, should he miss an installment (in California a creditor can garnish up to 50 percent of a buyer's wages!); (3) repossession laws which permit the seller to exact continued payments, even after the article has been repossessed from the purchaser; (4) "add on" provisions in installment contracts which make previous purchases, even though they have been paid for, serve as security for new purchases. Thus, in the latter instance, a person may have liquidated a $1,000 debt for furniture, but have it seized and sold to satisfy a new debt for a TV set for which he has missed payments! Wage assignments are another device employed by sellers to trap the unwary. By signing such an agreement an employer is authorized to turn over a share of the debtor's wages to his creditor without a court judgment, should there be a default in the payments. Many consumers are virtually trapped into these unconscionable agreements which consign them to garnishment, loss of job and public dependency because of the insensitivity of our legislatures and civil courts. Only three states, Texas, Pennsylvania and Florida, have banned garnishment. In California, loan brokers employing the device of a second trust deed (similar to a second mortgage) on one's home, offer to consolidate the debts of a borrower. In a fairly typical transaction of a $2,900 loan secured by a second trust deed, the borrower only receives $2,345 net because the loan broker has taken $555 off the top in commissions and loan processing costs. Even after paying each monthly installment for the three-year period of the loan, there is a large payment or "balloon" left, which may be nearly as high as the original loan. When the borrower is unable to pay, he refinances, paying commissions and processing costs on the new loan, and starts all over again. Should he miss a payment, he has defaulted and can be foreclosed. It has been estimated by the *Wall Street Journal* that there are $1.5 billion in such loans in California alone. Second mortgages are also common in other parts of the country and are usually not hampered by the more restrictive regulations governing other kinds of debt. In addition, an outrageous doctrine of law protecting the "holder in due course" of consumer commercial paper serves as a cover for many consumer frauds. In some instances the seller and the finance company are in reality one and the same party, with the installment contract being "sold" to a finance company to take advantage of the fact that the usual defenses of fraud or defect in the article cannot be raised in many instances against a "holder in due course."

Our legal system has an amazing degree of confidence in the adequacy of lawyers and psychiatrists to hold the machinery of the system together. There is an almost innocent faith in the ability and capacity of these caretakers to make the criminal courts, civil courts, juvenile courts and mental hospitals function. The Supreme Court decisions in *Miranda* and *In re Gault* possess an almost indefinable naiveté, for they depend so much on the lawyer to bring them to the level of working reality. In the case of *Gault*, virtually all of the procedural safeguards of the adult courts were made to apply to the juvenile courts. Subsequently, in 1970 in the *Winship* case (397 U.S. 358), the evidentiary standards of "guilt beyond a reasonable doubt" rather than "fair preponderance" of the evidence was made to apply to proceedings in the juvenile court. Finally, in *McKeiver v. Pennsylvania* (403 U.S. 528) 1971, the Supreme Court, in rejecting the attempt to require a jury trial in the case of juveniles, admitted that the "fond and idealistic hopes" for the juvenile courts had not been realized. To date, then, juveniles have been accorded four major areas of procedural safeguard which were previously in question: (1) notice of charges; (2) right to counsel; (3) right to confrontation and cross-examination; (4) privilege against self-incrimination.

In any event, there has been an "agonizing reappraisal" of the very agency that had as its historic mission the saving of children. But the real problem of the juvenile court is not just a legalistic one (although it really was a dishonest ploy to claim all these years that in order to save children they did not require the constitutional safeguards afforded adult criminals.) The focus of the juvenile court problem is that, in the words of Albert K. Cohen, "like

Christianity the juvenile court philosophy has never really been tried." Certainly *every* child should have *every* constitutional safeguard that we apply to adults—and then some. Just to furnish him with a lawyer and the other safeguards is not the heart of the matter. The root of the problem is resources—money. With the emergence of the precarious nuclear family we have dumped virtually every problem in connection with child socialization into other institutional frameworks, especially the schools. When the others fail, the juvenile court becomes the trash heap of all the unsolved problems. Additional legal services are not the key issue at all. If anything, recent studies indicate that something uncomfortably close to cooptation of juvenile court lawyers occurs anyhow, so we are right back to the real issue—more resources to care for troubled children and, hopefully, less punitive oriented juvenile courts. The juvenile court should be researched more carefully, for the real scene of all the action is at intake, not during the formal court proceeding itself. That is where all the bargains are struck and the real decisions made. Intake is the court's subsystem, supposedly just screening all the cases, but in reality making many of the substantive decisions, often in rather high-handed, arrogant fashion without regard to due process niceties.

Like many other professional groups, lawyers tend to vary greatly in their skill, training, expertise, honesty, commitment, capacity for helping others and resistance to bureaucratic blandishments. Unfortunately, many of the lawyers engaged in criminal practice and minor civil matters such as consumer debt are marginal, lackluster in their training and often of dubious ethics; the quality of their performance leaves much to be desired. On the other hand, one of the most promising programs has been the federally funded legal services programs which attempt to deal with problems of the delivery of legal services to those who need it most. Too often, legal services to the middle mass and poor are too little and too late. For every lawyer of the "Nader's Raiders" variety there are a hundred factory-type firms which operate as subsidiary shadow governments, engaging in various forms of lobbying and influence peddling, in addition to traditional law practice.

The only other profession in which the legal system invests great hope is psychiatry. But here, too, we find a great variety of skills as well as a profession torn by the dissension of a multiplicity of healing faiths. Respectable psychiatric opinion no longer simply categorizes people as mentally ill or healthy, but locates them somewhere on a continuum of well–unwell, normal–abnormal. There is also growing ambivalence about the psychiatrist even being permitted in a courtroom. A growing body of evidence shows that our commitment procedures are haphazard, perfunctory and lacking in due process; examination procedures are superficial, and there is a strong presumption of mental illness, rather than a full, objective inquiry. We have also withdrawn our belief that people committed to mental hospitals receive the "treatment" for which we send them, or that a mental hospital is preferable to a prison. The reverse is true in too many instances.

One promising development which may put a damper on a judge's enthusiasm for commitment as an alternative to jail has been raised by a New York case, *Whitree v. State,* 290 N.Y. Supp 2nd 693 (1968). Victor Whitree, after pleading guilty in 1946 to third degree assault (a misdemeanor) was placed on probation for three years. During this probation period he violated probation and was sent to Bellevue Hospital where he was diagnosed as suffering from "paranoia, with alcoholism." He was committed to the Matteawan State Prison for the Criminally Insane in May

1947. He remained there until September 8, 1961, at which time he was discharged. Note that Whitree, who had been sentenced to a *maximum* of three years on probation, was confined as a result of "mental illness" for 14 years and four months. During his entire stay at the hospital he was the subject of only one diagnostic conference (on September 10, 1947), with a diagnosis of "psychosis with psychopathic personality, paranoid trends" as its conclusion. At the time of his discharge 14 years later, his diagnosis was the same except for the word "improved," being added. While incarcerated at Matteawan, Whitree was assaulted on a number of occasions by hospital employees and other inmates; he was kicked in the mouth, struck in the testicles and beaten; and on one occasion hot coffee was poured over him, causing first degree burns on his face and chest. He received numerous fractures and lost several of his teeth. Whitree received $300,000 in damages because of the negligence of the state in failing to provide adequate medical care. The court in a harsh opinion called Whitree's case the "epitome of cynicism" and his diagnosis as "improved" "a symbol of his medical and psychiatric nontreatment." This case is but one instance of a growing tide of criticism of the concept of psychiatry in the courts and of committing people for treatment in lieu of prison. A quote from Thomas S. Szasz reflects my feelings on a final issue in connection with law and psychiatry—that of "criminal responsibility."

Neither the M'Naghten Rule, nor the Durham Rule, nor the American Law Institute Rule is "humanitarian"— for all diminish personal responsibility and thus impair human dignity; nor is any of them "liberal"—for none promotes individual freedom under the rule of law. The centuries-old practice of using mental hospitalization as a means of punishing "offenders" has received fresh impetus in our day through the rhetoric of "scientific psychiatry." Contemporary concepts of "mental illness" obscure the contradictions between our pursuit of conflicting policies and objectives—individualism because it promises liberty, and collectivism because it promises security. Through the mental health ethic, psychiatry thus promotes the smooth functioning of the bureaucratic mass society and provides its characteristic ideology. According to this ideology, loss of liberty may be either punitive or therapeutic: If the individual offends because he is "bad," loss of liberty is punishment; but if he offends because he is "sick," it is therapy. From this perspective, deviance is seen as sickness rather than badness and the individual appears as a patient rather than as a citizen. This is the view from the Therapeutic State.

I believe that progress in legal psychiatry now depends not on defining more and more offenders as mentally ill, but on a fresh approach to the relationship between law and psychiatry. To be effective, this approach would have to clarify the dual role of psychiatry. The psychiatrist would be identified as the defender of the individual or the protector of the state. There would have to be an acknowledgment of the realities of the present day law enforcement and the public mental hospital would have to be recognized as an auxiliary of the prison system. A realistic system would have to safeguard the civil rights of the individual from psychiatry. The person would be guaranteed the same protection against loss of liberty in the mental hospital as he is against loss of liberty in prison.

Our society's prison problem can best be summarized as follows. A prison population of about 1,300,000 is warehoused for a sum somewhat in excess of $1 billion, but only five cents out of every dollar is spent on "rehabilitation" or "treatment" programs. Most of these institutions are maximum security facilities, populated by inmates who have been subjected to great disparities in sentencing practice, overpenalized by harsh penal laws or an indeterminate sentence system administered by parole boards whose determinations are often cruel and arbitrary and subject to political considerations. The punishments of prison are well known—the deprivation of sex, poor food, boredom, censorship, lack of meaningful work or rewards for performing labor, rapes and homosexuality, other forms of violence practiced by both prisoners and guards, cruel punishments for minor infractions, punishments imposed without any regard to due process, lack of or limited access to mail, books, counsel, news and information, bathing facilities and clothing. Men and women are demeaned and dehumanized by the denial of even minimal regard for their integrity as human beings. Since most prisons have substantial black populations and almost totally white administrations, there is often a violent racist undertone. The law and order notion that mere warehousing of human beings cures or corrects anyone is belied by the fact that almost 70 percent of the prison population repeats criminal activities.

The one group for which the law and order advocates reserve their greatest admiration and in which they invest the greatest confidence is the police. The American police experience has been a cross-breeding of two traditions, the French military posture and the British image of the public servant. The pattern of enforcement in the area of drug distribution and use reveals the underlying weaknesses of reliance upon police discretion for law and order. The area of police discretion is one of the gray areas that cause a great deal of conflict. No matter how well trained, no matter what guidelines, no matter how close his supervision, the majority of the police officer's decisions will still be characterized by a measure of subjectivity, idiosyncratic selection and ideological interpretation in defining a given situation. Perhaps the best method of controlling and reducing the possibly harmful consequences of such discretion is the establishment of a system of external review. A board of review composed of policemen would inevitably share the typical policeman's basic world view— a concern with maintaining organizational equilibrium (often threatened by civilian complaints)—and may ignore or fail to see the larger social implications of their decisions. It is perhaps significant that the police and their line organizations have resisted outside review while at the same time pressing their claims for professional status. However, they have been highly selective in their pursuit of professionalism. While they earnestly desire the privileges, perquisites, involvements and status of the professional, in the area of "civilian review" they continue to cling tenaciously to bureaucratic secrecy and immunity.

Pressure to set statistical records in justification of police budgets has been overwhelming. Especially in narcotics cases police objectivity becomes a problem. Narcotics-related cases in the criminal courts of the larger cities constitute an important part of the caseload, and are an interesting example of police craftsmanship. Police testimony to establish "probable cause" in narcotics cases where none existed has often sounded like a badly written script: "As I approached the defendant, he dropped an envelope and he indicated that it was heroin and that he had purchased it for his own use. I thereupon placed him under arrest." For awhile drug addicts in major cities all over the country were observed to be dropping glassine envelopes on the pavements as policemen approached. This sort of arrest situation became stereotyped to the point where they were jocularly referred to as "dropsy" cases.

Police operations in the areas of sex, gambling, alcohol and drugs also involve selective enforcement, depending on the state of internal and external pressures on departments. The problems relating to drug traffic and drug consumption are a useful example of the way in which reliance on criminal law and criminal process to manage social problems ultimately corrupts the enforcement mechanism and defeats any intended ameliorative purpose.

Since World War II the penalties for sale and use of drugs have doubled, then trebled and quadrupled; in some instances the death penalty is prescribed. Despite these harsh penalties, drug traffic and drug consumption have soared. When applied, the penalties are usually imposed on the user or his small-scale seller-supplier. But the most serious byproduct of the Draconian drug laws is the creation of an incredibly profitable illicit industry that serves as one of the core activities of organized crime, which is thereby encouraged to expand its activities. Concomitantly, a significant segment of police manpower and administrative time, prosecution and court resources have been committed to the futile task of managing the drug problem through use of the criminal sanction and the criminal process. The virtual monopoly enjoyed by organized criminals in the drug field, together with a mindlessly relentless enforcement pattern, have forced the price of the illicit drugs so high that addicted users must engage in robbery, burglary, shoplifting and similar crimes to meet their drug needs.

However, the most ominous development is entrenched enforcement bureaucracies at the federal, state and local levels, which have a vested interest in maintaining the present hopeless system, and have been able effectively to frustrate proposals for reform. Employing shrewd moral entrepreneurship and crusading zealotry, enforcement agents in the drug field have been able to swell their budgets and expand the boundaries of their control, even though their achievements have not been notable.

The most disturbing aspect of the activities of the drug enforcement bureaucracies makes itself felt in other areas of social life. Drug offenses are ordinarily difficult to detect. As a consequence the drug enforcement pattern has often occasioned the greatest amount of police malpractice, including unconstitutional searches and seizures, bugging and wiretapping, and entrapment. Equally reprehensible is the employment of drug addicts to trap other addicts. Police often use a quantity of narcotics in lieu of a money payment to encourage addicts to engage in this sort of activity. Police are often employed as undercover agents, posing as addicts and committing crimes themselves in the pursuit of a "good pinch." A quantity of narcotics is sometimes planted on the person or in the home of an individual the police may want to harass, coerce or embarrass into cooperating with them in connection with other matters in which they may be interested. The demonic pursuit of an admittedly small number of opiate users and sellers has already contributed to the erosion of constitutional protection. There will continue to be further pressures to weaken traditional safeguards, especially in the area of "no-knock" and elaborate preventive detention procedures. The threat posed by the addict and the drug traffic create a social and political climate in which we all become more vulnerable to the criminal process and its agents.

There are two other significant consequences of our irrational drug enforcement pattern. The drug enforcement bureaucracies and their supporters have effectively kept the medical profession from treating the addict and have, in general, discouraged imaginative and meaningful research in the treatment and cure of addicts, methadone programs and the development of heroin antagonists such as Naloxone and Cyclazocine Nalorphine, notwithstanding. The medical profession has been intimidated to the point that medical, biological and clinical decision-making has been surrendered to a group of enforcement agents who do not have scientific and clinical credentials. In their cruel harassment of drug users and physicians the enforcement bureaucracies have deliberately chosen to ignore the legal doctrine established by the Supreme Court in its interpretation of the Harrison Act, which treats addiction as a disease and the addict as a sick person for whom the medical profession could legally prescribe and treat in the course of private practice. Finally, there are indications that the police themselves have been corrupted by the highly profitable drug traffic, accepting gratuities as they have in the past in connection with gambling. Any illicit activity which is so profitable inevitably corrupts the would-be enforcers of unenforceable community standards.

The enactment of serious proposals for a more humane and administratively feasible civil-medical management of drug use is a long way off, since we refuse to recognize that there will always be a substantial number of individuals who will need a wide variety of drugs to help them endure the psychic and emotional pain of living. But it might be well to prepare ourselves for the not too far-fetched possibility, given our technological skills, that one of the so-called ethical drug companies will come up with a commercial version of "soma" to replace marijuana, alcohol, etc., which will be nonaddictive and will not interfere with intellectual and social functioning. What do you do with a drug of that kind in a self-flagellating culture such as ours? There is also the complication of our present attitudes which have made the drug enforcement pattern such an important part of our criminal process. (In New York City, for example, almost 30 percent of the caseload of the criminal courts is directly or indirectly related to drugs and their use.) Will the enforcement agencies want to give up this "business" for more difficult enforcement problems?

We live in dangerous times and our insecurity mounts because we have failed to invest in people. There is no guarantee that the "American way of life" will survive. If the slogan of "law and order" is to mean anything, it must be translated into a viable system of judicial and administrative practices. Such a system could, hopefully, override the injustices and inequities which generate the anger and desperation of individuals who want to destroy the last remnants of the democratic ethic that produces criminality, marginality and even illness. Unless the poor and the weak who constitute the bulk of our court and mental hospital caseload receive the kind of protection and resources now available only to the affluent, the knowledgeable and the powerful, it is useless to prate about "law and order." The existing system of justice in America promotes and reinforces class warfare by indicating to those at the bottom that they have no real stake in our society. Until more resources and fresh perspectives are committed to it, our present legal system will be a shoddy substitute for social justice, just as smog substitutes for breathable air. But what is needed is not just an overhaul of our legal, judicial and correctional machinery. Of more basic relevance to the stability of our society is an equitable share of our gross national product for the bottom poor and the middle mass, a rehousing of our nation, a viable system of medical services, minimum incomes for all, an equitable tax structure, new approaches to education and child care, and occupational opportunities that would deal with the basic grievances of many who lash out in anger.

Our nation is in danger of becoming an Aristotelian timocracy—a government of, by and for the wealthy. Such a government acts mainly to protect the monied and the powerful, and seldom acts for the disadvantaged groups in society. We may be certain of continued conflict over the distribution of wealth and power in America. If the affluent continue to thwart the bottom poor, we may look forward to increases in crime as the bottom poor desperately attempt their own income redistribution. If the middle mass simply tries to gain a larger share at the expense of the bottom poor, we can expect the worst possible civil disturbances, transcending anything we have ever experienced. In short, a nation that can mobilize its talents and resources to achieve miracles of technology, but will not invest in its own people, is in the process of destroying itself. In the words of President John F. Kennedy, "They who make peaceful revolution impossible make violent revolution inevitable."

The Tipped Scales
Of American Justice

STUART S. NAGEL

The Fourteenth Amendment to the Constitution of the United States asserts that no state or local government shall "deny any person within its jurisdiction the equal protection of the laws." The due process clause of the Fifth Amendment by judicial interpretation provides a similar restraint on the federal government. Other clauses in the Bill of Rights guarantee the right to a lawyer, a grand jury indictment, a speedy trial, and a trial by jury. Do all defendants in American courts get the full benefit of these guarantees?

Many criminologists, lawyers, and other observers say that they do not. The equality before the law guaranteed by the Fourteenth Amendment often turns out in practice to be much like the equality proclaimed on George Orwell's *Animal Farm*—all men are equal, but some groups are more

A more detailed analysis of the data presented in this article may be found in Stuart S. Nagel, "Disparities in Criminal Procedure," 14 *U.C.L.A. Law Review* (1967) 1272-1305.

equal than others. Justice, some observers say, may have a blindfold, but it may also have a price, a complexion, a location, and even age and sex; and those with enough money, the right complexion, in the right court, and even sometimes of the right age and the right sex, can often get better treatment. The "least equal" in America are generally those the Fourteenth Amendment was apparently designed specifically to protect—the Negro, the poor, and the ignorant.

The Supreme Court, in an opinion in 1956, stated that "there can be no equal justice where the kind of trial a man gets depends on the amount of money he has." The Attorney General's Committee on Poverty and the Administration of Federal Criminal Justice, headed by Professor Francis A. Allen, then of the University of Michigan Law School, in its 1963 report documented the charge that the poor suffer in the courts because of their poverty. The committee recommended reforms in the bail system, in legal representation, in appeals, and at other steps in the long ladder from arrest to release or conviction.

These propositions would seem to be further supported by common sense. Bail, lawyers, appeals, parole, frequently require money and professional help which are in short supply among the poor. Policemen, prosecutors, judges, and jailors are all human products of our times and nation and, therefore, like the rest of us, are capable of error, prejudice, and "taking the easy way." Our trials are based on the adversary system, in which two more or less evenly matched sides are supposed to meet in the cockpit of a courtroom, under rules designed to insure fair play, and contend until the side with the stronger case wins. How can the indigent, the ignorant, and the victims of discrimination hope to be strong adversaries?

In answer to this question, many prosecutors, law enforcement officers, and editorial writers contend that discrimination in the administration of justice is minor and relatively unimportant. What they believe is much more important—and more damaging—is that safeguards for defendants have already thrown the scales of justice out of balance, and more safeguards could make it almost impossible to get convictions.

Perhaps the picture is muddied partly because not enough broad reliable research has been done on the American system of justice, based on a large, nationwide sample. What has been needed was an analysis of a lot of data taken at all stages of criminal procedure, from all over the country, and including both federal and state cases. This article is based on such an analysis with a concentration on grand larceny and felonious assault cases.

Disparities in justice may appear at any stage of the criminal process—and most groups suffer both apparent advantages and disadvantages from them. For instance, in larceny cases non-indigent defendants are more apt to get probation or suspended sentences than indigent ones, but are also more apt to draw longer sentences if they don't get probation, possibly because of the larger amounts of money which they steal. Also, one defendant's handicap may be another's special privilege. An adult male who does not get a grand jury hearing is possibly being denied a fundamental right; a woman or juvenile who doesn't get one is possibly being given special, informal treatment.

Let us examine these stages briefly, and see what safeguards at each level can mean to an accused.

■ PRELIMINARY HEARING. The preliminary hearing is the first stage on which data are available. The main purpose of a preliminary hearing is to allow the presiding official (police magistrate, justice of the peace, or judge) to decide whether there is enough evidence against the accused

915 federal cases involving either grand jury or the prosecutor alone, 344 involved only the prosecutor—although
of these only half the defendants formally waived the right
to a grand jury hearing.

■ DELAY. The American Law Institute Code of Criminal
Procedure provides that if a defendant is held for more
than three months without trial due to no fault of his own,
then he must be set free without danger of rearrest for the
same crime, except for extremely extenuating circumstances.
A long delay before trial, especially in jail, can penalize
the innocent or over-punish the guilty, as well as make witnesses less available and reliable.

The federal data unfortunately do not distinguish between those who await trial in jail and those who can afford to wait at home. Nevertheless it does reveal that, inside or out, there was, for almost half the cases, more
than two months delay from arrest until release or trial
(whichever came first). In the state cases, of the 405 *not*
released on bail, 162 were kept in jail more than two
months. (Two months was chosen as the watershed for all
cases, half being delayed less, and half more.)

■ TRIAL BY JURY. Generally, there is less chance that
twelve jurors will agree unanimously on conviction than
one judge (especially a so-called "hanging judge"). Therefore a defendant usually has a greater chance of acquittal
before a jury. In addition, if he is a member of a disadvantaged group (uneducated, working-class, or Negro) he
stands a much better chance of encountering somebody like
himself on a jury than on the bench.

On the other hand, our data show that seeking a jury
trial may mean greater delay. It may also mean that if the
defendant is found guilty, he is less likely to get probation than if he only had a bench trial. (The stiffer penalties for those convicted by juries may reflect the possi-

bility that the more severe cases come before juries.) But on balance, the chance at a trial by "a jury of his peers" is a strong safeguard of the rights of a defendant.

Nevertheless, in the state data, 63 percent of those cases going to trial did so without a jury; 48 percent of federal trials were held without juries.

■ CONVICTION AND SENTENCING. About four of every five tried defendants, state and local, are found, or plead, guilty. The approximately 20 percent found not guilty, of course, had been put to the expense and anxiety of criminal proceedings. Of those considered guilty, 83 percent pleaded guilty—25 percent to lesser offenses than the original charge, possibly after negotiating with the prosecutor. Almost half the defendants found guilty were given suspended sentences or probation. Slightly more than half of those convicted and sentenced received sentences of more than one year.

These are the major stages in standard criminal procedure. And it is within this framework that disparities because of poverty, race, sex, age, and residence must be understood. The question is not whether the "average" accused person gets complete justice but whether some people and some groups suffer (or benefit) more or less than others—and if so, how and why.

Let us examine some of these disparaties.

■ ECONOMIC CLASS. In the state data, "indigent" is defined, generally, to mean not able to afford one's own lawyer—a legalistic rather than a sociological definition. The poor, then, must usually have court-appointed lawyers, or none. In the federal cases, where indigency is not specified, the poor may be defined as those with assigned counsel.

In the pre-sentencing stages, 34 percent of indigents up for felonious assault in state courts did not get preliminary hearings—compared to 21 percent of non-indigents. This to justify further action. If he decides there is not, then an innocent person may be spared considerable humiliation, expense, delay, and inconvenience. The hearing is preliminary to the prosecutor's formal accusation or to a grand jury indictment, which it can prevent. The preliminary hearing also has other advantages for an accused: (1) it deters the use of the third-degree; (2) it allows counsel to appear and plead for the accused, particularly with regard to bail; (3) and it reveals the fact that the accused has been arrested and detained, so that *habeas corpus* (which can bring about immediate release), right to a copy of the complaint, and other guarantees can be secured. In short, the preliminary hearing is a safeguard for the rights of the accused; and its denial is a limitation to those rights.

Of the 1,168 state cases coming from counties that have provisions for preliminary hearings and on which information was available, the accused received no preliminary hearing in 434. In 357 of these he waived his right to a preliminary hearing—possibly without realizing its importance; the rest were recorded as "no preliminary hearing, reason unknown." Information as to the preliminary hearing was not available in the federal data.

■ BAIL. The next important protection for a defendant is the right, or the ability, to be released on bail. Bail reduces his hardship, especially if he is innocent, and gives him a better chance to investigate and prepare his case. Of the 1,552 state cases on which information is available, 44 percent (689) were not released on bail. Of these, 562 were eventually found guilty, 71 found not guilty, and information was not available for 56. Of the 71 not convicted, 20 had stayed in jail for two months or less, 13 for over three months, and we have no information for 38. Five of those not convicted, nor released on bail, in effect served jail terms of six months or more although found guilty of nothing.

■ DEFENSE COUNSEL. Lawyers generally concede that few persons (including lawyers) are capable of properly preparing and arguing their own cases—especially when confined. Having a lawyer, preferably of your own choice, is therefore a fundamental right.

All the state cases were felonies, punishable by more than a year in prison. Yet 183 of the 1,561 cases had no lawyer at all, and only 13 of these were recorded as having waived counsel. (Under the Supreme Court ruling in the famous case of *Gideon versus Wainright*, decided in 1963, all indigent state defendants must hereafter be assigned counsel for any felony. The 1962 data for this study, however, precedes Gideon.) In federal court, all defendants must have counsel of some kind, and the cases were divided according to whether the lawyer was the defendant's own. At least 390 of the 1,151 federal defendants did not have a lawyer of their own choosing.

A lawyer is considered essential for investigation, negotiation with the prosecutor, examination of witnesses, and the presentation of legal and factual arguments to judge and jury. A court-appointed lawyer is better than none, and often better than some, but he can easily suffer from lack of experience, sympathy, enthusiasm, and especially finances and time, since he will probably be appointed late, and may have to take much expense money out of his own pocket.

■ GRAND JURY. What percentage of cases went before a grand jury? Like the preliminary hearing (and the trial) the grand jury process is designed mainly to protect and to minimize the harm done to the innocent. The alternative is to let the prosecutor alone judge whether the accused should be held for trial. The state data did not separate those indicted by a grand jury from those who were not. Of the was also true, if not as markedly, in state grand larceny cases. Bail, since it requires the ability to raise money, shows the greatest disparity between those who have money and those who do not. About three-quarters of all indigent state cases did not raise bail and stayed locked up, with all this means in unearned punishment and inability to prepare for trial, while 79 percent of non-indigent assault cases, and 69 percent of larceny, did raise bail and got out.

In *having a lawyer,* an interesting reversal occurs; In most states one must be poor to have assigned lawyers, the rich hire their own, and it is the middle group that may be the most apt to be undefended. (Since the *Gideon* decision, as noted, merely having a lawyer is perhaps no longer a major disparity; what *kind* of lawyer, of course, is something else.)

In the state cases, the indigent were delayed in jail awaiting trial more than the non-indigent. This, obviously, is related to their relative inability to raise bail. In the federal figures delay is measured irrespective of whether or not the defendant is in jail—and here the indigent have *shorter* waits. A court-appointed lawyer would be inclined, apparently, to put in less time and trouble on his case than a private lawyer, and not be as apt to ask for delays; he might also want to get his bail-less client out of jail as soon as possible, and so be less likely to delay the trial.

The federal data show that the indigent are much less likely to have a grand jury indictment than the non-indigent. Perhaps they lack knowledge and are more easily persuaded to waive this right. Perhaps also this ignorance, coupled with appointed attorneys' desires to be rid of their cases, accounts for their relatively high frequency of bench, rather than jury trials. The state indigents also have proportionately fewer jury trials—but here the difference between them and the non-indigent is much less, perhaps because state juries are usually presumed to be of a lower class than federal juries, and middle-class defendants may show less preference for them.

About 90 percent of all indigents studied were found guilty. Though the percentage of non-indigents found guilty was also high, it was consistently lower (averaging about 80 percent). The greatest disparity was in the federal cases, where all indigents had court-appointed lawyers, and this may indicate that poorer representation had something to do with the higher rate of conviction. The poor also tend to feel more helpless, and may be more easily persuaded to plead guilty.

Not only are the indigent found guilty more often, but they are much less likely to be recommended for probation by the probation officer, or be granted probation or suspended sentences by the judge. Of the defendants on whom we had data in this study, a sizeable majority of indigents stayed in jail both before and after trial, unlike non-indigents.

The federal data show that this is true also of those with *no* prior record: 27 percent of the indigent with no prior record were *not* recommended for probation against 16 percent of the non-indigent; 23 percent indigent did *not* receive suspended sentences or probation against 15 percent non-indigent. Among those of both groups with "some" prior record the spread is even greater.

Why these class disparities? They reflect, at least partly, inferior legal help. But even when the lawyer works hard and well, the indigent faces the handicap that he is, and looks, lower class, while those who determine his destiny —probation officer and judge—are middle-class. Therefore, apart from the other disabilities of the poor, class bias among judicial personnel may work against them.

■ SEX. Are women discriminated against in criminal proceedings as in other walks of life? The findings are much less definite for sex than for poverty, partly because the sample was too small. (Women simply do not commit as many larcenies—and especially assaults—as men.) What differences do emerge seem to be in favor of women, especially in sentencing. It is apparently assumed that women cannot—or, chivalrously, should not—endure as much as men. On the other hand, it is possible that women can be persuaded to give up their rights more easily, and that procedures with them tend to be less formal.

Men are much less likely to be released on bail they can afford than women. In trial, women are more likely to be found innocent, and if guilty more likely to be put on probation or given suspended sentences. Studies in women's prisons have shown that women develop fewer defenses against the pains of incarceration than men and perhaps suffer more, and it is possible that judges and juries know or sense this. Or perhaps they simply find the idea of women in prison, away from their families, offensive.

■ RACE. Most Negroes are poor. A great many poor people are Negroes. So the figures about indigency and race must overlap. But they are not identical, and the differences are important. Generally, the poor suffer even more discrimination than Negroes in criminal justice; and Negroes may suffer more from lack of money than from race.

For instance, a Negro is more likely to get a preliminary hearing than a poor man. He is not as likely as the white defendant to be released on bail, but much more likely to be released than the indigent defendant. Since many Negro defendants are also indigent, the Negro is slightly more likely to have a lawyer than a white defendant, given the indigency prerequisite for receiving a court-appointed lawyer. When the Negro has a lawyer, his lawyer is much more likely to be court-appointed than the lawyers of white defendants. In the federal larceny cases, 52 percent of the

Negroes did not have their own lawyers as contrasted to 25 percent of the whites.

Like the indigent, the Negro awaiting trial with his court-appointed lawyer tends to have *less* delay than the white defendant. In fact, being subjected to delay seems to be a sign of high status rather than discrimination. Delay while released on bail may be desired by the defendant because it can benefit the guilty defendant by prolonging his freedom and weakening the memories of witnesses.

The Negro is much less likely than the white to have a grand jury indictment in either federal assault or larceny cases. If he goes to trial he is even more unlikely to have a jury trial. Indeed, 86 percent of the Negroes in federal assault cases failed to receive a jury trial, contrasted to a 26 percent figure for white defendants. It appears that the constitutional rights of a grand jury indictment and of trial by jury are mainly for white men. Perhaps Negroes believe white juries to be more discriminatory than white judges. But it is also possible that Negroes commit the less severe larcenies and assaults, and so do not as often require grand or petit juries.

Negroes, compared to whites, are particularly discriminated against when it comes to probation or suspended sentences. This is evident in the assault convictions, but is more dramatic for larceny; 74 percent of guilty Negroes were imprisoned in state larceny cases, against only 49 percent of guilty whites; in federal larceny cases the score is 54 percent to 40 percent. With prior record held constant, the disparity still holds up.

Why the difference in treatment between Negro assault and Negro larceny? Are not crimes against the person usually considered more reprehensible than those against property? The answer possibly is that larcenies by Negros are more often (than assaults) committed against white men, who are more likely to be worth robbing; but assaults occur most frequently within one's community, in this case against other Negroes. Disparities in sentencing may therefore be double, determined not only by the color of the skin of the criminal, but of his victim too.

It is interesting to note that there is a greater race disparity in federal probation *recommendations* than in probations *granted*. This may be because probation officers deal more subjectively with people, while judges (who are also better educated) tend to put more emphasis on objective factors, like the nature of the crime and the law.

On the other hand, of those actually imprisoned, the Negro defendants (particularly in larceny cases) tended to receive lighter sentences. This may be because, like the indigent defendants, they tend to steal smaller amounts; but it is probably also because the mild white offender is more likely to escape imprisonment altogether.

Generally, and surprisingly, discrimination against the Negro in criminal proceedings was only slightly greater in the South than in the North. It was, however, consistently greater in the South at all stages, pre-trial, trial, and sentencing. Discrimination in the South, predictably, was also greater at the state level than the federal level, possibly because federal judges are more independent of local pressures than state judges.

■ AGE. Younger defendants (below 21 in the state data, 22 in federal) generally are less likely to receive the safeguards the older defendants do, but are more likely to get lighter sentences.

Thus 66 percent of the young did not have their own lawyers in federal assault cases compared to 36 percent of the older defendants. They are less likely to face either grand or trial juries. There is, however, no substantial difference in preliminary hearing or bail. Much of the lack of formal procedure may actually be an advantage, reflecting a protective attitude by the courts toward the young (as toward women), and the belief that informality of procedure diminishes the "criminal" stigma, and leads more easily into rehabilitation. This is, of course, the rationale behind separate juvenile courts. The lack of a personal lawyer probably also reflects some poverty—people 21 and under seldom have much money of their own.

Young defendants are more likely to be recommended for probation, more likely to get it (or suspended sentences), and those few who do go to prison generally receive shorter sentences. (The one exception—longer sentences for youthful federal larcenists who are imprisoned—is probably unrepresentative because of the small sample, or perhaps because only the most hardened cases actually go to federal prison.) Younger people, of course, usually have shorter prior records, and this could count for some of the disparity; but the main reason is probably the belief that the young (again like women) are not as responsible, are more easily rehabilitated, and suffer more hardship in prison.

■ URBAN VS. RURAL, SOUTH VS. NORTH. The sample does not distinguish between *defendants* from the North or the South, the city or the farm—but it does distinguish between *courts* in different locales. Which were the fairest? The answer might sometimes surprise those who automatically accept the stereotype of Northern-urban civil-libertarianism, as opposed to Southern-rural anti-civil-libertarianism.

In the state data, an urban county was defined as one with more than 100,000 population; the federal data used a similar but more sophisticated definition. For both, "South" meant the original eleven states of the Confederacy. The six border states were considered neutral, and the "North" encompassed all the rest. As it developed, most cases (especially the larcenies) were tried in urban courts.

DISPARITIES IN CRIMINAL PROCEDURE TREATMENT

	DISADVANTAGED GROUPS (Indigents, Negroes, & Less Educated)	PATERNALIZED GROUPS (Juveniles & Females)	INDUSTRIALIZED GROUPS (Northern & Urban Defendants)
SAFEGUARDS FOR THE INNOCENT	Unfavorable, especially as to bail, but favorable as to being provided with a lawyer.	Unfavorable for juveniles especially as to jury trial, but unclear for females.	Unfavorable as to preliminary hearing and delay, but favorable as to providing lawyers. Mixed as to jury trial depending on the crime.
ASSAULT SENTENCING	Unfavorable, especially as to the probation officer decision.	Favorable, especially at the federal level.	Unfavorable as to whether to grant probation, but favorable as to length of imprisonment.
LARCENY SENTENCING	Unfavorable (more so than assault) as to whether to imprison, but favorable as to length of imprisonment.	Favorable, especially at the federal level.	Relatively favorable treatment.

(Based on 1,949 state cases and 981 federal cases from all 50 states for the years 1962-63 in which the defendant was charged with a single charge of assault or of larceny.)

Generally, North-South differences in treatment were greater than urban-rural differences.

In preliminary hearing and bail, urban-rural differences were small and inconclusive, but North-South differences were large and consistent—and not to the credit of the North. Thus 38 percent of Northern assaults had no preliminary hearing in spite of laws providing for them, compared to only 10 percent in the South. The South is more traditional toward law and custom, perhaps. The bail difference may also be due to the fact that more Northern defendants were classified as indigents.

Not having any lawyer at all was disproportionately rural and Southern; of the eleven Southern states, eight did not have laws providing for compensated counsel. (*Gideon vs. Wainwright* originated in a Southern state, Florida, and the South will now have to change its ways.) But in the federal cases, where assigned counsel was available, the rural and Southern defendants were *more* apt to have their own hired lawyers than in the cities and the North. That more defendants were labeled indigent in the North, and lawyers cost more there, may be an explanation.

The urban and Northern courts are more congested; defendants wait longer for trial. In the state assault cases, 56 percent of urban defendants sat in jail for more than two months, contrasted to 31 percent of rural defendants, and there is a similar 25 percent spread for federal larceny cases. Much has been written about congestion and delay in urban civil cases, but delay in criminal cases also needs attention, especially in the Northern cities.

In assault cases, jury trials and grand jury indictments are more common in the South than in the North; in larceny cases, however, it is the other way around. (The findings are similar in rural and urban courts, although not as consistent.) Urban and Northern courts are more likely to *imprison* for *assault*; the rural and Southern, for *larceny*. Perhaps these disparities reflect the "frontier" morality still lingering in the open country and the South, in which a man is expected to be prepared to personally defend his honor (and therefore assault is not so terrible) but a crime against property is something else again.

In the congested cities and the North, perhaps, crimes against the person seem more terrible, whereas property tends to be considered corporate and impersonal. Moreover, people in settled areas are more conditioned to rely on professional police, not personal defense and retribution. No great differences exist North and South, urban and rural, in percentages of convictions. But there is a good deal of difference in length of sentences. Rural and Southern courts are harsher, at least at the state level—66 percent of Southern state larceny sentences were for more than a year, contrasted to 35 percent in the North. Assault shows about the same spread. Rural-urban differences are parallel, if less marked. Southern states make the greatest use of capital punishment.

■ FEDERAL VERSUS STATE. Because of different constitutions and judicial interpretations, federal defendants have greater access to the grand jury and to counsel (when the data was collected) than state defendants. Delays are much shorter at the federal level. Shorter delays mean less need for bail, and the grand jury hearing diminishes the importance of the preliminary hearing. A slightly higher percent of federal trials are tried before juries.

Both federal and state trials end in guilty findings (or pleas) about 80 percent of the time; both find assault defendants guilty less often than larceny defendants. Probation and suspended sentences are more common in federal court—but, perhaps because the milder cases are already winnowed out, federal assault sentences are longer.

As detailed earlier, disparities unfavorable to Negroes are slightly greater in the states. Juveniles are more likely to be deprived of safeguards at the federal than the state level—but also given lighter sentences. In the broad outline, however, the same disparity patterns show up in both.

At risk of oversimplification, the major findings of this study are summarized in the accompanying chart.

Significant disparities in the administration of justice do exist. Some groups are more likely than others to receive preliminary hearings, release on bail, better lawyers, grand jury proceedings, jury trials, acquittals, shorter sentences.

Some of these differences are justifiable. The severity of the crime and the prior record, should affect the sentence (though not due process). Women and juveniles should perhaps be given more consideration. Some crimes may have greater importance in one place than another, and minor adjustments made accordingly. Nevertheless, the majority of disparities discussed in this article are probably not socially justifiable and run contrary to our democratic philosophy and to those laws which are supposed to guarantee due process and equal treatment.

What can be done about it? Remedies vary with the specific disorder. But these discriminations in the courts partly reflect the same discriminations in our society. The indigent would not get different treatment if there were no indigent; Negroes would not be discriminated against as Negroes if there were no race prejudice. If general American performance matched American oratory and promise, equality in the courts would come quickly enough. Thus the problem of criminal procedure disparities is inherently tied to attempts to remove distinctions that are considered undesirable between the city and the country and the North and the South, and to attempts to further emancipate women, as well as to decrease the numbers of the indigent and the uneducated, and to eliminate general racial discrimination.

Meanwhile, what is being done with regard to a more piecemeal attack on specific disparities?

Partly as the result of the recommendations of such groups as the Attorney General's Committee on Poverty and the Administration of Federal Criminal Justice, the Vera Foundation in New York City, and the National Bail Conference, the federal courts have been releasing many more people considered trustworthy *without bail,* pending trial. There is some evidence that state courts are starting to follow suit. Illinois now has a law requiring that most defendants waiting trial be released if they can afford a 10 percent down payment on the bail bond—the interest usually charged by commercial bondsmen. Philadelphia, New York, and St. Louis have followed the Vera recommendation to set up bodies that investigate defendants and advise judges whether they are good risks for release without bail. The fact is that judges have almost always had the authority to forego bail for trustworthy defendants— but few have been willing to use it with what little information they could pick up from the bench. In these cities at least they are using it now, and with increasing frequency.

Since *Gideon versus Wainwright,* all felony defendants can probably be assured of *some* kind of representation. In addition, a large scale campaign to provide *competent* counsel has been started by the National Legal Aid and Defender Association, and the American Bar Association. The Administrative Office of the U.S. Courts is currently conducting an educational program to encourage more rational sentencing practices and a statistical program to show more clearly just what those practices are. Though the evidence is very spotty, there does seem to be a general trend, especially in the large cities, toward better trained and better educated policemen, probation officers, and court officials. The civil rights movement, by focusing publicity on disparities, is also bringing change.

Bringing the facts to light can expedite needed change. The disparities exist partly because the facts have been denied, ignored, disbelieved, or simply unknown to a large public. The facts are available, and they keep accumulating. We may reasonably hope that when a similar study is done five or ten years from now it will show less disparity in the administration of criminal justice.

May/June 1966

Lawyers with Convictions

ABRAHAM S. BLUMBERG

The criminal trial—in a vision based not only on plays and novels, but also on a number of Supreme Court decisions—is believed to be a kind of highly civilized trial by combat. Two attorneys—one championing the people, the other championing the accused—robe themselves in the majesty of the law and battle before a stern impartial judge who considers their performances in light of the special rules of the law and grants victory to the best man.

This is a dramatic picture. But if we look closely at the reality of a large number of criminal trials, we find drama of a decidedly different kind. It may be a miracle play or a farce or a tragedy, depending on the point of view.

The defendant in a criminal court almost always loses. Most often—nine times out of ten is a good rough measure—he is found guilty. Does the prosecution have the best men, or are the police amazingly efficient? The prosecution does have good men, and the police do have competent investigators, but still we must look a little deeper to find out why losers lose.

Often, the source of their defeat has been sought in deprivations and social disabilities such as race, poverty, and social class. Researchers have attempted to learn how the deprived regard the legal system and how the system regards the deprived. But what of the legal system itself? What are the values of the judges and lawyers who work in the criminal courts? What is their thrust, purpose, and direction?

I am most concerned here with the "lawyer regulars"— those defense lawyers, including public defenders, who represent the bulk of defendants—and not with those lawyers who come to court occasionally because someone for whom they have written a will or deed has gotten into trouble. These clients end up in the hands of the regulars when their troubles are serious.

The private regulars are highly visible in the major urban centers of the nation; their offices—at times shared with bondsmen—line the back streets near courthouses. They are also visible politically, with clubhouse ties reaching into judicial chambers and the prosecutor's office. The regulars make no effort to conceal their dependence upon police, bondsmen, jail personnel, as well as bailiffs, stenographers, prosecutors, and judges. These informal relations are essential to maintaining and building a practice. Some lawyers are almost entirely dependent on such contacts to find clients, and a few even rely on an "in" with judges to obtain state-paid appointments which become the backbone of their practices.

A defense lawyer willing to go to trial can accomplish a great deal for his client, even a client technically guilty of some crime. Say the man has been arrested with a roomful of stolen furs, a satchel filled with burglar tools, a burglary record, and no alibi for the night of the crime. If the prosecution charges him with burglary, but the defense can show there was no forcible entry, then no burglary has been committed. The prosecution might try to convict on a number of lesser charges—theft, possession of stolen property, or possession of burglar tools—but in the process, the defense lawyer may have thrown up so much reasonable doubt as to get his man off. The prosecution is liable to other mistakes as well. They may have used faulty search warrants or attempted to introduce other illegal evidence; they may tamper with the witnesses or the jury; they may simply put on a bad case.

In order to accomplish these gains for his client, the defense lawyer must go to trial. However, going to trial is out of character with his role as a member of the court system. This holds true for both public and private attorneys. As members of a bureaucratic system the defense lawyers become committed to rational, impersonal goals based on saving time, labor, and expense and on attaining maximum output for the system. For the defense lawyer this means choosing strategies which will lead to working out a plea of guilty, assuring a fee, and shrouding these acts with legitimacy. The accused and his kin, as outsiders, cannot perceive the mutual dependence of the prosecutor and the defense lawyer, himself often a former prosecutor. These two need each other's cooperation for their continued professional existence. Even in bargaining over guilty pleas, their combat tends to be reasonable rather than fierce.

The defense lawyer in many ways plays the confidence man. The client is cast as the mark. The lawyer convinces him that pleading guilty will lead to a lesser charge or a lesser sentence, and the eager client agrees, forgetting that in pleading guilty, he is forfeiting his right to a trial by jury and getting a presentence hearing before a judge.

The lawyer's problem is different. He is not concerned with guilt or innocence, but rather with giving the client something for his money. Usually a plumber can show that he has performed a service by pointing to the unstopped drain or the no longer leaky faucet as proof that he merits his fee. A physician who has not performed surgery, advised a low-starch diet, or otherwise engaged in some readily discernible procedure may be deemed by the patient to have done nothing for him. Thus, doctors may order a sugar pill or water injection to overcome the patient's dissatisfaction in paying a fee "for nothing."

The practice of law has a special problem in this regard. Much legal work is intangible: a few words of advice, a telephone call, a form filled out and filed, a hurried conference with another attorney or a government official, a letter or brief, or some other seemingly innocuous or even prosaic activity. These are the basic activities, apart from any possible court appearance, of almost all lawyers at all levels of practice. The client is not looking for this, but rather for the exercise of the traditional, precise, and professional skills of the attorney: legal research and oral argument on appeals; court motions; trial work; drafting of opinions, memoranda, contracts, and other complex documents and agreements.

Despite the client's expectations, whether the lawyer has offices on Wall Street or in his hat, most legal activity more closely resembles the work of a broker, salesman, lobbyist, or agent. The product is intangible.

The members of a large-scale law firm may not speak as openly of their contacts, their fixing abilities, as does the hustling, lone-wolf lawyer. The firms trade instead upon thick carpeting, walnut paneling, genteel low pressure, and superficialities of traditional legal professionalism. There are occasions when even the large firm is defensive about the fees because the services or results do not appear substantial. Therefore, the recurrent problem in the legal profession is setting and justifying the fee.

Although the fee at times amounts to what the traffic and the conscience of the lawyer will bear, one further observation must be made about the size of the fee and its collection. The criminal defendant and his presumed loot are soon parted. Frequently the defense lawyer gets it in payment of his fee. Inevitably, the dollar value of the crime committed affects the fee, which is frequently set with precision at a sum which bears an uncanny relationship to that of the net proceeds of the crime. On occasion, defendants have been known to commit additional offenses while out on bail in order to meet their obligations for payment of legal fees. Defense lawyers teach even the most obtuse clients that there is a firm connection between paying up and the zealous application of professional expertise, secret knowledge, and organizational connections. Lawyers, therefore, seek to keep their clients at the precise emotional pitch necessary to encourage prompt fee payment. Consequently, the client treats his lawyer with hostility, mistrust, dependence, and sychophancy in precarious mixture. By keeping his client's anxieties aroused and establishing a relationship between the fee and ultimate extrication, the lawyer assures a minimum of haggling over the fee and its eventual payment.

As a consequence, all law practice in some degree involves a manipulation of the client and a stage management of the lawyer-client relationship so that there will be at least an *appearance* of help and service. At the outset, the lawyer employs with suitable variation a measure of puffery which may range from unbounded self-confidence, adequacy, and dominion over events to complete arrogance. This is supplemented by the affectation of a studied, faultless mode of personal attire. In larger firms the furnishings and office trappings will serve as the backdrop to help in impressing and intimidating the client. In all firms, solo or large scale, an access to secret knowledge and to the seats of power is implied.

The lack of a visible end product offers a special complication for the professional criminal lawyer. The plain fact is that the accused in a criminal case almost always loses, even when he has been freed by the court. All the hostility resulting from arrest, incarceration, possible loss of job, and legal expense then is directed toward the lawyer. Thus, it can also be said that the criminal lawyer never really wins a case. The really satisfied client is rare, since even vindication leaves him feeling hostile and dissatisfied. He didn't want to be arrested in the first place. Even the rare defendant who sees himself as a professional criminal and views legal fees as business expenses thinks that the overhead should be cut down. It is this state of affairs that reinforces the casting of the lawyer as a con man.

The risks of nonpayment of the fee are high. Most of the clients are poor, and most of them are likely to end up in jail, where their gratitude will be muted. It is no surprise that criminal lawyers collect their fees in advance. The fee is one of three major problems the lawyer must solve. The second is preparing the client for defeat and then cooling him out when it comes, as it is likely to do. Third, he must satisfy the court that his performance in negotiating the plea was adequate. Appellate courts are more and more looking over the trial judge's shoulder. Even the most unlikely cases may be finally decided by the Supreme Court. The next drifter accused of breaking and entering might be another Clarence Gideon.

To be sure of getting his fee, the criminal lawyer will

very often enter into negotiations with various members of
the accused's family. In many instances, the accused himself is unable to pay any sort of fee or anything more
than a token fee. It then becomes important to involve as
many of his relatives as possible. This is especially so if
the attorney hopes to collect a substantial fee. It is not
uncommon for several relatives to contribute toward the
fee. The larger the group, the greater the possibility that
the lawyer will collect a sizable fee.

A fee for a felony case which results in a plea, rather
than a trial, may range anywhere from $500 to $1,500.
Should the case go to trial, the fee will be larger, depending upon the length of the trial. But the larger the fee the
lawyer wishes to exact, the more impressive his performance must be. Court personnel are keenly aware of the
extent to which a lawyer's stock in trade involves precarious staging of a role which goes beyond the usual
professional flamboyance. For this reason alone the lawyer
is bound in to the court system. Therefore, court personnel
will aid the lawyer in the creation and maintenance of that
impression. There is a tacit commitment to the lawyer by
the court organization, apart from formal etiquette, to aid
him. This augmentation of the lawyer's stage-managed
image is the partial basis for the quid pro quo which exists
between the lawyer and the court organization. It tends to
serve as the continuing basis for the higher loyalty of the
lawyer to the court organization while his relationship with
his client, in contrast, is transient, ephemeral, and often
superficial.

The lawyer has often been accused of stirring up unnecessary litigation, especially in the field of negligence. He
is said to acquire a vested interest in a cause of action or
claim which was initially his client's. The strong incentive
of possible fee motivates the lawyer to promote litigation

which would otherwise never have developed. The lawyers have even encoded two crimes with fine medieval names to limit this activity. *Barratry* is persistent incitement of litigation, and *champerty* is taking part in a suit without justification in exchange for a cut of the proceeds. The criminal lawyer develops a vested interest of an entirely different nature in his client's case: not to promote the litigation, but to limit its scope and duration. Only in this way can a case be profitable. Thus, he enlists the aid of relatives not only to assure payment of his fee, but to help him in his agent-mediator role of convincing the accused to plead guilty, and ultimately to help him in the "cooling out" if necessary.

It is at this point that an accused defendant may experience his first sense of betrayal. While he had perceived the police and prosecutor to be adversaries, and possibly even the judge, the accused is wholly unprepared for his counsel's role as an agent-mediator. In the same vein, it is even less likely to occur to an accused that members of his own family may become agents. Usually it will be the lawyer who will activate the family in this role, his ostensible motive being to arrange for his fee. But soon the latent and unstated motives will assert themselves. The lawyer asks the family to convince the accused to "help himself" by pleading guilty. Appeals to sentiment are exploited by a defense lawyer (or even by a district attorney) to achieve the specific end of concluding a particular matter with all possible dispatch.

The fee is often collected in installments, usually payable prior to each court appearance. In his interviews and communications with the accused or with members of his family, the lawyer employs an air of professional confidence and inside-dopesterism to assuage all anxieties. He makes the necessary bland assurances and manipulates his client, who is usually willing to do and say things, true or not, which his attorney says will help him. Since what he is selling—influence and expertise—cannot be measured by the client, the lawyer can make extravagant claims of influence and secret knowledge with impunity. Lawyers frequently claim to have inside knowledge in connection with information in the hands of the prosecutor, police, or probation officials. They often do have access to them and need only to exaggerate the nature of their relationships to impress the client. But in the confidence game, the victim who has participated is loath to do anything which will upset the lesser plea which his lawyer has conned him into accepting.

The question has never been raised as to whether "copping" a plea, or justice by negotiation, is a constitutional process. Although it has become the most central aspect of the process of criminal law administration, it has received virtually no close scrutiny by the appellate courts. As a consequence it is relatively free of legal control and supervision. But, apart from any questions of the legality of bargaining, in terms of the pressures and devices that are employed which tend to violate due process of law, there remain ethical and practical questions. Much of the danger of the system of bargain-counter justice is concealed in secret negotiations and its least alarming feature, the final plea, is the only one presented to public view.

In effect, in his role as double agent the criminal lawyer performs a vital and delicate mission for the court organization and the accused. Both principals are anxious to terminate the litigation with a minimum of expense and damage to each other. There is no one else in the court structure more strategically located or more ideally suited to handle this than the defense lawyer. In recognition of this, judges will cooperate with attorneys in many important ways. For example, they will continue the case of an accused in jail awaiting plea or sentence if the attorney requests it. This may be done for some innocuous and seemingly valid public reason, but the real purpose is pressure by the attorney for the collection of his fee, which he knows he may lose if the case is concluded. Judges know of this none too subtle method of dunning a client. The judges will go along on the ground that important ends are being served. Often, however, the only end being served is to protect a lawyer's fee.

Another way the judge can help an accused's lawyer is by lending the official aura of the bench as a backdrop to an all-out performance for the accused in justification of his fee. The judge and other court personnel will serve as supporting players for a dramatic scene in which the defense lawyer makes a stirring appeal in his behalf. With a show of restrained passion, the lawyer will intone the virtues of the accused and recite the social deprivations which have reduced him to his present state. The speech varies somewhat, depending on whether the accused has been convicted after trial or has pleaded guilty. The incongruity, superficiality, and ritualistic character of the performance is underscored by a visibly impassive, almost bored reaction on the part of the judge and other members of the court retinue. Afterward there is a hearty exchange of pleasantries between the lawyer and district attorney, wholly out of the context of the adversary nature of the hearing. The courtroom players are not "method" actors.

The fiery passion of the defense is gone, and lawyers for both sides resume their offstage relations, chatting amiably and perhaps even including the judge in their restrained banter. Even a casual observer is put on notice; these individuals have claims upon each other.

Criminal law practice is unique since it really only appears to be private practice but is actually bureaucratic practice. Private practice is supposed to involve an organized, disciplined body of knowledge and learning. Individual practitioners are imbued with a spirit of autonomy and service. Earning a livelihood is incidental. But the lawyer in the criminal court serves as a double agent, serving organizational rather than professional ends. To some extent the lawyer-client confidence game serves to conceal this fact.

The "cop-out" ceremony is not only invaluable for redefining the defendant's perspectives of himself, but also in reiterating his guilt in a public ritual. The accused is made to assert his guilt of a specific crime, including a complete recital of its details. He is further made to say that he is entering his plea of guilty freely and that he is not doing so because of any promises that may have been made to him. This last is intended as a blanket statement to shield the court bureaucrats from any charges of coercion. This cuts off any appellate review on grounds that due process was denied as well as cutting off any second thoughts the defendant may have about his plea.

This affirmation of guilt is not a simple affair. Most of those who plead guilty are guilty and may be willing or even eager to say so in order to be charged with a lesser crime or receive a lesser sentence. The system serves the guilty better because they are glad to get half a loaf in return for playing along. But the innocent—subject to precisely the same pressures—get no reward from a negotiated plea. In any case, the defendant's conception of himself as guilty is ephemeral; in private he will quickly reassert his innocence. The "cop-out" is not comparable to Harold Garfinkel's "status degradation ceremony" because it has no lasting effect on the interrelations of the defendant and society. Rather, it is a charade. The accused projects the appropriate amount of guilt, penance, and remorse; his hearers engage in the fantasy that he is contrite and merits a lesser punishment.

Defendants begin dropping the guilty role very soon. Many do so in their interviews with the probation officer immediately after the plea but before sentencing. The first question the probation officer routinely asks is: "Are you guilty of the crime to which you pleaded?" I have gathered the responses of 724 male defendants to this question. The research was done in 1962, 1963, and 1964 in a large metropolitan court handling only felonies. The men were charged with crimes ranging from homicide to forgery, but most of them pleaded guilty to misdemeanors after negotiation. At this early stage, 51.4 percent claimed innocence in some fashion. In practice when a prisoner claims innocence, the probation officer will ask him to withdraw his plea and stand trial on the original charges. This threat is normally sufficient to provide the system with a second affirmation of guilt.

Very few choose to go on trial again. They are very likely to be convicted if they do. Between 1950 and 1964 in the court I studied, from 75 to 90 percent of the actual adversary trials ended in conviction. In all years less than 5 percent of all indictments ended in adversary trials.

In the present system it would appear that once an individual is indicted, there is very little chance of escaping conviction.

The unrehearsed responses to the probation officer tell us a great deal about how defendants feel about their negotiated pleas. Only 13.2 percent straightforwardly admitted their guilt and of these, 10.3 percent added exculpatory statements such as, "But I should have gotten a

better deal (from the lawyer, prosecutor, police, judge)."
The large group claiming innocence, 373 men, were for
the most part interested in underscoring their "goodness"
for the probation officer.

These innocent respondents employed varying degrees
of fervor, solemnity, and credibility. In the main they were
pragmatic, saying, "I wanted to get it over with," or "You
can't beat the system," or "They have you over a barrel
when you have a record." This pragmatic response covered
20.3 percent of the sample. "I followed my lawyer's advice," was the claim of 12.7 percent. Nearly as many defendants—11.8 percent—said they had been manipulated
or conned by lawyer, judge, police, or prosecutor. The
smallest number—2.1 percent—traced their plea to a "bad
report" by the probation officer or psychiatrist in investigations before hearing the plea. Only a very few were defiant
outright; just 4.5 percent (or 33) claimed that they had
been framed or betrayed.

By far the largest grouping in the sample were those
who were fatalistic, neither pressing their innocence nor
admitting their guilt. This 34.8 percent (248) explained
their pleas by saying, "I did it for convenience," or "My
lawyer told me it was the only thing I could do," or "I
did it because it was the best way out." This last group
seemed to feel that they, like Joseph K. in Kafka's *The
Trial,* are caught up in a monstrous apparatus which may
turn on them no matter what they do, no matter whether
they say they are innocent or guilty. These men adopt a
stance of passivity, resignation, and acceptance. Interest-
ingly, in most instances it was their lawyer who crystallized
the alternatives for them and who was therefore the critical
element in their decision to plead guilty.

In order to determine the critical elements in all 724
cases, the men were asked who first suggested the plea of

guilty and who most influenced their final decision to enter this plea. The results are listed in Table I:

TABLE I—DECISIONS TO PLEAD GUILTY

Agent-Mediator	First Suggestion		Most Influence	
	No.	%	No.	%
Judge	4	0.6	26	3.6
Prosecutor	67	9.3	116	16.0
Defense counsel	407	56.2	411	56.8
Probation officer	14	1.9	3	0.4
Psychiatrist	8	1.1	1	0.1
Wife	34	4.7	120	16.6
Friends and relatives	21	2.9	14	1.9
Police	14	1.9	4	0.6
Fellow inmates	119	16.4	14	1.9
Others	28	3.9	5	0.7
No response	8	1.1	10	1.4

It is popularly assumed that most guilty pleas are a result of pressure to confess from the police or more elaborate coercion from the prosecutor. In my sample, however, only 43 men, or 5.94 percent, had confessed before they were indicted, and as Table I shows, the defense attorney was by far the most potent source of guilty pleas, particularly if it is recalled that most of the pressure from family and friends to plead this way is likely to be generated by the defense attorney. The bureaucratic system cannot rely on idiosyncratic police pressures for confessions and retain its efficiency, high production, and rational-legal character. The defense counsel is a far more effective source of pleas, living as he does astride the world of the court and the world of the defendant. Even though fellow inmates were frequently the first to mention such a plea, defendants still tended to rely strongly on their counsel as the ultimate source of influence for a final decision.

Therefore, I asked the 724 defendants at what point in their relationship the defense counsel first suggested a guilty plea. Although these men cited many sources of influence, they all had lawyers, and of course they were not likely to plead without concurrence by or at least consultation with their lawyers. In the court I studied there are three basic kinds of defense counsel: private, legal-aid (a private defender system which receives public funds and has taken on the coloration of a public defender system), and court-assigned (who may later be privately retained).

The overwhelming majority related a specific incident of an early suggestion that they plead guilty to a lesser charge if this could be arranged. Of all the agent-mediators, it is the lawyer who is most effective in manipulating the defendant, notwithstanding possible pressures by police, prosecutor, judge, or others. Legal-aid and assigned counsel

TABLE II—STAGE AT WHICH PLEA WAS FIRST
SUGGESTED OR DISCUSSED

Meeting	Private	Legal-Aid	Assigned	All	%
First	66	237	28	331	45.7
Second	83	142	8	233	32.2
Third	29	63	4	96	13.3
Fourth or later	12	31	5	48	6.6
No response	0	14	2	16	2.2
TOTAL NUMBER OF CASES	190	487	47	724	100.0%

are apparently more likely to suggest the plea in the initial interview, perhaps as a response to pressures of time and, in the case of the assigned counsel, the strong possibility that there is no fee involved. In addition, there is some further evidence in Table II of the perfunctory character of criminal courts. Little real effort is made to individualize the defendant. Although the defense lawyer is an officer of the court he mediates between the court organization and the defendant; his duties to each are rent by conflicts of interest. Too often these must be resolved in favor of the organization which provides him with his professional existence. In order to reduce the strains and conflicts imposed, the lawyer engages in the lawyer-client confidence game so as to make his situation more palatable.

Based on data which are admittedly tentative and fragmentary, the furor over confessions, whether forced or voluntary, is not statistically meaningful. Criminal law enforcement has always depended, and will continue to do so in the foreseeable future, on judicial confessions—that is, pleas of guilty—rather than confessions hammered out in the squeal room of a police station.

The Gideon, Miranda, and Escobedo decisions were greeted with such lively delight or anguished dismay that outsiders must have thought that the Supreme Court had wrought some magnificent transformation in the defense lawyer. Actually, the court in these cases was perpetuating the Perry Mason myth of an adversary trial, while in the lesser courts of the nation, the dreary succession of 90 percent negotiated pleas continued. These "trials" are highly reminiscent of what George Feifer described in *Justice in Moscow*. The Soviet trial has been termed "an appeal from the pre-trial investigation." All notions of the presumption of innocence are completely alien, and as Feifer states: ". . . the closer the investigation resembles the finished script, the better. . . ."

I do not mean to be pejorative. Feifer finds the Soviet trial preferable in some ways because it judges the criminal and not the crime, but in the American form, the "irrelevant" factors of background and record are considered only after the finding of guilty, not before as in Russia and much of Europe.

The Escobedo and Miranda decisions protecting against defendant confusion in the hands of the police and the

Gideon decision assuring counsel for felony defendants are popular in and out of legal circles, but my experiences and observations suggest that a poor defendant with a lawyer may not be much better off than a poor defendant without a lawyer. These decisions have not changed the nature of the court bureaucracy and, if anything, the pressure for guilty pleas and the drive for efficient production may grow even stronger, and the position of the defendant as a bureaucratic client further hampered by race, poverty, and class may become weaker and weaker.

Courts, like many other large modern organizations, possess a monstrous appetite not only for individuals, but for entire professions. Almost all those coming under an organizational authority find their definitions, perceptions, and values have been refurbished in terms largely favorable to the particular organization and its goals.

Thus, the Supreme Court decisions extending the right to counsel may have an effect which is radically different from that intended or anticipated. The libertarian rules will tend to augment the existing organizational arrangements, enriching court organizations with more personnel and elaborate structure, and making them an even more sophisticated apparatus for processing defendants toward a guilty finding.

July/August 1967

Winners and Losers: Garnishment and Bankruptcy In Wisconsin

HERBERT JACOB

The prospect of being dragged into court for not paying one's debts or else pleading bankruptcy in order to evade them looms in the future of thousands of Americans every year. But whether the courts will be the last resort of debt collectors and debt dodgers depends on numerous influences ranging from the attitude of individual communities regarding indebtedness to the life-styles of debtors and creditors.

The courts are the most important contact many citizens have with the government. But whether this political instrument is used to seize wages of those owing money or to help others evade payment by declaring them bankrupt is related to income, the type of debt incurred, job status, to some degree race, and the manner in which the community where the action is taking place views itself.

To find out who uses the courts for garnishment and bankruptcy proceedings, we searched the court records of four Wisconsin cities—Madison, Racine, Kenosha, and Green Bay. In Green Bay, where the number of such proceedings was small, all debtor-creditor cases for a year were recorded. A random sample was taken from the other cities' files.

In all, 454 debtors were interviewed. Another 336 creditors and 401 employers returned completed questionnaires. Interviews with selected attorneys, creditors, collection agencies, and court officials added to the information. From these sources emerged profiles of creditors and debtors and their use of the courts.

Debtor-creditor conflicts usually involve the refusal of the debtor to pay what the creditor feels is due him. The debtor may feel he was cheated or that the creditor didn't live up to the agreement. Unemployment, ill health, a family emergency, or pressure from other creditors to repay them first are other common reasons that people don't pay bills. Sometimes, the debtor simply forgets or no longer wants to pay. In each case, the probability of conflict is high, for most creditors pursue the debtor until he pays. Only when collection costs rise above the amount owed, will most creditors write off the loss.

The typical creditor is a finance company, department store, service station, television repair shop, landlord, hospital, doctor, or even lawyer. A few creditors are personally involved insofar as they themselves extend credit, lend money, or have extensive personal relations with their customers and make a personal effort to collect the loan. Most collectors do not make loans, but are employees of large collection organizations and view collecting as a routine matter.

When most private actions to collect debts fail, the courts stand ready to help creditors: (1) If an article were purchased through a conditional sales contract, the creditor may repossess, sell it, and get a deficiency judgment for the difference between the resale price and the amount still owed on the item from the debtor. (2) The creditor may obtain a judgment so that he can use the sheriff's office in collecting the amount due. The sheriff can seize for sale any articles not exempt under the state law. (3) When, as in many cases, the debtor owns no goods that satisfy the judgment, most states allow the creditor to attach the debtor's wages through wage garnishment. In some states like Wisconsin, creditors may seize the debtor's wages through garnishment even before they obtain a judgment against the debtor.

Under garnishment proceedings, a summons is sent to the debtor's employer, who is then obligated to report whether he owes the debtor any wages. If he does, he must send those wages to court. The debtor may recover some of his wages for living expenses but the bulk of the funds satisfies the debt. A creditor may garnishee his debtor's wages repeatedly until the debt is paid.

Debtors, in turn, have a number of extralegal remedies they can use. In a country where there is free movement and different state laws regarding creditor-debtor relations, the easiest thing for a debtor to do may be to move. Or he may defend his nonpayment in the judgment suit, though this is expensive and rarely successful. But debtors increasingly use a more successful legal measure—promising repayment through a court-approved amortization plan.

Such plans may be available under state law (as in Wisconsin) or through Chapter 13 of the Federal bankruptcy statute. Under the Wisconsin statute, a debtor earning less than $7,500 per year may arrange to repay his debts in full within two years if his creditors consent. During this time, he is protected from wage garnishments and other court actions that seek to collect the debts listed. New debts, however, may be collected as before through judgments or wage garnishments. Under Chapter 13 of the Bankruptcy Act, amortization usually allows the debtor three years to pay. During this time, interest accumulation is stopped and all creditor actions against the debtor are prohibited. New debts as well as old ones may be included in the repayment plan although new debts may be incurred only with the approval of a court-appointed trustee. Chapter 13 also provides for partial payment in satisfaction of the debt.

Bankruptcy provides the final legal escape for the debtor. Bankruptcy is available under Federal law to both the business and nonbusiness debtor. A debtor need not be penniless; he only needs to have debts which he cannot pay as they fall due. Under bankruptcy proceedings, the debtor makes available to the court all nonexempt assets that he possesses for repayment to his creditors.

Nonbusiness bankruptcies usually involve no assets that can be distributed to creditors. After this has been established, the Federal court discharges the debts of the bankrupt and he is no longer legally obligated to repay. (Tax debts, alimony, and child support payments as well as debts incurred through fraud cannot be discharged.) The only limitation to this remedy for debtors is that it may be used only once every six years.

Only a tiny proportion of credit transactions turn into conflicts between creditor and debtor and only a small proportion of those are eventually brought to court. It is therefore important to identify the conditions under which some people seek to invoke governmental sanctions in their efforts to collect or evade debts. *Four sets of conditions* are readily identifiable and are the subject of analysis here.

■ *Socioeconomic conditions:* A recession (even if slight and local) following a period when credit was freely extended is likely to produce more creditor-debtor conflicts than continued prosperity or a long recession. Likewise, the type of economy in an area is important. Subsistence economies, either in rural or urban slums, do not involve much consumer credit. Factory workers whose employment or earnings are erratic are more likely to be in credit difficulties than white-collar workers whose employment is steadier and whose wages, although lower, are more regular. The availability of credit is also significant. Those living in small towns or cities with few banks and lending institutions may find it more difficult to get credit and also find themselves less tempted to borrow than those living amidst a plethora of lending institutions, constantly inviting them to borrow.

■ *"Civic" or "public" culture of a community:* Some communities have more conservative lending policies than others. Large blocs of citizens may not borrow because they are older and not used to it or because they come from ethnic groups unaccustomed to living on credit. Alternatively, some communities are composed of groups who borrow heavily. In some communities, using the courts comes easily; in others, it involves a morally and culturally difficult decision.

■ *Availability of court action:* In some communities, court action is unlikely because no court sits in the town—all actions must be started in a distant town making litigation inconvenient as well as expensive. Also, some courts are more stringent about requiring representation by lawyers than others. In one town, attorneys may be more available for collection work than in others. Finally, litigation costs vary from town to town, as local judges interpret state laws regarding fees in different ways.

■ *Ability of potential litigants to use remedies:* Different members of a community vary considerably in their ability to use available remedies. They need to know about them.

They need the requisite financial resources. They need to be convinced that court action is really appropriate in their situation and to be free of the psychological restraint of shame and the social restraint of retaliation.

In the cities studied, money lenders (principally finance companies), and retailers were the heaviest users of wage garnishments. Hospitals, doctors, and dentists were the third most frequent users in three cities, while in the fourth, landlords were. All other creditors accounted for less than one-third of the wage garnishments docketed in small-claims court.

Creditors, however, do not use wage garnishments in identical ways. Their readiness to use the courts occurs under very different conditions. Finance companies, for example, have the most developed collection system. Ten days after a payment is due, they consider the debtor delinquent and begin efforts to collect. A large repertoire of collection methods are called into play, including overdue notices, telephone calls to the debtor, personal calls to his home, telephone calls to his employer, calls to co-signers of his note (if any), seizure of the collateral for the loan (if any), and wage garnishment. Most of these steps are carried out with minimal assistance by outsiders since their internal organization is structured to accommodate them. Consequently, finance companies almost never use collection agencies. And although they garnishee frequently, they do so only after a long chain of attempts to collect.

Doctors and hospitals are in a different position. Medical ethics downgrade commercial success, and patients reinforce this de-emphasis. Most patients expect a bill; few expect a bill collector to follow. Medical services are something they feel entitled to, regardless of their ability to pay, and therefore even when medical clinics and hospitals

have business offices, they do not usually use them for extensive bill-collecting purposes.

Most doctors are not organized for nor do they depend
on credit profits. Yet collectively, they probably extend as
much credit as finance companies do. As professionals,
they dislike spending time collecting delinquent bills. Generally, they wait three months before they consider a bill
delinquent. They then send one or two reminders to the
patient. They do not call him at home or at work. They
have no co-signer through whom to exert pressure; they have
no purchases to repossess. They do not even have the time
to go to court themselves, so they usually turn delinquent
accounts over to a collection agency or attorney. One or
two more impersonal attempts are made to collect before
the issue goes to court for a judgment and/or wage garnishment. Typically, the doctor and the hospital receive
only half the proceeds collected by the agency, the other
half being the agency's fee. Most maintain that they pay
little attention to what the collection agency does to collect
a bill and are unaware that they are garnisheeing their patients' wages. Some say they resort to collection agencies for
tax reasons only, since they believe the Internal Revenue
Service does not permit them to write off a delinquent
account as uncollectable unless court action was attempted.

Retail merchants stand between finance companies and
medical men in their use of wage garnishments. Large
stores with thousands of accounts have about the same organizational capability of collecting debts as finance companies. Small merchants have to use collection agencies.
Like doctors, most retailers do not consider accounts delinquent until 90 days after payment is due and they also
have no collateral to repossess since most retail sales are for
soft goods. When hard goods such as TVs and refrigerators

are sold on credit, the notes are sold by the retailer to a finance company. Retailers, moreover, are sensitive to their customers' opinions of them. Nearly 25 percent of the retailers interviewed were afraid that if they were frequently involved in direct wage garnishments they would lose customers. Almost 50 percent of the doctors expressed similar fears, but no finance company and very few banks and credit unions mentioned this as a reason for not using garnishments more often.

Willingness to use government help in collecting delinquent accounts thus seems to depend, in part, on the organizational resources of creditors, on their dependence on credit for profits, and on restraints produced by customer or patient alienation. Finance companies frequently use the courts because they possess the organizational resources, depend entirely on credit profits, and have little to fear since their customers generally have no other place to borrow. Doctors, hospitals, and retailers differ on all these points from finance companies and, insofar as they differ, are less likely to use the courts. Many, however, are indirectly drawn into court actions by the collection agencies they employ because collection agencies have the same characteristics as finance companies: the organizational resources to sue, their existence depends on collecting, and they have no fear of customer alienation.

The size of the debt is another important variable in the use of the courts. Most bills leading to wage garnishments are relatively large. Only 16 percent involved less than $50. Most were $50-$99, the median was $100-$149. About 20 percent were between $400 and $500, the upper limit of small-claims actions.

Most creditors find that costs are too high for debts of less than $50 to risk wage garnishment proceedings. It costs up to $35 (half in court fees and half in attorney's fees) to collect a bill by garnishment. If the creditor is successful in assessing the garnishment, the debtor pays the court fees. But if the garnishment is unsuccessful—if the creditor puts the wrong employer down on the summons or if he garnishes when the employer does not owe his employee any wages (for example, the day *after* payday rather than the day before)—the creditor must pay the full costs.

Since most debtors earn less than $100 a week, most debts far exceed the amount that can be collected by a single garnishment. Under Wisconsin law, the employer must usually pay the debtor $25 if he is single and $40 if he has dependents before he turns wages over to the court for payment to the creditor. Thus, most garnishments capture $60 or less out of which both the original debt and the court and attorney fees must be paid. In many cases it would take at least three garnishments to satisfy the debt and few debtors are likely to remain on their job beyond two such proceedings. Either they are fired because of the garnishments or quit in order to escape them. Most creditors therefore use wage garnishment to force the debtor to come in and make an arrangement to repay more gradually. As we shall see later, however, these generalizations about the users of garnishment proceedings are not entirely accurate for every city studied, with the locale making a considerable difference.

While creditors are often organizations, the debtors we studied were always individuals. Bankrupts had most often purchased large items such as cars (generally, used cars), appliances, TVs, furniture, and encyclopedias in the three years before going bankrupt. Garnishees, however, reported such purchases far less frequently, mentioning only two luxury items with consistency—home freezers and air conditioners. Medical debts were common to all; 82 percent of the bankrupts and 92 percent of the garnishees reported they were behind in their medical bills. Garnishees were more often protected by medical insurance. While 84 percent said some of their medical bills were paid by insurance, only 66 percent of the Chapter 13's and 57 percent of the bankrupts had similar protection.

Significantly, debtors in our sample who sought court relief were very similar to those who did not. Although

Table I

INDEBTEDNESS OF BANKRUPTS, CHAPTER 13's
AND GARNISHEES

Indebtedness	Bankrupts *(N = 196)	Chapter 13's (N = 72)	Garnishees (N = 168)
Up to $999	.5	9.7	25.6
$1000-4999	56.6	73.6	52.4
$5000-9999	20.4	12.4	10.1
Over $10000	22.9	4.2	11.9

* Number of cases

garnishees generally had a lower level of indebtedness, and many bankrupts were hopelessly mired in the quicksand of credit, most owed about the same amount of money —between $1,000 and $5,000. (See Table I)

■ Slightly more than half the bankrupts had incomes below $6,000, less than the median family income for the four Wisconsin cities in 1959. Like the garnishees, the vast majority were above the official "poverty" line of $3,000. Most of the Chapter 13's and garnishees reported incomes above $6,000. (See Table II) The most striking difference between the three groups is the frequency of home ownership, with garnishees owning homes more often. This difference may in part be attributed to the loss of homes by bankrupts in the bankruptcy proceedings.

■ As Table III indicates, garnishees who did not go

through bankruptcy court often had larger numbers of wage garnishments levied against them than did bankrupts or Chapter 13's. In fact, many of the bankrupts and Chapter 13's reported neither actual garnishment nor threatened garnishment prior to court relief from their debts.

What then distinguishes those who seek government aid to evade debts from those who don't? Indebtedness and assets do not clearly differentiate the three groups, nor do education and occupation. Most debtors, 84 percent to 87 percent, had at least some high-school education. Most were blue-collar workers—craftsmen, foremen, factory workers, or laborers. A small proportion, ranging from 10 percent of the Chapter 13's to 15 percent of the bankrupts were white-collar workers.

Age, however, separates the three groups. Younger debtors go bankrupt more frequently than older ones. Sixty-two percent of the bankrupts were less than 30 years old. Only 43 percent of the Chapter 13's and 37 percent of the gar-

Table II

SELECTED ASSETS OF DEBTORS:
TOTAL FAMILY INCOME, HOME OWNERSHIP

Income	Bankrupts	Chapter 13's	Garnishees
Less than $3000	6.2%	6.1%	5.4%
$3000-5999	47.4%	30.7%	33.9%
$6000-9999	40.7%	57.0%	48.2%
Over $10000	5.7%	6.1%	12.5%
Number of cases	209	65	168
Home Ownership			
Own or buying	21.2%	36.4%	42.1%
Number of cases	212	66	171

nishees were so young. *A majority of the bankrupts were young men in the early years of their family life who had built up high levels of debt, purchasing most of the items needed to establish a household.* Most did not have more than two children living with them. By contrast, the garnishees were a much older group with well-established homes; often their children had already left home so that they too were usually supporting households with two children or less.

Moreover, a relatively high proportion of the debtors were Negroes. While only 2.5 percent of the total population were black, 16 percent of the garnishees, 12 percent of the Chapter 13's, and 9 percent of the bankrupts were Negroes. This is not surprising given the generally high

Table III

ACTUAL AND THREATENED GARNISHMENT

Actual Garnishment	Bankrupts	Chapter 13's	Garnishees
None	44.3%	45.3%	—
1-2	28.8%	22.7%	58.1%
3-5	15.6%	17.3%	30.4%
More than 5	11.3%	14.6%	11.5%
Number of cases	214	75	174
Threatened Garnishment			
Yes	55.6%	72.7%	50.3%
Number of cases	214	77	176

income of Negroes in the four cities and the likelihood that Negroes are more tempted to overpurchase, because of their previously deprived status and because of the hard-sell techniques. That fewer Negroes take advantage of court relief from their debts results from their being among the least efficacious members of society and that they may know courts only from criminal proceedings.

Neither indebtedness, income, education, nor age distinguish Negroes who seek court relief from debts from those who don't. The difference is principally occupational status, with craftsmen and foremen going to bankruptcy court and mainly factory workers being garnished.

A number of characteristics seemingly related to the oc-cupational status of Negroes are present among the whole sample of debtors. High-job status Negroes are relatively well-integrated at their work place and probably better in-tegrated into the general community than lower-occupation status Negroes. Furthermore, they are probably better linked in communication networks through which they may learn about bankruptcy than are lower-status Negroes. These inferences can't be tested here because the number of Negroes in the sample is too small for more detailed analysis. But these hypotheses should also hold true for the entire group of debtors.

The data indicate that there are significant differences between garnishees and bankrupts in the quantity of infor-mation they had and the direction of advice they received about their financial distress. Bankrupts were apparently much better integrated into the legal system than gar-nishees since twice as many bankrupts as garnishees saw an attorney about a previous garnishment. In addition, those who saw an attorney in the two groups received different advice. Only half the bankrupts were advised to make ar-rangements to pay their creditors while 75 percent of the garnishees were given that advice. More than 40 percent of the bankrupts were advised by their attorney to go into bankruptcy; less than 20 percent of the garnishees received such advice. Combining the effects of the propensity to see a lawyer and the advice lawyers gave, we find that almost half of the bankrupts were told to take advantage of bank-ruptcy, while only 5 percent of the garnishees received such advice from a lawyer.

Bankrupts also received different advice from their friends than the garnishees. Far fewer bankrupts reported that their friends advised "doing nothing" or paying their creditors off. Many more reported being advised to see an attorney about their garnishment and a significant proportion (17 percent) were told about bankruptcy, whereas not a single garnishee reported being told about bankruptcy by a friend.

Other data also indicate the importance of integration into a communication network which facilitates the decision to go into bankruptcy. The second most frequent response to "Why did you decide to go into bankruptcy?" was advice from various quarters—most often that advice came from their attorney. In addition, when we asked them where they learned about bankruptcy, lawyers were the most frequently mentioned source of information. Friends, relatives, and people at their place of work followed. The overwhelming proportion of our sample learned about bankruptcy from personal sources rather than from impersonal communications. Indeed, the media were not specifically mentioned by a single one of the almost 200 bankrupt respondents. A final indicator of the importance of personal communications comes from the fact that more than half the bankrupts knew someone else who had gone through bankruptcy.

These data indicate that bankrupts were integrated into the legal system by a communication network which was conversant with bankruptcy proceedings. Although bankrupts varied greatly in their socioeconomic characteristics, they were linked in a loose communication network. They apparently learned about bankruptcy with relative ease and received support from the various people from whom they heard about bankruptcy. All of this contrasts sharply with the experience of garnishees. Garnishees, although in financial difficulty, were shut out of that network. Thus they did not learn about bankruptcy, were not encouraged to use it, and were not in contact with the professionals who might facilitate their use of it.

Neither creditors nor debtors used the courts to the same extent in the four cities studied. Nor did the variation in

Table IV

GARNISHMENT AND BANKRUPTCY ACTIONS
FOR 12 MONTH PERIOD:

	Madison	Racine	Kenosha	Green Bay
Garnishments	2860	2740	813	130
per 1000 pop.	22.6	30.7	12.0	2.1
Bankruptcies	112	100	63	32
Chapter 13's	37	18	5	7
Total BK-13 per 1000 pop.	1.17	1.32	1.0	.62

garnishment and bankruptcy rates in the four cities conform to social, economic, or partisan factors. (See Table IV) Each of the cities had approximately the same degree of prosperity during the period studied. The proportion of families with incomes in the range where garnishment and bankruptcy most frequently occurs ($3,000-$10,000) was almost identical for Madison, Racine, and Kenosha. Green Bay had slightly more such families but this scarcely explains its *lower* garnishment and bankruptcy rate. All cities had small nonwhite populations. Racine has the largest Negro community consisting of 5.4 percent of its population. Only .9 percent of Green Bay's population was nonwhite, principally Indian. And though there are no available figures on the amount of credit extended in the four cities, the differences in retail sales for the four do not explain the differences in garnishment and bankruptcy rates.

The only factor clearly explaining the different rates of garnishment and bankruptcy in the four cities might be called the "public" or "legal" culture. Excluding garnishment and bankruptcy, the frequency with which civil court cases are initiated in the four cities closely follows debtor case rates. (See Table V) The highest rate occurs in Racine, with Madison, Kenosha, and Green Bay following. As expected, the criminal rates differ since they are initiated by public officials. Civil cases, for the most part, are initiated by private citizens. All civil litigation reflects, it then seems, a set of peculiar institutional and cultural patterns that are not evident in the standard socioeconomic indexes ordinarily applied to these cities.

Robert Alford and Harry M. Scoble's study of these four cities and their municipal decision-making processes

Table V

CIVIL AND CRIMINAL CASES IN FOUR COUNTIES, JULY 1, 1964-JULY 1, 1965

Civil Cases	Dane (Madison)	Racine	Kenosha	Brown (Green Bay)
County and Circuit Court	1691	817	1203	803
Small Claims Court (minus garnishment)	4203	3024	743	233
Civil Case Rate 1000 pop.	26.5	27.0	19.5	8.2
Criminal Cases (excluding ordinance)	3195	1020	867	722
Rate/1000 pop.	15.8	7.2	8.6	5.8

suggests that they represent distinct political cultures. They label these cultures as (1) *traditional conservatism* (Green Bay), government is essentially passive, a caretaker of law and order, not an active instrument for social or private goals; (2) *traditional liberalism* (Kenosha), "the bargaining process may even extend to traditional services . . .;" (3) *modern conservatism* (Racine), government is legitimately active, but furthering private economic interests that *liberalism* (Madison), "a high level of political involve-ment . . . may itself exacerbate conflicts. . . ." Alford and Scoble concentrate on the liberal-conservative dimensions of the four cities, by focusing on the kinds of public de-cisions made and the range of participation in the decision-making process. When we examine litigation rates, how-ever, the cities cluster on the traditional-modern dimension. It appears that Green Bay and Kenosha share low litiga-tion rates because of more traditional public cultures, while Racine and Madison share higher litigation rates because of their more modern public culture. Data from our interviews provide supporting evidence for this conclusion.

Less frequent use of public facilities to settle private conflicts is congruent with the concept of a traditional American public culture. Depending more on personal and less on bureaucratic ways of settling disputes, the tradi-tional culture leads to dependence on personal contact be-tween the principals.

Taking a debtor to court is a highly impersonal pro-ceeding involving the use of public officials as intermedi-aries and arbiters. Interview data indicate that in Green Bay and Kenosha firms and professionals collecting delin-quent accounts depend more on the use of personal con-tacts, telephone calls to the debtor, or informal arrange-ments with employers. In Green Bay, where the garnish-ment rate is lowest, attorneys and creditors often asserted that the city was small enough for everyone to know every-one else, making court action unnecessary. But Green Bay has only 5,000 fewer inhabitants than Kenosha (where no respondents mentioned the intimacy of the town) and is only one-third smaller than Racine which has the highest garnishment rate. Nevertheless, the exaggeration of its small size is significant, since the perception of Green Bay as a small town fits the description of its traditional culture.

The lower garnishment rate also fits Alford's description of these traditional cities as ones in which the business elite does not look upon government as an instrument to obtain private objectives. Passive government and informal bargaining typify many public situations in Green Bay and Kenosha, with the debt-collection process being just one manifestation. In Madison and Racine, creditor-debtor conflicts, like public disputes, more frequently reach official government agencies—in this case, the court—for formal adjudication.

Alford's characterization of these cities leads us to look for differences in the degree to which the people are fiscally traditional.

For the most part, these expectations are confirmed by the debtor interviews. Slightly more debtors in Green Bay than elsewhere thought banks were the best place to borrow money and an overwhelming proportion thought finance companies the worst source of loans.

But Kenosha does not fit the expected pattern, falling instead between Madison and Racine in both ratings. The same is true for actual behavior of the debtors: Fewer Green Bay debtors reported finance companies as their biggest source of loans; the highest proportion using finance companies was in Racine. On another behavioral indicator, more Madison debtors showed an inclination to approve borrowing for a wider range of items than Racine, Kenosha, or Green Bay debtors. The ordering of the cities followed our expectation closely though not exactly: Madison, Racine, Kenosha, Green Bay. Finally, a related indicator showed Green Bay debtors to be more aware of interest rates on their loans than Madison, Kenosha, and Racine debtors—traditional norms of consumer behavior emphasize cost rather than immediacy of purchase. These data support Alford and Scoble's characterization of Green Bay and Kenosha as traditional and Madison and Racine as modern. The patterns distinguishing the public decision-making styles of these cities apparently spill over to private use of judicial agencies by both creditors and debtors.

Traditionalism also affects the legal culture. Only in Green Bay did most of the attorneys handling garnishment cases send out letters to the debtors prior to initiating the court action despite the cases having been extensively worked over by the creditor's collection department or a collection agency. Attorneys in Green Bay were more concerned about avoiding formal court action than attorneys in the other three cities, who reported that they immediately filed for court action unless they knew there had not been an active effort to collect.

Everything cannot be explained by cultural differences between the communities. The higher incidence of Chapter 13 proceedings as compared to bankruptcies in some of the cities is due to different evaluations of Chapter 13 by attorneys and to pressure exerted by the referees in bankruptcy. Where Chapter 13 proceedings are most frequent (in Madison and Racine), debtors report that lawyers often give them a real choice between it and bankruptcy. In Kenosha and Green Bay, lawyers rarely talk about Chapter 13 to bankruptcy clients and since these clients rarely heard of Chapter 13 from other sources, fewer used it.

Differences in attorney behavior are largely accounted for by the pressures they feel from the referee in bankruptcy and their relation to the Chapter 13 trustee, who handles the debtors affairs while he is under the plan. In Madison, the lawyer's preference for Chapter 13 proceedings can be traced to active campaigning in favor of it by the Madison Referee in Bankruptcy. Racine's higher Chapter 13 rate reflects the fact that the trustee was a fellow

Racine attorney, readily available on the telephone for consultation. Kenosha attorneys who also had to use the Racine trustee felt that Chapter 13 cases were beyond their control. They hesitated to incur the slight charge for a call to neighboring Racine. They preferred amortization under state law (although it provided less protection for the debtor) because they could maintain control over the proceedings and keep in close contact with the debtor who might later bring them higher fees in an accident or divorce case. Green Bay and Madison attorneys almost never used Wisconsin's amortization proceeding and did not speak of it as a lure to attract clients in better paying cases.

With only four cities, it is statistically impossible to estimate how much of the variation is explained by the political culture, by the legal culture, and by what appear to be accidental variations. Nevertheless, the wide variations discovered among four cities are significant.

This exploration of court usage in wage garnishment and consumer bankruptcy actions shows none of the usual political links between governmental action and private demands. To look for partisan biases of the judges (or referees), for evidence of other attitudinal biases in their decisions, for the linkage between the judicial selection process and court decisions, for the role of other political activities in this process, we would come away convinced that wage garnishment and bankruptcy are totally nonpolitical processes. Only an examination of patronage shows political processes at work, since the referees may appoint at will Chapter 13 trustees and trustees for all bankrupt estates. But Chapter 13 cases don't generate a great deal of revenue for the trustees and most straight bankruptcies by consumers involve either no or very limited assets so that the trustees benefit little from the cases. In the usual *partisan* sense, the processes examined are indeed nonpolitical.

Nevertheless, the courts are very political. Garnishment and bankruptcy cases invoke government power for private ends. Garnishment redistributes millions of dollars each year from the wages of debtors to the accounts of creditors. Bankruptcy results in the cancellation of other millions of dollars of indebtedness. The use of these court procedures also involves frequent harassment and considerable stigmatization. Although garnishment and bankruptcy are considered "private" proceedings, they significantly affect the distribution of material and symbolic values by government in the United States.

Thus it is politically significant that only a few of all eligible creditors and debtors use garnishment and bankruptcy proceedings. It means that government power is used to buoy what many consider to be the socially least desirable form of consumer credit—that extended by finance companies. The experience of wage earners with garnishment is likely to undermine their confidence in the courts as institutions which treat them justly and fairly. On the other hand, the use of bankruptcy by the minority of those eligible for it limits its benefits to the small group which happens to be well integrated into the legal system. Translating these findings to larger cities, it seems likely that in ghetto areas garnishment has even more disadvantageous effects in supporting undesirable credit and bankruptcy is even less used by the masses of alienated consumers who crowd the inner core.

The political process described is quite different from the electoral or legislative political processes political scientists ordinarily study. Instead, it resembles the administrative process which is becoming increasingly significant. The use of agricultural extension services, the use of counseling and educational services by the poor, the use of higher-education facilities by the young raise problems similar to those of court usage. None of these, however, involve, as wage garnishment and bankruptcy do, the dramatic use of the government coercive power for private objectives.

Government power can be invoked through far more routine ways than campaigning in elections. The consumption of government services is based on far different objectives than the ordinary use of government power through partisan means. Court actions, as well as other administrative decisions, frequently affect the core of people's personal behavior, their life-style, or fortune. They can color people's perception of the government and generate support for or alienation from it. We need to know what individuals and groups use such services and how they use them.

May 1969

FURTHER READING SUGGESTED BY THE AUTHOR:

Buy Now, Pay Later by Hillel Black (New York: Pocket Books, 1961) is an expose of credit schemes.
The Poor Pay More by David Caplovitz (New York: Macmillan-Free Press, 1963) describes the credit problems of impecunious consumers.

Double Standard
of American Justice

STUART S. NAGEL / LENORE J. WEITZMAN

Are women treated equally in American courts? Or does
sexism tip the scales of American justice against women
when they are defendants and litigants before the bar? In
the literature dealing with women's rights, researchers have
found that "in several states, higher penalties are imposed
on a woman who commits the same crime." However, this
conclusion is based on those few state statutes and appellate test cases which describe the law on the books
rather than law in action. Our research will focus instead
on the law in action. We will ask if, in practice, women are
sentenced to more time in prison than men for the same
crimes. Are women favored or disfavored in criminal,
personal injury and divorce proceedings? How does the
presence of women jurors and judges affect the relative
treatment of male and female litigants?

Analogies are frequently drawn between the treatment
of women and blacks in many areas (e.g., employment) of

American society. Is this similarity applicable to the courtroom? A comparison of black-white and male-female
sentencing practices is examined for comparative insights.

Women as Criminal Defendants

In 1962, Lee Silverstein of the American Bar Foundation (ABF) compiled data on 11,258 criminal cases, using
194 counties located in all 50 states as his sample. While
the main focus of his study was on procedures for providing attorneys to indigent defendants, Silverstein also
gathered information on the race, sex and age of the
defendants and the treatment they received at all stages
of the criminal justice process—from preliminary hearing
through sentencing.

Two basic patterns of discrimination emerge. The first—
the disadvantaged pattern—involves unfavorable treatment
of defendants who are poor, black or have only elementary
education. These defendants in socially inferior positions
receive unfavorable treatment at virtually all stages of the
criminal justice process, including 1) receiving a preliminary hearing, 2) being released on bail, 3) having a hired
attorney rather than assigned counsel or no attorney, 4)
being subjected to relatively shorter pretrial detainment
while in jail if not released on bail, 5) receiving a jury
trial, 6) being dismissed or being acquitted, 7) receiving
probation or a suspended sentence if convicted and 8) receiving a relatively short sentence if jailed.

The second discriminatory syndrome—the paternalistic
pattern—particularly applies to juvenile offenders and involves unfavorable treatment only in the area of safeguards
for the innocent, such as having an attorney or a jury trial.
It involves favorable treatment, however, in being kept out
of jail pending trial, in not being convicted and in not
being sentenced to jail if convicted.

Both the disadvantaged and paternalistic patterns of discrimination against women are apparent to some degree in the ABF findings. However, when female criminal defendants are compared with their male counterparts, the resulting treatment pattern most readily fits the paternalistic mold. Paternalistic discrimination against and for women, as in the case of juveniles, is found in both grand larceny cases and in felonious assault cases, although women are somewhat more likely to be jailed when they commit assault. Due perhaps to the fact that assault is considered a more masculine type of crime than larceny, women's and men's jail sentences correspond more closely in these cases.

To the extent that male and female larceny and assault cases are comparable, the data suggest that the difference in treatment may be explained by a judicial attitude which assumes women (and juveniles) to be weaker, and therefore more likely to be harmed by pretrial and postconviction jailing.

Although blacks and indigents are particularly discriminated against when it comes to being released on bail, in the larceny and assault cases studied, the opposite holds true for women (Table 1). Of the 63 female larceny defendants, 76 percent were released on bail, while of the 771 male larceny defendants, only 50 percent were released on bail—a 26 percent difference. This practice works to avoid keeping juveniles and women in jail pending trial or after conviction. The same pretrial jail-avoidance phenomenon is evident in the assault cases, where there is a 19 percent difference.

Likewise, the data show that women receive more lenient treatment if they are convicted in grand larceny cases; 64 percent of the women received a suspended sentence or probation, as compared to only 43 percent of

TABLE I: HOW THE TREATMENT OF FEMALES DIFFERS FROM MALES AS DEFENDANTS IN CRIMINAL CASES

		DEFENDANTS Receiving Treatment		
GRAND LARCENY CASES				
	Females	%	Males	%
BEING JAILED				
Released on bail	63	76	771	50
Had less than 2 months delay of those awaiting trial in jail	10	60	231	67
Case dismissed or acquitted	71	24	841	13
Received suspended sentence or probation of those convicted	47	64	656	43
Received less than one year imprisonment of those imprisoned	9	33	241	45
FORMAL SAFEGUARDS				
Received preliminary hearing	42	57	606	55
Had or given a lawyer	61	90	781	87
Received a jury trial of those tried	18	47	283	31
FELONIOUS ASSAULT CASES				
BEING JAILED				
Released on bail	43	77	615	58
Had less than 2 months delay of those awaiting trial in jail	6	17	152	49
Case dismissed or acquitted	45	36	638	23
Received suspended sentence or probation of those convicted	25	44	415	36
Received less than one year imprisonment of those imprisoned	9	89	172	57
FORMAL SAFEGUARDS				
Received preliminary hearing	31	74	451	73
Had or given a lawyer	42	88	620	89
Received a jury trial of those tried	24	19	262	45

the men. A related although weaker difference is also apparent in the felonious assault cases studied.

Of those defendants who actually received jail sentences, there are too few (20 or less) women in the sample who were jailed pending trial or imprisoned after conviction to make a meaningful comparison possible on length of imprisonment. Possibly as a means of avoiding imprisonment and the stigma of a criminal record, fewer women are convicted than their male counterparts. The study shows that 24 percent of the women were acquitted or had their larceny cases dismissed, as compared to only 13 percent of the men. A similar difference is present in the assault cases cited.

Convicted defendants given indeterminate sentences were not included when computing the number imprisoned because these sentences lack the necessary precision for comparison. Of the 363 women sentenced in the total sample, 27 percent received indeterminate sentences, while 35 percent of the 5,898 men's sentences were indeterminate. Although these sentences are usually associated with such crimes as murder and arson (which men are more likely to commit), men usually receive a slightly higher percentage of indeterminate sentences than do women for the same type of crime. Such sentences generally have higher maximums than fixed terms and may result in longer prison stays.

When it comes to formal safeguards for the innocent, judicial treatment is mixed. When women defendants are compared with men defendants in either larceny cases or assault cases with respect to having a lawyer, no discriminatory pattern emerges. Likewise, no discrimination is evident with regard to receiving a preliminary hearing, although this is probably not as important a safeguard for the innocent as are having counsel or receiving a jury trial.

(Of these three safeguards, only preliminary hearings have not been made a due process right for adults by the Supreme Court.)

However, women—in conformity with the paternalism hypothesis—are more likely to receive informal treatment with regard to not receiving a jury trial, at least in the assault cases, where the percentage difference between men and women is 26. This disparity is contrary to the best interests of women, because juries are generally less likely to convict than are judges. To be convicted by a jury normally requires the unanimous agreement of 12 persons, a task harder for the prosecutor to achieve than that of convincing a single judge. The University of Chicago Jury Project research indicates that while both juries and judges tend to favor women in their criminal verdicts, juries do so to a greater extent.

Although the numbers are small, a comparison of women by race indicates that white women are less likely to be jailed before or after conviction than are black women, and they are also less likely to have a lawyer to represent them. This is because they are less apt than blacks to be so poor that they are appointed counsel by the court. And while black women (unlike black men) receive more favorable treatment than do white men with regard to being jailed before or after conviction—in this case, sexual paternalism and racial discrimination are mixed—there is no consistent pattern whereby black women receive or do not receive a jury trial. Therefore, white women seem to fit the paternalistic mold more neatly.

The ABF data, then, indicate that women are substantially less likely to be held in jail before or after trial, but are more likely to lack a jury trial. While all the differences discussed were sufficiently significant that they could not readily be attributed to chance, some of them might be attributable to the fact that women commit grand larcenies and felonious assaults on a less grand scale than men do, and that therefore they have less at stake to merit a jury trial and less guilt to merit a severe sentence.

It is interesting to note that male juveniles and female adults are treated about equally. Although the male juveniles are less likely to have an attorney, a jury trial or a preliminary hearing, the female adults are more likely to be kept out of jail before and after conviction.

In addition to assuming that women are weaker and more open to harm from jailing, judges may also give shorter sentences to women than to men convicted of similar crimes because they think this weaker nature also makes women less dangerous to society, more easily deterred from repeating their crime and more speedily rehabilitated. Custodial care, deterrence from further crime and rehabilitation being the official goals of imprisonment in any case, women are thus already assumed to be in a position of conforming to them. Women and especially juveniles are also less likely to be hardened criminals—in the sense that they are somewhat less likely to have prior criminal records.

Likewise, judges might feel that both juveniles and women should be treated in a more fatherly, less legalistic way, and that jury trials and defense counsel interfere with this paternalistic informality.

The few statutes which provide different sentences for women and men for the same type of crime generally provide more indeterminate sentences for women, just as juvenile statutes provide more indeterminate sentences for juveniles. The legislators who pass these laws probably believe that women and juveniles are more accessible to rehabilitation than are adult males, and that indeterminate sentences contingent on progress made in prison will facilitate rehabilitation. (However, we know that indeterminate sentences usually result in a longer period of incarceration.) Testing this explanation would require determining the legislators' attitudes, although the judges who apply criminal statutes allowing for discretion are probably more instrumental to the increase or decrease of sexual discrimination than are the legislators who write them into law.

Women as Personal Injury Plaintiffs

In personal injury cases, where the defendant is usually an insurance company rather than an individual man or woman, the difference in the sex of the plaintiffs who have suffered personal injuries may be an important variable. How do sex differences affect treatment received?

There are separate stages at which discrimination can occur in personal injury cases—the first being whether or not the injured party files a complaint.

In Alfred Conard's 1964 study of the economics of personal injury cases in the state of Michigan, he compiled data on the background characteristics of automobile accident victims who subsequently became personal injury claimants. His key sex data (Table 2) show that of the seriously injured male accident victims, 38 percent filed suit, whereas of the seriously injured female accident victims, only 30 percent filed suit. This difference might be due to a higher rate of precomplaint settlements for women or to less severe injuries sustained by them. An even more telling explanation might be that women are encouraged to be less aggressive in asserting their legal rights in personal injury cases.

Once the suit is filed, the next stage is establishing the defendant's liability to pay something to the injured plain-

TABLE II: HOW THE TREATMENT OF FEMALES DIFFERS
FROM MALES AS VICTIMS AND PLAINTIFFS
IN PERSONAL INJURY CASES

	Female Plaintiffs	Male Plaintiffs
SUIT FILED		
Suit filed by seriously injured victim	30%	38%
LIABILITY ESTABLISHED		
Claim was paid in bodily injury cases	80%	77%
Victory in jury trial cases (to plaintiffs of all ages)	61%	62%
Victory in jury trial cases (to adult plaintiffs)	69%	76%
AVERAGE AMOUNT AWARDED		
Award in jury trial cases (to plaintiffs of all ages)	—2% below average	+1% above average
Award in jury trial cases (to adult plaintiffs)	—2% below average	+6% above average
Award for loss of victim's services (to spouse plaintiffs)	$5,585	$6,524
Award for victim's death (to spouse plaintiffs where victim employed age 21-29)	$67,524	$39,820
Award for urinogenital injuries	$11,835	$31,966

tiff. The 1970 Department of Transportation study of personal injury claims (which used nationwide data) shows that there is virtually no difference between men and women in the likelihood of their winning claims (see Table 2). It is interesting to note that there is a lower victory rate in cases which go to a jury decision as compared to cases heard by a judge or settled without coming to trial—possibly because the nontrial cases more clearly favor the plaintiff—but there is no differentiation related to whether the plaintiffs are men or women.

A discriminatory pattern begins to appear if one leaves out minors and compares only adult male plaintiffs with adult female plaintiffs, since adult males win 76 percent of their jury trials and adult females only 69 percent of theirs. Sexual discrimination seems less prevalent in the comparison between boy and girl minors (especially preteenage minors) because the tendency is to class them simply as "children." The data reveal, however, that adults, whether male or female, have a better chance of winning their cases than children of either sex, probably because children frequently contribute through negligence to their own injuries, and juries tend to identify more closely with adult defendants than with child plaintiffs.

Once liability has been established, the next stage involves determining the amount of money to be awarded. Again there is little difference in the average amount awarded to male and female plaintiffs when adults and minors are grouped together, although a small percentage difference may involve a substantial number of dollars. However, the pattern of amounts awarded is again more favorable to men when only adults are compared: men received 6 percent above the average personal injury award for similar cases of injury with similar compensation for medical expenses and lost wages, while women averaged 2 percent below this figure.

The more interesting male-female comparisons relate to specific kinds of personal injuries. For instance, when husbands sue for loss of consortium (affection and sex) caused by their wives' injuries they collect more than when wives sue for loss of consortium caused by their husbands' injuries. This is so even though when women sue for their own injuries, they tend to collect less than men do. Our data also shows that there are more than 11 times as many suits by husbands for the loss of their wives' services as by wives for the loss of their husbands' services—another odd phenomenon. Does this represent the fact that more wives than husbands suffer personal injuries, or is it rather a reflection of outmoded legal tradition? It would seem to be the latter, for in fact, these 28 suits in which the wife is plaintiff represent a sizeable increase over the three such cases shown in the 1964 Jury Verdict Research Report, and in some states the law still permits only husbands—and not wives—to sue for loss of a spouse's services—a holdover from the time when wives were considered part of their husbands' property—and one's property cannot sue for damages to the owner of the property. It may also have been felt unseemly for a woman to sue for the loss of the sexual services of her husband.

The generally larger amounts awarded to male plaintiffs for their personal injuries may be in part explained by the greater earning power of males, which may be temporarily or permanently reduced by the injury. This greater earning power may reflect employment and educational discrimination against women over which personal injury juries have no control. In cases where the injury results in death, male victims are clearly valued more highly than women in terms of monetary awards; because of this, women seem to be favored as plaintiffs. However, it must be remembered that where a wife-plaintiff is seeking to collect for a killed husband rather than a husband-plaintiff for a killed wife, one is mixing favoritism as to the victim's sex with discrimination as to the plaintiff's sex.

Differences in the amounts awarded to male and female plaintiffs for injuries not generally related to an individual's work capacity cannot be readily explained in terms of differential earning power. Urinogenital injuries fall into this category, and the inequality pattern here is greater than with any other type of bodily injury. In the sample studied, the average male plaintiff who wins a urinogenital injury case collects $31,966, while the average female plaintiff collects only $11,385. This represents an absolute difference of $20,131 or 170 percent. Monetary awards for injury to male genitalia run almost three times as high as those for injury to female genitalia—a direct indication of an apparently sexist value system in American courts.

Some of the difference may be accounted for by the fact that urinogenital damage was usually more severe and more likely to be permanent among the male plaintiffs. Because the child-bearing capacity of women is especially valued in American society, a more useful comparison would be between women who lose their capacity to bear children with men who lose their potency.

An overall view of the findings seems to reveal a pattern in which adult women are less likely than men to file suit, to establish liability and to receive a relatively high award, especially for certain types of injury. In this regard, the pattern of discrimination against women resembles that of black plaintiffs rather than juveniles. The victory rate for black plaintiffs was 57 percent as compared to a general rate of 61 percent and a rate of 46 percent for children under 12. Damage awards to black plaintiffs averaged 15 percent lower than the general level of awards. If children collect anything in court, they tend to get either very small or very large awards. This uneven distribution gives them an average award close to that of the general population. In personal injury cases, children, blacks and women, in that order, do worse on liability than adults, whites and men. Given this order of discrimination on a victory-rate continuum, women plaintiffs are thus closer to blacks than to children in the treatment they receive. On a damages-awarded continuum, however, women are closer to children than to blacks, with blacks farthest behind.

The basic issue in personal injury cases is whether the

plaintiff succeeds in collecting money for damages. Since women are usually less favored in economic matters in our society, a similar pattern of negative discrimination should be evident in personal injury cases. This has, on examination, turned out to be correct. The paternalism hypothesis, which made some sense in relation to the treatment of women as criminal defendants, cannot be applied in the same terms to personal injury plaintiffs, because they are not in jeopardy of being placed in jail or stigmatized with criminal records. It could, however, be defined here as favoritism toward the weak in imposing negative sanctions, but disfavoritism in awarding or enforcing monetary awards. If it is so defined, we can legitimately say that the discrimination women experience fits both the disadvantaged and the paternalistic patterns. Its causes are probably the traditional subordination of women in the family, employment and educational discrimination, the rationing of scarce monetary resources, and even, in some cases, a Freudian castration fear and other sexual anxieties, as indicated by the huge discrepancy in awards for loss of urinogenital functions. As contemporary pressures for societal and legal change steadily erode these causal factors, differential victory rates and damages awarded should become more nearly equal.

Women as Divorce Litigants

The predominant impression among the general public is that divorce cases are a manifestation of female domination or even exploitation of men, because normally only women litigants seek and obtain alimony or child support. Despite this prevailing opinion, the facts about women as divorce litigants could well be said to show actual male domination and even exploitation.

In a sample of divorce cases in 22 states taken in 1963,

wives were plaintiffs in 72 percent of the cases. Yet, even where women are the formal plaintiffs, existing data indicate this is often really a nominal status, and in reality it is the husband who has taken the de facto rather than the de jure initiative in dissolving the marriage. William Goode, on the basis of extensive interviews with a sample of 425 divorced women in 1956, concluded that "the husband more frequently than the wife is the first to desire a divorce, and it is the husband more often than the wife who adopts (whether consciously or not) a line of behavior which forces the other spouse to suggest a divorce as the appropriate solution."

Among the poor, desertion by the husband is a frequent substitute for divorce and is a major cause of eligibility for welfare aid. In the year 1967, 76 percent of the 1.3 million Aid to Dependent Children families in the United States had fathers absent from the home. Once again the man appears to be the active partner in the dissolution of the family.

The fact that wives seem to have better formal grounds for divorce and thus become the plaintiff-complainants may possibly show greater provocation on the part of husbands. An alternative explanation is that both husband and wife recognize that the wife has a better chance of winning the case. In divorce cases where decrees were granted, the wife as plaintiff lost only about 2 percent of the time, whereas the husband as plaintiff lost about 10 percent of the time. Although women have become more independent as a result of increased employment opportunities, they are still more economically dependent upon their husbands than their husbands are on them and would therefore tend to resist divorce were it not for their husbands' provocation, which may take the form of cruelty, nonsupport, desertion or some other ground.

In descriptions of the divorce trial process, there are many references to the often degrading paternalistic procedures to which women litigants are subjected. Begging for alimony may be particularly degrading, even if alimony is considered 1) income accrued as a result of inadequately compensated wifehood and motherhood and 2) payment for obtaining educational rehabilitation and training. Seeking child support may also be a frustrating ordeal, even if the judge recognizes the concept as covering both some of the considerable work the mother must do in caring for her children and some of the many out-of-pocket expenses involved in raising the children which the husband has fathered. Although it might at first glance appear to be a victory when the wife obtains custody of and responsibility for the children, which she does in about 95 percent of cases, husbands in fact admitted that about 85 percent of the time they agreed with the custody decrees.

A double standard of morality may also prevail in custody disputes, condemning extramarital activities by wives but tolerating them on the part of husbands. In some states, the double standard actually allows husbands to obtain a divorce on sexual grounds which are not allowed to wives—as, for example, a common provision that allows husbands to divorce wives who were pregnant at the time of the marriage, whereas there is no comparable legislation allowing wives to divorce husbands who have made other women pregnant at the time of the marriage.

The real test of possible discrimination in the judicial process comes not at the stage of initiation or filing suit, nor even at the stage of judgment, but rather at the stage of that judgment's enforcement. To a lesser extent, this reasoning also applies to criminal and personal injury cases, but a far higher percentage of the results of such cases are determined at the prejudgment stage. In addition, there seems to be no data available on the collection of personal injury damages by sex—as distinct from the awarding of damages—nor on the paroling of convicts by sex. We do however have some data on the monetary judgments awarded to women divorce litigants.

Table 3 illustrates the probability of a divorced woman being able to collect any child-support money. It is based on data gathered by Kenneth Eckhardt from a sample of fathers who were ordered to pay child support in divorce decrees in a metropolitan county in Wisconsin in 1955. Within one year after the divorce decree, only 38 percent of the fathers were fully complying with the support order. Twenty percent had only partially complied, and in some cases partial compliance constituted only one payment. Forty-two percent of the fathers had made no payment at all. By the tenth year, the number of open cases had dropped from 163 to 149 because of the death of the father, termination of his parental rights or the maturity of the children. By that year, only 13 percent of the fathers were fully complying and 79 percent were in total noncompliance.

If noncompliance with child-support orders is so great, we can reasonably expect it to be even greater with alimony orders, although alimony orders are in fact relatively infrequent. In a 1956 analysis of 12,000 Chicago divorce cases, the wife requested post-divorce alimony in only 7 percent of the cases. In 1922, the last year the United States Census Bureau kept alimony data, their figures showed alimony decreed in only 15 percent of a nationwide sample, although women were considerably less independent at that time.

Of 172,000 minor children involved in divorces in Chicago in the period 1949-50, one-third were awarded no child support at all. It should also be noted that the original child-support orders given by a court probably do not meet the full support needs of the children. Some of the orders may also be further judicially reduced when the husband remarries or when his financial status otherwise worsens. Thus, if only a minority of husbands are paying anything at all, and those husbands are paying only a substantially less than full support order, this means in practice that most of the actual child support is being carried by the mother or by the state.

In spite of potential sanctions such as contempt of court, civil action and criminal prosecution and despite the considerable incentive to the state to avoid unnecessary welfare payments, legal action is seldom initiated against the nonpaying father. This is especially the case as the children grow older and probably require even more support money. Yet Table 3 shows that only 19 percent of the 101 nonpaying fathers at the end of the first year had legal action taken against them, and in the tenth year only 1 percent of the 128 nonpaying fathers were faced with legal action. Indeed, monetary divorce awards may well be the least complied with and the least enforced of criminal or civil court orders.

The explanation for the lack of enforcement is not that the fathers are unable to comply. Support orders take into account the father's ability to pay. In fact, working-class fathers, though less financially well off, are more likely to be prosecuted than are middle-class fathers, because their ex-wives are more likely to be on welfare, and they themselves are more likely to have criminal records. The explanation for general nonenforcement of support orders probably lies in the pro-male bias of the prosecutors, judges and legislators who could more effectively enforce the law if they cared to. Some of the nonenforcement may also be due to the greater complexity of nonsupport cases (espe-

TABLE III: THE POSSIBILITY OF A DIVORCED WOMAN COLLECTING ANY CHILD SUPPORT MONEY

Years Since Court Order	Number of Open Cases	Full	Compli-ance Partial	No	Non-paying Fathers*
One	163	38%	20%	42%	19%
Two	163	28	20	52	32
Three	161	26	14	60	21
Four	161	22	11	67	18
Five	160	19	14	67	9
Six	158	17	12	71	6
Seven	157	17	12	71	4
Eight	155	17	8	75	2
Nine	155	17	8	75	0
Ten	149	13	8	79	1

* Nonpaying fathers against whom legal action was taken.
Based on data from Kenneth Eckhardt, "Deviance, Visibility, and Legal Action: The Duty to Support," 15 *Social Problems* 470, 473-74 (1968).

cially where there is a question of interstate enforcement) and to the less current nature of nonsupport decrees, as compared to the crush of other cases.

A realistic remedy for the nonenforcement of child-support orders may lie not in the more vigorous prosecution of errant males—although in some flagrant cases this might be merited—but in the imposition of some system of social insurance to cover the situation and preserve the dignity of those concerned. The concept of survivorship under Social Security could be expanded to include children of a deserting or divorced father, as well as of a deceased father. Other social alternatives include child allowances, the negative income tax or an expanded Family Assistance Plan. A national program of wholesome, well-run daycare centers and a government stimulation of possible employment opportunities would also enable those women who wish to work to support themselves and their children to do so, rather than have to ask for child support or welfare.

Effect of the Sex of the Jury

The amount and direction of inequality between treatment of male and female litigants may be affected by whether the judge is a man or a woman and the predominance of male or female jurors. While there is a significant lack of female judges and a corresponding lack of data comparing them with male judges in their treatment of male and female litigants, it may be possible to extrapolate some findings about male and female jurors to male and female judges. (The concern here is with the effect of the sex ratio of judicial decision-makers on discrimination against women as litigants. Studies that deal with the effect on sentences or awards in general are not directly relevant. However, such studies do show that housewives are less punitive in burglary and possibly in other theft cases too, but more punitive in father-daughter incest and possibly other male-female sex crimes.)

There are five meaningful hypotheses which one can formulate about the effect of the jurors' own sex on their treatment of male and female defendants in criminal and personal injury cases. (Since jury trials are a rare occurrence in divorce cases, they will not be considered here.) One hypothesis might be called the attraction-of-opposites hypothesis, predicting that men will favor women and women men. "If you are representing a personable young man," advises John Appleman in his *Successful Jury Trials* (1952), "try to seat kindly old ladies in the jury box. If you are presenting an attractive young woman, have as many male jurors, old or young, as possible."

Second is the chivalry hypothesis, which predicts that

men will favor women and women will also favor women, because women need special treatment. A third, the brain-washing hypothesis, says men and women both favor men because they have both been indoctrinated to believe men are more valuable. Fourth is the equality hypothesis, which says men favor neither sex, and women favor neither sex. This is the implicit or explicit hypothesis in those court cases which have held that it is not a denial of equal protection for a state to systematically decrease the chances of women serving on juries. Fifth is the likes-attract-likes hypothesis, which says men favor men and women favor women.

With regard to criminal cases, the most relevant data appear in a study by Arnold Rose and Arthur Prell. In 1953, they asked a sample of students taking courses in introductory sociology and social psychology at the University of Minnesota what sentences they would hand down if they were serving as judges or jurors in a variety of hypothetical fact situations. One situation involved a male convicted of a certain crime. Another, placed elsewhere on the list of situations, involved a female convicted of the same crime. The male respondents tended to give the male defendant a lower sentence than the female defendant, whereas the female respondents tended to give the female defendant a lower sentence than the male defendant. In other words, men tended to favor males and women tended to favor females. To the extent that this finding can be extrapolated to real juries or real judges, it confirms the likes-attract-likes hypothesis.

There is data available from the Jury Verdict Research Corporation on the way actual juries have treated females as distinct from males in personal injury cases, taking into consideration the sex of the jury. The study answers two questions: "If I know the sex of the plaintiff, what can I predict with regard to victory and damages before male-dominated and female-dominated juries?" and, "If I know the dominant sex of the jury, what can I predict with regard to victory and damages for male and female plaintiffs?"

Both parts of the study show that controlling for the sex of the jury makes no significant differences with regard to establishing liability. Both parts, however, show that controlling for the sex of the jury does make a substantial difference with regard to the average amount awarded. For instance, male-dominated juries gave awards to male plaintiffs that were 12 percent above the average to be expected for the type of injury, medical expenses and lost wages, whereas male-dominated juries gave female plaintiffs awards 17 percent below the average expected. Female-dominated juries reversed the direction of favoritism between female and male plaintiffs, further reinforcing the data that the likes-attract-likes hypothesis is the valid one, at least for average amounts awarded.

Discrimination, or at least inequality, between men and women seems to be greater in the amount of damages awarded than in the establishment of liability. This may be attributed to the fact that extremely large awards, those over $100,000 for instance, tend to be rendered for work accidents that result in crippling injuries—and relatively few women are injured in such circumstances. But some of the liability-damages difference may be because the differential earning power rationale only applies to assessing damages, not to establishing liability, and male jurors may place more emphasis on that rationale.

Much of the difference may also be attributed to the greater subjectivity involved in determining the extent of damages, which allows prejudice to enter more readily than in the more legalistic decision involved in establishing liability. Likewise the greater inequality present at the bail and sentencing stages in criminal cases, as compared to the pretrial procedural safeguards, may also be partly attributable to the relatively greater subjectivity and lesser legalistic restraint involved in the setting of bail and sentencing.

Because the disparities in the treatment of male and female litigants can be affected by the sex of the decision-makers, this should be further reason for society to seek out more women judges and jurors, in addition to the reasoning that emphasizes more democratic representation. To obtain more women judges, we must encourage more women to become law students and lawyers who will in due course be eligible to become judges. As for jurors, a majority of states by law still allow women to be more easily excused or exempted from jury service than men, and women are therefore probably underrepresented on the juries of those states.

Although women are more easily exempted from jury service in most states, local administrators and judges play a crucial role in applying jury selection laws. A Pennsylvania study showed an imbalance toward male jurors in Lancaster County, an imbalance toward female jurors in Philadelphia County and approximate equality in Allegheny County—all under the same state law.

From this general review, we can conclude that women as litigants do not receive the same treatment as men. In criminal cases women are much less likely to be jailed before or after conviction and are more likely to lack a jury trial than are men charged with the same crime. In personal injury cases, adult women are less likely to win than are adult men, and they collect awards that are substantially smaller, especially for certain types of injuries and especially before male-dominated juries. In divorce cases, where there is always a woman on one side and a man on the other, the woman seems to win on the basis of a simple analysis of divorce decrees; but these decrees become meaningless when we look at the collection records.

These findings seem consistent with how women are treated in American society in general. There is a kind of paternalistic protectiveness, at least toward white women, which assumes that they need sheltering from such manly experiences as being jailed or being treated in an overly formal fashion in family law or criminal cases. At the same time, when it comes to allocating scarce valuable resources, such as personal injury monetary awards or money for child support, women are more likely to be slighted.

More equal treatment might be achieved by increasing the public awareness of the disparities in the treatment of male and female litigants and by increasing the representation of women as jury and judicial decision-makers. Needed, however, are more specifically focused changes within the legal system, which will in turn improve the legal process for men and women alike.

For example, the remedy for the disparities in the jailing of women lies not in lessening the frequency of their release on bond, or increasing their postconviction term of imprisonment, but in providing pretrial release for all persons—regardless of sex—mainly on the basis of the likelihood that they will in fact appear for trial. Likewise, society needs to provide postconviction sentencing for everyone, regardless of sex, again, mainly on the basis of whether that person is likely to be rehabilitated or deterred from future crime by a period of imprisonment.

Along related lines, the remedy for disparities in personal injury awards and child-support collections probably does not lie in lowering the damages awarded to males or in prosecuting wayward nonpaying fathers more vigorously. Instead, society should perhaps seek collective action, such as no-fault insurance and an expanded Social Security program.

Neither these measures nor any others, however, will be sufficient in themselves. Nothing will successfully eliminate the discrimination that exists against women litigants—save the complete eradication of discrimination against all women in our society.

March 1972

FURTHER READING SUGGESTED BY THE AUTHOR:

"Women as Litigants" by Stuart S. Nagel and Lenore J. Weitzman in the *Hastings Law Journal* (Winter 1971), contains more data on the subject of the article.

Women and the Law: The Unfinished Revolution by Leo Kanowitz (Albuquerque, N.M.: University of New Mexico Press, 1967) is good on what the law is, but weak on empirical data.

Radical Lawyers: Their Role in the Movement and in the Courts edited by Jonathan Black (New York: Avon Books, 1971) contains good chapters dealing with legal aspects of women's liberation.

"Women's Servitude Under Law" by Ann Garfinkle, Carol Lefcourt and Diane Schulder in *Law Against People: Essays To Demystify Law, Order and the Courts* edited by Robert Lefcourt (New York: Vintage Books, 1971) contains a good summary of some aspects of legal discrimination against women.

The Moral Career of a Bum

JAMES P. SPRADLEY

More arrests occur in the United States for public drunkenness than for any other crime; during 1965, of six million arrests, nearly two million were for this charge. The President's Commission on Law Enforcement and Administration of Justice has commented that this system of criminal justice "burdens police, clogs lower criminal courts and crowds penal institutions throughout the United States," an observation borne out in Seattle, where 70 percent of all police man-hours are spent on this type of offense and 80 percent of the jail population throughout the year are the chronic alcoholic offenders.

Any person arrested for public drunkenness in Seattle may post a bail of $20 and be released in a few hours, and

From *You Owe Yourself a Drunk: An Ethnography of Urban Nomads,* by James P. Spradley. © 1970 by Little, Brown and Company, Inc. Reprinted by permission of the author and publisher.

most of those who post bail do not appear in court, preferring to forfeit their bail. Some chronic offenders spend
hundreds of dollars each year in this manner. Those without sufficient funds to post bail must appear in Seattle
Criminal Court, where it was reported that during 1967
nearly 65 percent of all cases were those charged with
public drunkenness, or an average of about 70 persons per
day. Ninety-seven percent of those appearing in court are
found guilty and sentenced to serve time in the city jail
for their crime.

The effect of this system upon the individual, especially
those who cannot post bail, is often held to be partially
therapeutic by many members of our society. On June 17,
1968, the Supreme Court of the United States ruled, in the
case of *Powell v. Texas,* to uphold the laws which make
public drunkenness an offense in every state of the Union.
One of the majority opinions stated the following reasons
for this decision:

Jailing of chronic alcoholics is definitely defended as
therapeutic, and the claims of therapeutic value are not
insubstantial. As appellees note, the alcoholics are removed from the streets, where in their intoxicated state
they may be in physical danger, and are given food,
clothing, and shelter until they "sober up" and thus at
least regain their ability to keep from being run over
by automobiles in the street.

Not everyone agrees with this modestly positive evaluation, however, least of all the drunks themselves. They
know they are caught in a revolving door, and it is time to
listen to their view of it. Consider the case of Mr. John
Hallman, a long-time resident of Seattle: he was first
arrested for public drunkenness in 1947 and two years later
declared by the courts to be a "common drunkard"; during
the 21-year period from 1947 to 1968, he was convicted
over 100 times for this crime; he received many suspended

sentences and posted $165 in bails which he forfeited; and there were 74 charges of public drunkenness during this period on which he was sentenced to jail. He was given a total of 5,340 days for these convictions, or *more than 14 years.* If he had posted $20 bail each time it would have cost him $1,480. In this man's experience, then, a year of his life was worth only about $100! During 1966 he received two six-month sentences which he could have avoided for only $40.

Why do urban nomads encounter the police, get arrested, plead guilty and do time in an almost never-ending cycle? They do, of course, violate local ordinances that prohibit drunkenness, drinking, begging, sleeping and urinating in public. But what they do is much less significant than who they are. These men do their life sentences on the installment plan because they have been discredited and stigmatized by other Americans.

No man begins life as a bum, nor were these men socialized into the world of tramps as children. At one time in their adult life they had a variety of respected identities—they were fathers, husbands, students, sons, employers and employees. Many attended high school; some went to college. One informant who had been a tramp for several years was a graduate of Harvard University. Others had owned businesses or worked at skilled trades. Nearly half of these men had once maintained a family.

The conception a man has of himself and his place in the world is, in part, socially constructed. Like the brick and mortar that go into creating a building, so the edifice of the human self is constructed one building block at a time. While new dimensions of self-identity may be acquired throughout the life span, dramatic change in personality can occur only if these former identities are subjected to radical manipulation.

The revolving jail house door is for the drunks "making

the bucket"; it is a *rite de passage,* the actions, timing and spatial ordering of which are intertwined in a complex array of symbolic meanings that ceremonially tell the urban nomad and those in his world who he is no longer and who he is becoming. We shall focus here upon the "stages of making the bucket," using the categories that tramps employ to order their experience throughout this rite and to anticipate and prepare for what is ahead.

Stage 1: Street. One of the most important ways in which members of any society learn a new identity is through a process of being labeled by others, especially those who hold power over their lives. Not all labeling activity by others is significant, of course, but when a man's concept of himself is shaken because of his own loss of control over doing those things that society considers important, he is especially vulnerable to the labels others use for him.

For the urban nomads, as I shall call them, the most significant "others" are the police. One man recalled, "That bull said I was just a wino and a bum that wasn't worth being tossed in a shit ditch." The label of tramp was often used in a manner which implied the inferiority of such an identity. "Get going, you fuckin' tramp. Can't you hear your own name, ass-hole?" Many other discrediting labels such as "you wino son-of-a-bitch," "ding bat," "fucking dehorn," "drunken bum," "cocksucker," "Skid Road bastard," "fuckin' tramp" and "phoney ass" were among those reported by my informants. Tramps are often threatened as well: "Shut up or we will put you in the pads and beat the shit out of you."

A man may also be stigmatized by the police by having other aspects of his identity thrown up before him as evidence that he is only a bum. There is, for example, a large population of Indians in the city of Seattle, and many find companionship in the Skid Road district and often get charged with being drunk in public. In many ways they are considered beneath all others. One man said, "That bull called me a fucked-up chief and stated that liquor rights should never have been given to these fuckin' Injuns." Another remembered an officer saying to him, "They didn't play cowboys and Indians long enough; they should have killed all of you bastards off."

Whatever the reasons for this labeling behavior, most tramps are aware that it goes on and come to the same conclusion as the man who stated, "In many cops' minds a drunk isn't human."

Stage 2: Call Box. Personal and social identity are not only structured by the roles we play and the names we use, but also by objects of personal property. For the tramps, rings, watches, money, wallets, identification papers, address books and clothing help to give form and structure to *who* one is, and their loss is significant. Although they may be robbed at any point during the entire ritual of making the bucket, the first fleecing often takes place at the call box.

When a man is arrested by a policeman on his beat, he is taken to the call box where a paddy wagon or police car is summoned to take him to jail. In the interim he undergoes a thorough search and may lose some of his belongings; in a sample of 100 men, 23 percent of the men indicated they had been robbed by a policeman while he was shaking them down at a call box.

Even if they make it to jail without being robbed, their possessions are not safe. When the wagon takes them off to jail, they hope against the odds that their possessions will be in their property box when they are released, but as one man recalled, "They took a watch and ring from me in 1968 and told me it would be in my property at the jail. I never got them back."

In addition to being despoiled of his property, a man

at the call box is almost always robbed of his autonomy at a deeper psychological level. His world has been invaded by someone with the authority to treat him in a manner designed to show him that he is utterly powerless, certainly not that he is innocent until proven guilty. The street corners on Skid Road have a different meaning to tramps than they do to others in American society. They are not merely dingy public places; they are the living rooms and private meeting places for urban nomads. A man who has recently arrived in town will hang around a street corner hoping to meet an old friend or find a new one. Therefore, when a man is required to place his hands over his head and allow an officer to invade his clothing and other domains of privacy, while at the same time threatening him, it is done in full view of other tramps.

Stage 3: Paddy Wagon or Police Car. Although the drive to the jail may involve only a few blocks, a man does not always get there after he is picked up in the paddy wagon; 23 percent of the sample reported the police had stopped them or picked them up, taken their money or other property and then let them go. Because they are not arrested on such occasions, this form of shakedown is considered to be an involuntary payoff to the police. Only 6 percent of the sample reported they had ever made a *voluntary* payoff. Some have stories such as this man's: "In 1968 they picked me up in a prowl car and took me down on Skid Road back in an alley and searched me, took my money, drove me around for awhile and then let me out way down on Skid Road in a back alley. They drove off without returning my money."

It is almost impossible to verify these incidents by legal means, but enough tramps have experienced this official thievery for it to have become part of their general cultural knowledge. The strategies tramps use to make themselves invisible when they sleep are also used to protect their personal property. Like chameleons, they are careful to conceal any hint that they have valuable possessions. Some men reported they would dress in old clothes "like a bum" in order to avoid become a candidate for jackrollers and thieves.

Stage 4: Elevator. The elevator from the basement of the Public Safety Building to the sixth floor where the jail is located is especially dangerous for the tramp. He is entirely cut off from the view of everyone except the police— not even a disinterested passerby can influence what takes place. Although it is a short trip, the bull can easily push the stop button between floors. As the elevator slowly rises, the reality of imprisonment sweeps over the tramp with an immediacy that suffocates any self-assertive wishes he may still harbor. The two bulls at his side, like uniformed bars of a cell, cannot be seen as human beings to whom he can respond, for any reaction on his part other than a plastic passivity may be interpreted as resistance. The tramp may not himself have been worked over in the elevator, but he has certainly heard of it from his fellow urban nomads.

Although being clubbed or smashed against a wall symbolically reminds a man that his body, the most intimate dimension of his self-concept, is vulnerable, it also has another important meaning. Like a rehearsal before a dramatic performance, it forcefully instructs the tramp to play the part of a dependent and passive actor within the bucket. The longer a man has been in the world of tramps, the more he learns to respond as if he were an animal whose master had broken his will. Labels, threats, physical abuse and thefts of property in themselves are hard for any man to take, but more significant is the implicit message in these actions: they clearly identify for the tramp those who hold power over his life then and during the coming months he may spend in jail. If he refuses to acknowledge his deferential role, further steps will be taken, as they were with the man who recalled:

In 1967 he shook me down, took my wallet, looked in it, took $11. Put my wallet back and I said, "Since when do you look for a gun or a knife in a man's wallet?" He split my head, and it took four stitches.

Stage 5: Booking. When the elevator door opens, a man sees to his left the gun rack where the officers will deposit their weapons. Before him is a row of closely spaced steel bars that lurch into motion with the sound of a buzzer pressed from behind the booking desk. As the steel gate opens he is ushered across a waiting area of 20 or 30 feet in diameter to a high counter with several windows. For each man the officer fills out in quadruplicate a property record and booking sheet. Although there is space for the prisoner to sign and verify the property record, almost 70 percent of my informants indicated they were not usually allowed to do this, and 98 percent of the sample indicated they had never received a receipt.

When I questioned tramps about thefts from their property boxes, 40 percent reported their occurrence. One man recalled this story:

I was in jail and had no money, and there was a fellow who owed me $12, and so I wrote and asked him for it and told him to send it registered letter. I got the letter, but the money wasn't in it. When I got out I didn't have no money in my property box. I said, "I've got a registered letter here saying I was sent $12. I'm not leaving until I get it." The bull said, "You don't have no money." The sergeant came by just then, asked what it was and looked at the letter and went back to the property box and then came out and said, "Oh, here's your $12. It was in the wrong property box."

One factor of which tramps are most keenly aware in the entire ritual of making the bucket is that at every point they receive different kinds of treatment than those they refer to as "citizens" or "uptown tramps." A well-dressed man is seldom robbed, beaten or cursed because he is likely to cause trouble.

The booking desk has one further significant effect on these men who are undergoing an identity change, and that is creating a "record." This record becomes part of the court file on each man, and it is used to determine the severity of his sentence. Later it may be much more widely disseminated, as was noted in the study of the Seattle Police Department made by the International Association of Chiefs of Police in 1968. Any success at passing as an average citizen, whether it be for employment, housing or friendship, may crumble when others discover his record. Although *he* may know that many of his arrests were simply due to his visibility in the Skid Road area, it is not easy to convince others that this was the case.

Stage 6: Padded Drunk Tank. From the booking desk it is a short distance down a hallway to the padded drunk tank, so called because a thin layer of cork covers the floor, to cushion the men as they sleep off a drunk or await the next stage of the ritual. Most men have very few memories of this tank because they spend little time there, or they are too drunk to remember what transpired. Only one of my informants got a second (sober) glimpse of the padded drunk tank. A young merchant seaman, who was 29, had arrived in Seattle and was arrested several times. While waiting for his appearance in court, the following incident occurred:

I was in the cement drunk tank with about 40 guys. They had some visitors coming through the jail, and they took several of us out of the cement drunk tank and gave us each two blankets and put us in the padded drunk tank. It had a rubber floor. They brought us in food, they heaped our trays with stew for dinner at 4:30, and the visitors came through and everything looked great.

Tramps are aware of such subterfuge, and it is one of the reasons they believe no one can discover their plight and that you "can't change City Hall."

Stage 7: Mug and Print Room. Any man who has made the bucket more than once knows that here is the watershed at which the poor are separated from the not so poor. After a man is sober enough to be processed in this room, he also is sober enough to post a bail of $20, walk out of the jail a free man. He has bought his way out for $20. He has purchased a clean slate, a new sense of self, an *immediate* opportunity to assert himself and release all the pent-up hostility he may have felt toward the system—all for only $20. And he can continue bailing himself out forever if he has the resources or friends who will pay. But what does this say to the man who sees others post their bail, who tries to phone a friend or bondsman for the needed money, only to fail and enter the drunk tank with the knowledge that he could have been free if he had not been poor—a poverty which may have been incurred only a few hours earlier at the hands of his captors?

Stage 8: Cement Drunk Tank. Events have moved rapidly for the tramp who has gone through the first stages of the ritual. From the street to the call box, into a paddy wagon and up the elevator, through the booking desk process and on into the padded drunk tank for a few hours of sleep. X-rays and pictures follow in quick succession. And then suddenly, as the heavy door closes on the cement drunk tank, time seems to wind backwards.

The cement drunk tank is not a comfortable place to

spend several days, and 90 percent of my sample reported having spent two or more days there. There are no bunks in this room, meant to hold about 35 men, and only one toilet and washbasin. Only 3 percent of the sample reported ever receiving a blanket. The lights are left on 24 hours a day, and there is nothing resembling privacy; but the most abhorrent part of this experience is the crowding, which makes it impossible for a man to protect himself from being contaminated by others. One man described these conditions in graphic terms:

That's all right if you're a young fellow, you can take it. It's miserable, but you can take it. Sometimes, I don't know what the reason for it is, it doesn't make sense for you at all, but I've been in there when there is standing room only, in one of those concrete cells, for two or three days. There's barely room to sit down. You certainly can't lie down without putting your face in someone's dirty socks or something like that. And this is when there are two or three other tanks available that are completely empty. There's no reason why they don't take half of them and put them in another one, except they don't want to bother to clean it up.

In fact, the physical discomfort in itself is not unbearable; after all, tramps have slept on cold hard cement before without a blanket. But now they have lost control of their lives, and as they lie there waiting for court, the drunk tank reminds them of this as nothing else could.

A man's most immediate needs are often for cigarettes, food and information about the state of his property. He has lost the control over all of these items. Although food is served three times a day, it is never enough. If he has been able to smuggle some money into the drunk tank in his clothing, he can pay a trusty 50 cents or a dollar to "hustle" him a cup of coffee or get something from his property, but he can never depend on this. The trusties often steal, but the men cannot complain to the bulls since it is against the rules to have money. Moreover, the bulls will often not even protect them against other prisoners in the drunk tank. One man recalled:

I remember about three years ago I was working in a logging camp and had just come to town, and I ended up in the drunk tank. I woke up, and I caught some guy trying to steal my shoes in the drunk tank. He was taking them off my feet, see, so we got into it, and he had two or three buddies in the drunk tank, and I started hollering for the bull, the jailer, and they put the finger on me, see, that I started it. I tried to tell the jailer that the son-of-a-bitch was trying to steal my shoes. I'd sobered up by that time, and that big jailer, he says, "You come out here." He took me over into an empty tank, and I knew what was comin' then. He slammed the door shut, and he walks up to me and says, "You think you're pretty tough, huh?" I seen it coming, you know, and held my breath, and he hit me in the guts as hard as he could. He didn't even knock me down. I just stepped back two or three feet, and he kind of looked at me, you know, and that was it. He didn't knock me down the first time, so he left me alone, and I said, "What in hell did you do that for?" He didn't answer me, but if I had swung on him, which I could have done, well then they'd have brought in two or three more, you know, and really whipped my ass."

Even though he is already in the drunk tank, in principle a man may still contact a bondsman, attorney, employer or friend who will help get him out of jail. But to contact the outside, he must of course use the phone. Eighty-five percent of my informants said they had been permitted to make one phone call, but the man who has no regular employment, family or permanent address finds the privilege of a single telephone call next to useless. He may need to contact several people until he finds one who will bail him out, get his money, pay for his room, get his clothing or assist him in some other way.

Stage 9: Court Docket. Time drags its feet in the drunk tank. The hours creep by, turning slowly into days and nights to be endured. The men think about food, count the hours until they will appear in court, rack their brains for someone who could bail them out, swap experiences of other jails, listen eagerly to newcomers with word from outside and wonder where they will travel when they are released. Uppermost in the minds of most men are thoughts of "beating their drunk charge."

The heavy door of the drunk tank opens at about 8:00 AM each morning, Monday through Friday, for the drunks to file out, walk down the hallway, through the main lobby past the booking desk, up the stairs and through a maze of corridors to the court docket. This room is much like the cement drunk tank except that it is smaller and filled with rows of steel benches where the men await court. On most days, just before court begins, a counselor for the alcoholism treatment center appears to explain their program and how a person can qualify for it. Most men are sitting sleepily on the benches or lying on the floor, some still fighting the pains of a hangover or withdrawal from a long drunk. They move out, then, in groups of about 25 into the small area to the right and front of the judge's bench, barricaded from the rest of the courtroom by a railing. They are crowded into this cramped space and told where to stand by the officer, where they remain, lined up three deep, pressed together, holding their hats in their hands, heads down, waiting for the judge to speak.

Stage 10: Courtroom.

You men have all been charged with drinking in public, drunk in public or begging which are in violation of the ordinances of the city of Seattle. The maximum penalty for these crimes is $500 fine and/or 180 days in jail. You have a right to plead guilty or not guilty. You have a right to consult a lawyer before you enter a plea of guilty or not guilty. If you want to consult a lawyer you must pay for your own attorney. The court does not have provisions for this. If you wish a continuance, please indicate when you return to court. On a plea of guilty you waive your rights to appeal to a higher court. On a plea of guilty your case will be continued for trial at a later date. Now return to the court docket and when you are called in you will enter a plea of guilty or not guilty. If you wish to make a statement you may do so.

The "rights spiel," as one man fondly dubbed it, takes less than a minute to complete. The group of men are then hurried back into the court docket to listen for their name again. When a man hears his name, he returns to the courtroom alone. He faces the judge's bench, separated by the railing and the prosecuting attorney for the city of Seattle who says, "You have been charged with the crime of public drunkenness, how do you plead?" If a man enters a plea of guilty, and over 90 percent of them do so, the prosecutor reads his prior record to the judge who will sentence him according to a preset formula based on his record. A man may plead guilty or not guilty, ask for a continuance, make a statement or request he be sent to the alcoholism treatment center.

The best way to beat a drunk charge is to have a good record, a strategy that has wide ramifications for the life style of tramps. In some courts there is a single sentence for anyone guilty of public drunkenness, but in Seattle, as in many cities, there is a sliding scale determined by a man's past record. A first offender, who may only be new to that court or who simply may have been out of action for six months or more, will get two days suspended. An eight-time loser may get as much as 90 days.

Whenever tramps discuss previous experiences in jail and court they explain them by making references to how many days they have "hanging" (the amount of time they know they will be sentenced to do). It is impossible to understand the actions a man takes, such as bailing out, asking for the treatment center or pleading guilty, unless it is also known how many days he had hanging.

The judge apparently gives sentences of increasing magnitude, with an occasional major suspended sentence, for two reasons: to reduce the recurrence of a man's drinking sprees and help him regain his health. Tramps, however, know they are arrested for many reasons besides their drinking behavior; it is their life style, only one feature of which involves drinking, that brings them into court. While the punishment of longer sentences may motivate some men to abstain from public drunkenness, it has a much more significant influence for most tramps; it motivates them to travel. In order to improve their record in court so as to reduce the amount of time they will do on their next conviction, tramps choose another alternative— leaving town. With each succeeding arrest in Seattle a person's record becomes more tarnished and the number of days he has hanging increases. But every tramp knows this slate could be completely erased by leaving town for six months.

The suspended sentence is an even more important stimulus to the mobility of tramps. When a tramp receives a suspended sentence of 90 days, he has escaped doing time, but only for the moment; back on the street he walks with the knowledge that he now has probably doubled the number of days he has hanging. If arrested again he may serve the suspended and the new sentence consecutively.

After a long period of incarceration, a man feels like "moving on" as an end in itself; he wants to enjoy his freedom to the utmost. But tramps also travel from one place to another because they become marked men who are arrested over and over again for their very presence in the Skid Road district. There is an intimate relationship between mobility and other features of their life style which involve drinking: alcoholic beverages function as a social lubricant at all levels of American society, but they fulfill this need in a special way for urban nomads. Nomadism creates a unique kind of loneliness and sense of isolation in an individual, and when he arrives alone in a new town he seeks to find others of his own kind to reduce such anxieties. Almost the only place where he can find acceptance, friendship and sociability is on Skid Road and in the bars located there. Bars are categorized among tramps in a variety of ways, but especially in terms of what one may find there in the way of friends, female companionship and work opportunities. For urban nomads, bars function as churches and clubs, employment agencies and dating centers, begging places, drinking and eating places and flops. Most of all, they are a place to find friendship, even if it is only of a fleeting nature. In a Skid Road bar one is not restricted in his behavior; he can perform in ways appropriate to this subculture and know he will be accepted; he can find out important information about jail and court and employment which other tramps will freely give him. One tramp who wanted to control his drinking behavior clearly saw the relationship between mobility and drinking. As he was about to be released from the alcoholism treatment center he commented: "My biggest problem when I get out next week is traveling. When I get in a strange vicinity I head for a bar. If I want to work, I go to a bar. That's where they come to hire a man." Skid Road and its bars, in addition to being a place to solidify new-found friendships with a drink, is also where most arrests for public drunkenness occur. And so we have come full circle: *urban nomads visit Skid Road and its bars because they travel; they are arrested because they live and drink in this area of town; and they travel because they are arrested.*

Some of the strategies used to beat a drunk charge are linked together. A man who requests a continuance does so in order to be able to bail out; similarly, a person who uses an alias does so to have a good record or escape the one he has created over the past months. As one informant stated, "If they have no previous arrest for a name they usually give a kickout. You've got to beat them some way." But few men use this dodge as it is too risky:

One Friday Sanders gave the name Johnson, as he had time hanging. They called for Johnson many times Friday, Saturday and Sunday. Monday morning when they called Johnson for court the officer who knew him spotted Sanders and told him he ought to kick his teeth in. Sanders had forgot what name he'd used.

The most widely used way to beat a drunk charge is a passive one—plead guilty and hope for the best. Ninety-four percent of the sample reported they usually pleaded guilty to a drunk charge even when they felt sure they were not really drunk at the time of arrest. Nearly 97 percent of the drunk cases heard in this court result in convictions. Tramps firmly believe that "you can't beat the charge," "you can't win the case" and "it doesn't make any difference what you plead—you are guilty anyway." Most men feel they actually have no other choice, and some believe they will get a lighter sentence.

Twenty-seven percent of the sample had, however, entered a plea of not guilty at one time or another, although only four men reported they had been acquitted. One stated, "The judge told me if I didn't think I was guilty to plead not guilty, which I did. He moved my case ahead 30 days, and I spent 30 days in jail, was found guilty and sentenced to 30 days." It is important to remember how these men feel about the drunk tank and the sense of isolation there. It is an almost unbearable thought to stand in court and know that if you plead not guilty you will return to that place. A man pleads guilty because he can be sentenced sooner and start "doing my time." The uncertainty of waiting for the outcome of trial and the fact that the days you wait for trial may be "dead time," not even counted as part of the sentence you finally receive, are perceived as punishments for entering an honest plea, and they provide sufficient motivation to enter a plea of guilty. One who pleads not guilty also runs the risk of offending the arresting officers who must take time to appear in court as witnesses. One man recalled: "If you plead not guilty you have the arresting cops against you, so you can't win anyway."

Finally, men plead guilty most of the time because they believe the courts are in collusion with the police against them. "All a cop has to do is say you were drunk—the judge never goes against a cop."

Tramps not only know the principles and rules of our legal system, they also know that the law enforcement agencies violate these rules as far as they are concerned: they are assumed to be guilty rather than innocent; they are rewarded for pleading guilty even when they are innocent; they have no way to provide themselves with a defense attorney; and they are punished if they go against the system by pleading not guilty. The network of protections for the innocent is stripped away from the process of criminal justice for these men, and in its place is an overwhelming pressure coercing them into violating their own integrity by agreeing with the verdict of the system.

One option usually open to a man attempting to beat a drunk charge is to make a statement. Only 16 percent of the sample reported they had ever asked to make a statement in court and not been allowed to do so. The tramp learns which factors influence the judge as he sentences a man to jail for public drunkenness, and the statement he makes will reflect these concerns.

Equal justice for all under the law is the maxim of this court, yet when we consider whom the judge sentences and who escapes, we must conclude that some men are more equal than others. The man who still has family responsibilities may talk of family ties in an effort to get a suspended sentence. He is aware that being a responsible family man is one of the things that separates urban nomads from the rest of society, and any indication that he is still trying to keep from being a bum will carry weight with the judge.

Many men indicate they have a job, but unless it is a rather permanent one or unless there are some other extenuating circumstances, they are still apt to get a sentence. The most effective kind of statement may be a promise to get out of town. In these cases, the men are offering the judge the only thing they have left in life—their mobility:

Prosecutor: Mr. Brown, you have been charged with drunk in public. How do you plead?

Mr. Brown: Guilty.

Judge: When were you released?

Mr. Brown: Last Saturday morning. Could I have a

break? I want to go pick apples. Last time, I got out of jail and walked around to where the bus to the apples was and when I got to the bus I was waiting in line to get on and the patrol car picked me up.

Judge: Will you go pick apples if I give you an opportunity?

Mr. Brown: Yes, I will.

Judge: 30 days suspended.

Such claims as "I was asleep in my car" or "I just got out of the hospital, and I've been taking pills. I had a couple drinks and fell asleep, but it was the pills that made me fall asleep" are commonly heard in court, but they do not often lead to a suspended sentence. At the least they offer a meager opportunity for a man to attempt to restore his damaged self-respect for having given in to the system and pleaded guilty.

During the past couple of years in Seattle, a new strategy for beating drunk charges has been added to the list: request the alcoholism treatment center. When the judge considers a man to be a good candidate, he then continues his case, waits for him to be psychologically and medically examined and finally recommended by the treatment center staff for acceptance. If he is acceptable, he will then be sentenced to the treatment center for a period of four months. Sometimes a man is anxious for treatment but does not indicate appropriate interest and goes to jail instead, as in the following case:

Prosecutor: Mr. Pace, you have been charged with drunk in public. How do you plead?

Mr. Pace: Guilty.

Judge: Do you have a drinking problem?

Mr. Pace: We all have drinking problems, but I've worked on mine.

Judge: Have you had any help?

Mr. Pace: Yes, I went to Alcoholics Anonymous, but

their rules are too stringent. They wouldn't allow working any night job or overtime. I talked to the probation officer, and he said try to take their advice.

Judge: Do you want assistance, or do you want to continue as you are?

Mr. Pace: It depends on how strong the treatment would be.

Judge: We have a new treatment center, but it's only for those who want help and will cooperate with the program. If you don't want to, you can go back to the city jail.

Mr. Pace: Well, I would like to go if their program isn't too stringent.

Judge: There can be no conditions on your going there. The sentence is 30 days in the Seattle city jail.

The treatment center is viewed by some men, however, as an easier place to do time than in jail, and in a sense they "beat their drunk charge" by going there. Very few tramps have become totally immune to the norms and values of American culture, and they often feel guilty, especially when they are arrested for a long drunk. Some men reported that the worst aspect of court was the way it intensified their feelings of shame and guilt without any opportunity to express this. One said, "It hurts my pride. It's degrading. You are on exhibition for everyone to see, not being able to express how sorry you really are for being drunk." In all these experiences—the public humiliation, the waiting, facing the judge without any means of defense, the physical discomfort involved—tramps feel that underlying the whole process they are looked upon by the officials of the society as objects to be manipulated, as something less than human. The worst thing about court is being "herded around like a bunch of cattle—dumb animals."

Stage 11: Holding Tank. Men who receive a sentence

walk back into the seventh-floor section of the jail and are placed in the holding tank after the court session is completed. The trusty officer joins them there, and a decision is made regarding the future role they will have in jail: trusty or lockup. This decision is probably the most significant factor in determining whether a man does hard time or easy time, since trusties have many advantages that lockups do not. They are put in several different kinds of tanks that are unlocked during the day. Some have freedom to move throughout most of the jail, and others may even go outside to work. Their greater freedom allows them to watch TV at certain times, and, most important, they have access to food and other resources in and out of the jail. It is difficult to determine the reasons why an individual may not become a trusty, but often there are not enough jobs, or a man may be too old and sick, while another may have run away the last time he was a trusty.

Stage 12: Delousing Tank. The men spend several hours in the delousing tank, and most of them felt it was the worst part of the entire process of making the bucket. As soon as the assignments are made in the holding tank, all inmates, both trusties and lockups, are taken a few feet down the hall to be deloused. There are 16 bunks in this tank with a small passageway between the bunks, a shower and toilet. The men are crowded in and ordered to strip off all their clothing. The nakedness that the men must now endure is felt to be degrading in itself, but the men also feel they may be contaminated by each other. And their clothes, if not lousy before, certainly will be after the treatment they get.

One machine with 30 men's clothes for delousing— some guys are better than looking at carnivals, wearing a couple of union suits, couple pair of pants. The clothes should be turned inside out where the seams show so the greybacks can't hide; some guys are filthy. If they're lousy and guys are so crowded together, everybody's contaminated. Them clothes should really be in that machine for maybe three hours so nobody gets lousy.

Many men reported that they felt very keenly about their clothing, and they are perfectly aware that the designation of bum is used for them largely because of their appearance. While they were in court, after lying in the drunk tank for several days, the state of their clothing caused them great embarrassment and concern. But all these feelings about clothes reflect the fact that as the self crumbles, men cling more desperately to the last vestige of any material objects which symbolize, in some sense, their personal identity and the world outside. Not only is the men's clothing stripped from their backs, but the best articles are sometimes stolen by trusties, and almost everything comes out of the heating machine in worse shape than when they went in.

Stages 13 and 14: Time Tank and Trusty Tank. For the lockup nothing so increases the amount of hard time a man does as much as hunger. One man said, "You can do hard time any place especially if there's poor grub or if you're sleeping on steel," and almost everyone agreed that in Seattle jail the grub was poor indeed and everyone was continually hungry.

The experience of doing hard time as a trusty or lockup is related to many other facets of life in the bucket besides food, however. It results, in part, from failure to maintain a compliant attitude toward the social and physical environment, failure to live a day at a time, losses of personal property and jobs on the outside and losses of clothing in the delousing process. In addition, a system of rewards and punishments within the jail contributes directly to the experience of doing hard or easy time.

While rewards are sought and favors are gratefully accepted from many policemen, the men are aware that they are granted only if one maintains a submissive attitude, and even at that, they are few and far between. The men are much more alert to the possibility of punishment, which may come in the form of withheld privileges, extra physical torment or being busted. In jail men have the privilege of writing letters, making a phone call each week, getting out of their cell for a brief period of exercise and using the money in their property to purchase candy and cigarettes through the weekly commissary. These privileges are not equally available to all men, and their withdrawal by the police is felt as a terrible loss.

The bulls may also punish more directly. The men usually refer to this as being put on "the bull's shit list" or having "a cop on your ass." One man recalled, "Even a trusty may do hard time if a cop is on your ass." Fifteen percent of the sample reported that they had been put on the bull's shit list for various reasons—"I refused to polish a cop's shoes," or "because I told them I was going to call the Civil Liberties Union about the sadistic treatment" or "by not calling him 'officer.' "

The final kind of punishment is being busted. Almost any person, whether lockup or trusty, can be busted to another less desirable place within the jail. There are six distinct places within the jail to which a man may be busted for misbehavior, for getting on the bull's shit list or for some unknown reason: the trusty tank, time tank, padded cell, drunk tank, stand-up cell and the hole. One man reported being busted to the drunk tank because he kept asking for medical treatment: "This is what I received to keep me quiet." Another said, "The nurse had this man busted on word from another trusty which was not true pertaining to his work in the dispensary, and he did 35 days there."

A few men will go to the drunk tank at their own request in order to do easy time. They want the extra food which those who are too ill and cannot eat will leave there for them, or they may want to avoid having to control their behavior carefully as they must when they are lock-ups or trusties. But no one goes voluntarily to the stand-up cell or the hole. Many men did not know of these places, but one man described the hole this way:

There was a small Indian man who I knew, and he got in a fight with a bull at the booking desk. They cuffed his hands behind his back and worked him over and then put him in the hole and left him there for two days. He said he passed his time by doing pushups. They stripped him naked, he had no clothing, and the hole is a little concrete cell about six-foot square. There was no light, and he was fed bread and water.

But overarching the concrete results of the rewards and punishment used to control the tramp's behavior are two other factors. A man summed up one, the dread of loss:

Well, one thing a man does not do in jail is talk unless he is spoken to. There is a constant fear of loss, because loss is a penalty. One way to penalize a man is simply to ignore him as he rattles the bars of his cage or the cell. For instance, a man might be going into DTs and need some medical attention, and so to attract attention of the guard he will shake the cell bars very loudly, because he is desperate for some kind of help, and he'll be pe-nalized by simply ignoring him.

Second, it should be pointed out that most men felt there was a great deal of unpredictability in the punish-ments they might receive. Everything depended on the vagaries of the officers' moods and especially which officer one encountered.

Stage 15: The Street Again. Whether a man is a lockup or trusty the days do pass until the inmate is doing short time—only a few days remain on his sentence. For some, the last few days are easy time, filled with the knowledge and expectation of release. For others, as their minds become filled with memories of the outside and they plan for the days ahead, it is not so easy. But eventually the morning arrives when a man knows he will be escorted from his cell, lay aside his identity as a lockup or trusty and become, if only for a few hours, a kickout. After being discharged he walks to the elevator and rides quickly to the ground floor, walks out of the building—a free man who will now take up his life as an urban nomad in other scenes of that world.

But jail is perhaps the most important scene in that world. Here the remaining shreds of respectable identity have been stripped away as they became participants in the elaborate ritual of making the bucket. Society, which has swept them out of sight and in the process cut them off from their former selves, now views them as bums or common drunkards. But in jail there has developed in these men an identity vacuum, along with powerful motivations to fill it, not only because of their material losses, but because inactivity, restraint and oversensitivity to the staff create pressures to act, to become and to gain a new sense of personal identity and a new set of values to replace what has been lost.

The novice who repeats this experience several times may first seek to escape it by travel to a new town, but once there he usually goes to Skid Road for ready acceptance. Sooner or later, for many men, the world and culture of the tramp become a viable alternative to replace what has been lost in the ritual of making the bucket. In that culture he may still be alienated from the rest of society—but *not from himself* or others like him. He will find acceptance as well as adaptive strategies for survival as an urban nomad. But more importantly, something else has been going on simultaneously during the days in jail—he has been learning the attitudes, values and skills which are required for survival in this new culture.

May 1970

FURTHER READINGS SUGGESTED BY THE AUTHOR:

Skid Row as a Way of Life by Samuel E. Wallace (Totowa, New Jersey: Bedminster Press, 1965), a sociological study of one skid row in a midwestern city, provides an extensive bibliography of other studies and also reviews the theories used to explain this subculture.

Asylums: Essays on the Social Situation of Mental Patients and Other Inmates by Erving Goffman (Chicago: Aldine, 1961) describes and analyzes what total institutions such as jails can make of the inmate and how the inmate can survive within them.

Lawyers for the Poor

DALLIN H. OAKS/WARREN LEHMAN

The Sixth Amendment to the Constitution requires that criminal defendants have access to a lawyer. That creates the problem of just how a lawyer should be obtained for the defendant who cannot afford to hire his own. Should the government pay private lawyers for taking on the criminal defense of the poor, or should it set up a bureau of full-time public defenders? If you take at face value the doctrine—necessary to the sound administration of the law—that all lawyers are equal, it would seem the only way to decide this issue is on the basis of efficiency and economy.

Illinois is a good state in which to test this hypothesis. Illinois has a so-called mixed system: There is a public defender available to all indigents charged with crime, but in some circumstances a defendant may have a private counsel appointed to him instead of the defender. It is possible, therefore, to see the two systems in operation before the same judges and juries and under the same laws.

The data for our comparative study are all of the felony cases in Cook County for the year 1964. In talking about these cases we refer to 5,579 indictments; actually this is a synthetic figure, properly called "defendants by indictment," for a defendant may be named in more than one indictment and one indictment may name two or more defendants. The 5,579 indictments represent 4,040 defendants.

For our comparison, we divided defense counsel into three groups. About 40 percent of all indictments (2,226) were of indigents served by the Cook County public defender's office. About 4 percent (213) were of indigents defended by members of the Chicago Bar Association's Defense of Prisoners Committee. Though the committee's members handled only about half of the appointed-counsel cases, its records provide the only evidence of the work of appointed counsel. The remainder of the indictments (56 percent or 3,140) were defended by other private attorneys and largely represent the quality and style of service given defendants who manage to employ their own counsel. Of this group 95 percent were hired and paid by their clients. The others were appointed and paid by the state but cannot be separated statistically.

Before examining the data, something should be said of the general characteristics of these three groups.

The Cook County public defender's office is one of the oldest and largest in the country. It was founded in 1930 after the Defense of Prisoners Committee had spent five years studying the problems of indigent defense. In 1964 the defender's staff consisted of 21 assistants. (In 1966 it had 28.) Eleven of these had principal responsibility for the 2,226 felony indictments disposed in 1964, or about 200 cases a year for each man—far more than any attorney in private criminal practice. Many assistant defenders are young. They often go on the staff right out of law school just for this rapid introduction to criminal trial practice. A graduate entering the service gets $7,200 per year, probably a little less than his fellow who goes to work for a general practice private law firm in Chicago. For the person interested in criminal law, it's a good way to start.

Criminal law practice is a very chancy business. There are few private attorneys making good livings from the private practice of criminal law. Not many criminals have the money to pay a lawyer well. And you can't just hang your shingle out, say "Practice limited to criminal law," and expect the Mafia to beat a path to your door. The ranks of private lawyers doing criminal work include the few top men in the city, baffled family lawyers whose clients have fallen into the hands of the police, hacks who find their clients in the halls of the Criminal Courts building, corporation lawyers whose clients ask them to perform the work as a service, and young men on the way up who mix criminal and civil practice in the effort to make their way in the law without the benefit of a firm to feed, train, and provide them clients. Private retained lawyers are, therefore, a heterogeneous group, working on retainer, bringing to their clients both the best and the worst in ability and experience.

The members of the Defense of Prisoners Committee are quite likely to be associates of downtown law firms who for reason of principle or for the excitement of trial work make themselves available through the committee for court appointments to defend indigents. Each younger attorney is paired in a team with a senior attorney. There are about 50 such teams, which during 1964 handled between them about the same number of cases as a single public defender. The members of this committee are entitled, as is any attorney appointed to defend an indigent charged with a felony, to a fee up to $150 paid by the county, or $250 if the charge carries a possible death sentence. Many of the members don't collect their fees.

The statutory fees hardly compensate a lawyer who takes the time from a lucrative private practice to handle a lengthy criminal trial. On the other hand, the pay is not bad for the lawyer who merely pleads his client guilty or who hasn't much else in the way of practice. There are at least a few lawyers who earn a significant part of their income in statutory fees for appointments to defend indigents. In 1964 one attorney collected fees for appointments in 20 capital cases and 4 other felonies. Another collected in 5 capital cases and 18 other felonies. That's 47 fees between them. By comparison, the 100 or so members of the Defense of Prisoners Committee collected 118 fees. Committee members also had fewer capital case appointments (23) than the two specialists in appointment (who had 25 between them). Because of the lack of data, these appointed private counsel had to be lumped together for this study with the heterogeneous group of private retained counsel.

We have found significant differences in the style of operation favored by each of these groups as well as differences in where they have both their success and their failures. Overall, the differences suggest less that one kind of counsel is better than another than that they perform somewhat different roles in the overall operation of the criminal justice system.

The cause of these differences is another question. Differing ability—the most obvious inference—is only one possibility and not necessarily the most likely. Many factors, the relative weight of which we could not ascertain, influence trial success. Public defenders, for instance, have much less control over their clients. A private lawyer can threaten to walk away from the case when his advice is not followed; the defender cannot. The types of crimes may not be equally distributed among the three groups. And we know that, in general, the chance a person will be convicted varies radically according to the crime he is charged with. (This happens both because some types of crimes—forgery, for example—are likely to come with better evidence and because for some crimes—such as drunkenness—there is little enthusiasm for enforcement.) For every Speck case, the public defender gets thousands of impoverished defendants who have committed unspectacular crimes without imagination or style.

The differences associated with who one's lawyer is appear even before trial. Cases can be dismissed before trial for a number of reasons—because a defendant out on bond fails to show up for trial (the indictment is reinstated when he's caught), because a prosecutor having obtained a conviction on one count decided to drop another, because a defendant has died. If these were the only causes, a difference in pretrial dismissal rates would not be important. However, it is possible for a lawyer to have a pretrial hearing to decide such a question as whether evidence was improperly obtained. A defense lawyer can win a case by a successful motion to suppress evidence crucial to the prosecutor's case. Successful suppression before trial is likely to lead to a dismissal.

Our figures indicate that public defenders and bar association committee members get dismissals in about the same proportion of cases—8 percent for the defender and 6 percent for the committee member. In contrast, private retained counsel get dismissals in 29 percent of their cases.

The significance of this difference is almost impossible to assess. Unfortunately, the tags that are put upon various types of dismissal don't correspond to the reasons for dismissal that would interest us most. One tag, SOL (stricken with leave to reinstate) is used both for bail jumpers and for at least some evidentiary dismissals. Another, nolle prosequi, is used for evidentiary dismissals, too, as well as for dismissals when the prosecutor wins another case against the same defendant.

One thing we do know is that something like 300 defendants jumped bail. The majority of these had to be clients of retained counsel simply because the public defender and bar association counsel got only 100 SOL's between them—retained counsel got 577. But it is probably also true that bail jumpers are disproportionately represented among the clients of retained attorneys. It is, after all, those who can afford to pay lawyers who are more likely also to be able to post bond and get out on bail. Even discounting bail jumpers, there appears some residual advantage at this stage for retained counsel; we cannot similarly discount the retained counsel's more favorable rate of nolle prosequis.

With pretrial dismissals discounted, there remained 4,469 indictments to be disposed either on guilty plea or by trial. The decision whether to plead guilty or go to trial is first of all a tactical one, almost an exercise in gamesmanship. There are, as we noted, differences in the odds of conviction at trial depending on what crime is charged. The odds favoring success at trial must be weighed against the likelihood that a stiffer sentence will be imposed on the defendant who is convicted at trial. It is the favored treatment given those who plead guilty that keeps the number of trials within reasonable bounds. From the defendant's point of view the problem is one of weighing the certainty of a lesser penalty against the possibility of a stiffer one. Lawyers (and experienced defendants) are very sensitive to this problem, and nationally there is a very close correlation between guilty plea rates and the likelihood of conviction for the crime charged.

On guilty plea rate there is also a large discrepancy, though in this case the appointed counsel look more like private retained counsel and less like the public defender: 82 percent of the defender's clients plead guilty; the rate for private counsel is 68 percent and for appointed counsel 69 percent.

TABLE I—OVERALL DISPOSITIONS

	Public defender	Bar Association committee	Private and other appointed counsel
Dismissals before trial	8.0%	6.0%	29.0%
Found not guilty	8.2	11.0	5.8
Found guilty	8.4	18.0	12.2
Guilty pleas	75.4	63.1	53.0

Our finding compares closely with that of Lee Silverstein who in *Defense of the Poor* reported for Chicago in 1962 a 15 percent difference in plea rate between clients of the defender and those with retained counsel. The similarity we discovered between plea rates of retained and appointed counsel, however, runs contrary to the experience in federal courts in Chicago. The *Report of the Attorney General's Committee on Poverty and the Administration of Justice* issued in 1963 indicated that clients of appointed counsel plead guilty far more often than those with retained counsel. At the time of the study there was no public defender system in federal court. The difference may well have resulted from appointed counsel getting all of the problem clients that are absorbed in the state courts by the public defender. The attorney general's committee suggested that appointed counsel may advise a plea when the defendant lacks resources for an adequate defense. Whatever the merits of that suggestion with federal defendants, we found no evidence that bar association lawyers had such an attitude about their state defendants.

While it is true that either work pressure or the desire to please the judge with whom one works every day may influence an assistant public defender to encourage guilty pleas where a counsel under less pressure would advise a trial, trial is not always in the interest of a defendant. He will, after all, be less severely treated if he pleads guilty. There are probably extraneous pressures on both appointed and retained counsel to go to trial where in the abstract an attorney might advise a plea. Some lawyers have suggested that the retained counsel, having taken a fee, may feel he is bound to "go to the mat" to show that he has earned it. And trial work is exciting. While we have no evidence, it is reasonable to suppose that the volunteer defender from the bar committee may have some bias for the satisfaction to be gained from trial work.

There are other factors that may be operating to vary the plea rate. Second offenders and others who have been exposed to jail talk while awaiting trial may be more knowledgeable about the advantages of pleading guilty. If the public defender has a higher proportion of such clients —as he believes—this would tend to increase the number of clients who are willing to plead. And once again the discrepancy might be influenced by differences in the distribution of crimes charged.

Finally, the discrepancy could result from an advantage to the defender in bargaining with the prosecution over the type and length of sentence. One experienced prosecutor advised us that assistant state's attorneys can make a more favorable recommendation for the clients of the public defender than they could for retained counsel. The supervisor in the state's attorney's office may question their motivation if they seem unduly lenient with retained counsel, especially prominent counsel; the same doubts don't arise when the beneficiaries of bargaining are the assistant public defender and his indigent client. This theory is supported by the fact that about one-fifth of the defender's pleas are on reduced charges and that he seems to be somewhat more successful in getting probation for his clients.

By weeding out more of his clients with guilty pleas, the public defender improves his chance for success, compared to private and appointed counsel, on the 18 percent of his indictments he actually takes to trial. In 1964 he won acquittals in 50 percent of his trials. Committee counsel, who tried 32 percent of their cases, earned a 38 percent acquittal rate. Retained counsel have the worst record—23 percent acquittals on the 31 percent of their cases that go to trial.

If you combine guilty plea and conviction rates, thus including all cases decided on the merits, committee counsel come out best with an acquittal rate of 12 percent; the public defender wins acquittal for 9 percent; retained counsel win for only 7 percent. The relative success rate changes once again if we include pretrial dismissals. On that basis, retained counsel look best with 36 percent of all indictments ending either in dismissal or a finding of not guilty. The corresponding rate for committee counsel is 18 percent and for the public defender, 17 percent. A good part of the apparent advantage of the retained counsel disappears, of course, when we discount those dismissals that are due to clients jumping bail. Still it would appear that in at least some cases faulty evidence means release before trial for clients who have retained lawyers and victory in trial for indigent clients. This difference, too, may contribute to the relatively poor trial record of the retained attorneys.

Overall acquittal statistics hide some other important differences in the behavior of different types of counsel. A counsel who decides to go to trial may choose to try the case before either a judge or a jury. There is a difference between counsel in relative preference for a jury trial. Committee counsel go before a jury in about two-thirds of their trials, retained counsel do so in one-third; the public defender goes before a jury in only 15 percent of his cases. One possible contributing factor is that committee counsel may choose a jury trial to gain experience. The public defender, on the other hand, is very busy and very conscious of the probable extra penalty accruing to a defendant who loses his case before a jury. Just as there is a penalty for going to trial rather than pleading guilty, there is also a penalty for choosing the more expensive and time-consuming jury trial rather than a bench trial. In one case the trial judge stated on the record that he would have sentenced the defendant to one year to life in the penitentiary, but because the defendant had put the state to "the trouble of calling a jury" and had falsely protested his innocence in testimony, "it will cost you nine years additional, because the sentence is now 10 to life in the penitentiary." The sentence was reduced by the Illinois Supreme Court. Few judges are so naive as to allow such statements to appear in the record, but that philosophy—if not in such exaggerated a form—undoubtedly influences sentencing by most judges. Were that not so, every defendant would demand jury trial.

The assistant public defender who is permanently assigned to a single courtroom may be more aware of any hostility his judge has to jury trial. And since he has a backlog of other cases before the same judge, he may be

TABLE II—SUCCESS IN BENCH AND JURY TRIALS BY TYPE OF COUNSEL

	Public defender	Bar Association committee	Private and other appointed counsel	All counsel
Bench trials: Acquitted	55%	48%	20%	34%
Convicted	45%*	52%	80%	66%
Number of Defendants	312	23	476	811
Jury trials: Acquitted	18%	33%**	30%	28%
Convicted	82%	67%	70%	72%
Number of Defendants	55	40	231	326

* Includes 3% found guilty of a lesser charge.
** Includes 10% that terminated in a "hung" jury.

more sensitive to the overall delay caused by demanding a jury.

Finally, the defender may hesitate to demand a jury trial because he is far more successful in bench trials. The defender in 1964 won 55 percent of his bench trials but only 18 percent of his jury trials. Committee counsel, by comparison, won 48 percent of their bench trials and 33 percent of their jury trials. The discrepancy in success rates is, therefore, not so great. Retained counsel are the only ones who do better before juries than before judges. They got only 20 percent acquittals in bench trials, but got 30 percent before juries—not quite as good a rate before juries as the bar association counsel. (It is only fair to add that the defender has won as many as 46 percent of his jury trials—in 1965—and that the figure varies greatly from year to year. Unfortunately, statistics for other types of counsel in other years are not available.)

Despite all these differences in what happens to defendants with each type of lawyer, there is a surprising similarity in the total of all clients, whatever type of counsel they have, who are convicted by plea or trial. Committee counsel have a conviction rate of 88 percent, the public defender 91 percent, and retained counsel 93 percent. One might say that the type of counsel makes little difference in whether or not one is found guilty. However, it is often a trap to assume that similar results are produced by similar causes.

We have reached the final point in the criminal process, the sentencing. Because there is no information on the comparative length of prison sentences or frequency of death sentences, the only comparison that can be made is with respect to how often a convicted felon is put on probation rather than given a jail sentence. We found that in 1964 the public defender obtained probation for 28 percent of his clients, compared with 14 percent for all other counsel. However, in a sample of 163 cases made two years earlier, Silverstein found that the public defender had a probation rate of only 18 percent compared with a 39 percent rate for retained counsel. Our result, based on a much larger sample, compares more closely to expectation. If a guilty plea can increase the chances for probation or lead to a lighter sentence, as is generally believed, then the public defender's style of representation should offer the best prospect for the average defendant. If the case is one which ought to be tried by a jury, retained or committee counsel would be better.

What we have shown is that the various types of counsel have rather different styles of defense and that these styles may be more or less appropriate for different defendants, depending upon their positions. Those against whom the evidence and law are clear would be ill served by the lawyer whose insistence on a full-fledged trial results in a stiffer penalty. The defendant trapped in a web of circumstantial evidence will want the full attention of the most able and unharried trial lawyer. So too will the one who believes a jury will never convict him.

It seems to us advisable to maintain parallel systems simply to provide diversity in style of representation, to provide the indigent a range of choice. But that is not the only reason. While there is no question of either the integrity or ability of assistant public defenders, it may be that the quality of public defense is maintained by the opportunity of the accused to reject the defender and demand a private lawyer. The private appointed lawyer can set a very high standard of indigent defense, operating without the pressures of volume that continually impinge on the defender. And they can and do take causes, devoting amounts of time, energy, and money that could not be asked of a public servant.

Finally, the appointed counsel have a special function as a result of their interest and ability in jury trials. In their study *The American Jury* Hans Zeisel and Harry Kalven Jr. suggest that the jury trial sets standards both for the bench and the opposing attorneys. They state that decisions to waive a jury trial or to plead guilty "are in part informed by expectations of what the jury will do. Thus, the jury is not only controlling the immediate case before it, but the host of cases not before it which are destined to be disposed of in the pretrial process." Through the jury the public gets a chance to express its views of criminal law enforcement. The indigents whose cases are deserving of consideration by this court of last resort are as entitled to its review as are those who can employ counsel.

We regret, therefore, any tendency—even in the name of economy—to reduce the role of the private lawyer in indigent defense. The evidence of the defender's economy is doubtful at best, and the private lawyer's participation in a spirit of public service may well be the touchstone of continued integrity in the treatment of the poor.

July/August 1967

FURTHER READING SUGGESTED BY THE AUTHORS:

The American Jury by Harry J. Kalven, Jr., and Hans Zeisel (Boston: Little, Brown & Co., 1966). A study of the operation of the jury and judge as finders of fact in criminal cases.

Defense of the Poor in Criminal Cases by Lee Silverstein (American Bar Foundation, 1965). A national field study on methods of indigent defense and attitudes of judges and lawyers.

The Rationing of Justice by Harold S. Trebach (New Brunswick, N.J.: Rutgers University Press, 1964). A general summary of the criminal process and indigent defense, written for the layman.

Store Front Lawyers
in San Francisco

JEROME E. CARLIN

A United States district court on April 22, 1968, invalidated California's residency requirements for persons seeking public assistance. Previously, applicants had to be residents of the state for at least one year before they could become eligible for benefits. According to the *San Francisco Chronicle* of April 25:

> The Reagan Administration will try to overturn last week's landmark Federal Court decision. . . . Health and Welfare Director Spencer Williams said the decision would add another 24 million dollars to welfare costs, and adds about 6,900 families and 12,000 other individuals to the welfare rolls.

On December 28, 1968, the *New York Times* printed the following story datelined San Francisco:

POOR WIN VICTORY IN A HOUSING SUIT

COURT HALTS COAST RENEWAL UNIT

RESIDENTS BACK PLAN

> A Federal Court has halted the funding of a $100 million urban renewal project here with a decision that is expected to affect similar projects across the country and

173

aid the poor in establishing legal rights for themselves. The court order prohibits the Department of Housing and Urban Development from supplying additional funds for the project until an acceptable plan has been approved for relocating uprooted families. . . . In taking the action to court, the Western Addition community group was [represented] by the San Francisco Neighborhood Legal Assistance Foundation. . . .

On August 12, 1969, the following appeared on the front page of the *Chronicle:*

BAY JUDGE ORDERS BOOST IN WELFARE

More money must be paid in rent allotments to people in the biggest welfare program in San Francisco and Alameda Counties, a Superior Court judge ruled here yesterday. Judge Alvin E. Weinberger further ordered the State Department of Social Welfare to take steps that will produce another increase in rent money across the State in a few months time.

He acted in a law suit brought by the San Francisco Neighborhood Legal Assistance Foundation on behalf of all persons receiving Aid to Families with Dependent Children (AFDC) in the two counties. Foundation lawyers charged that most AFDC clients are getting a monthly rent allotment less than the actual rent they are paying. Under State law, the Department's standards for rent must insure "safe, healthful housing." And the Department's own regulations require that its rent standards be based on "current actual costs for housing."

Judge Weinberger said the state and counties must live up to their own laws and regulations. . . .

The total sum required statewide would be $19 million per year. . . . This would pay the actual rent. How much more would be required after the Department hearings, to pay for safe, healthful housing is a matter of dispute. But the total increase could reach $50 million.

These have been some of the more newsworthy activities of a new type of professional organization. The San Francisco Neighborhood Legal Assistance Foundation is a federally financed, community-controlled legal service agency which has been aggressively advocating the rights of the poor since it began operation in October 1966. It is one of about 300 agencies throughout the United States funded by the Office of Economic Opportunity (OEO) to deliver more effective legal services to the nation's poor.

Since the foundation has probably gone farther than almost any of the other legal service agencies in carrying out this mandate and has served as a model for many other programs in the United States, it may be instructive to examine what it set out to accomplish, the extent to which it was able to achieve its objectives, and the problems it encountered. One of the most important issues that emerges from such an inquiry is the apparent incompatibility of the two principal goals of the organization: control by the client community and institutional change.

Having participated in the creation of the foundation, and having served as its head for the first three years of its existence, I will be presenting an insider's view that may well be biased and self-serving. I trust that my training as a sociologist and lawyer will serve to curb any major excesses.

The foundation is a private, nonprofit corporation with a governing board consisting of representatives of the local bar associations, law schools and the poverty community. The bylaws require that a majority of the board members be selected by the five poverty areas in San Francisco and that the board must also have a majority of attorneys. This is accomplished by having each poverty area select at least one lawyer representative. The board hires the coordinator, who is the chief executive officer of the foundation, and the directing attorney (chief counsel) for each of the five neighborhood law offices. The coordinator is responsible for carrying out the overall policies of the organization (which are determined by him and the board), for allocating resources among the various offices and departments and for hiring and supervising administrative and legal staff at the headquarters office (main office) of the foundation. Each chief counsel hires and fires his own staff of attorneys, secretaries, law students and aides.

In the fall of 1969 there were more than 120 paid staff persons working at the foundation, including 50 full-time attorneys and about 30 part-time law students. In addition, about 25 law students and ten social work students spent varying amounts of time at the foundation for credit under faculty supervision. Numerous private attorneys, on a volunteer basis, interview clients in the evening at a neighborhood office, make court appearances on default divorces or perform other services.

The staff attorneys are generally young—about a fourth came to the foundation right out of law school (mostly through the OEO-funded Reginald Heber Smith Fellowship and VISTA programs); only about a third had at least four years of practice experience before joining the foundation. Most attended top-ranking law schools; approximately a third graduated from an Ivy League law school (Harvard, Yale or Columbia). One out of four foundation attorneys is from a minority group; there are nine black lawyers.

The yearly budget of the foundation is over a million dollars, practically all of which comes from OEO in the form of an annual grant channeled through the local poverty agency, the Economic Opportunity Council of San Francisco (EOC). Although the foundation must deal both with OEO and EOC, it is essentially the former, and particularly the Legal Services Division within OEO, that has played the principal role in articulating and enforcing general guidelines for the foundation (and other legal service agencies) and evaluating performance.

OEO seeks to shape and control programs and promote certain national objectives, not only through the funding process, but also by means of nationwide training programs, research and back-up centers and fellowship programs that place bright young law school graduates in funded agencies. Many foundation lawyers (particularly those working in the main office) maintain close ties with other poverty lawyers throughout the country by taking an active part in these OEO programs as well as meetings of the National Legal Aid and Defender Association (which has become largely dominated by OEO lawyers) and other newly developed associations of poverty lawyers. In the national poverty law movement, OEO's Legal Services (in alliance with the American Bar Association, if not all or even most state and local bar associations) continues to play a leading role, giving solid support (with only few lapses) to program goals generally more advanced than most funded agencies are willing or able to realize.

Every month over a thousand new clients come into the five neighborhood offices of the foundation. A large majority of the clients are seeing a lawyer for the first time; most are on welfare; and half are in families with an annual income of less than $3,000 a year. About 15 percent of the clients are referred out—mainly to private attorneys or the public defender—because they fall above the foundation's income standard or they have a fee-producing or criminal case. The largest number of clients (about 30 percent) want help with a family problem, and half of these are seeking a divorce. The next biggest group are those having problems with administrative agencies: welfare, unemployment insurance, social security, immigration and naturalization (the bulk of the cases in the Chinatown office) and the draft. Problems with landlords and merchants (and their collection agents) each constitute about 15 percent of the cases.

Most of the family cases, including all divorce matters, are referred to the domestic relations unit, located at the main office, for more expeditious handling. This innovation has been adopted by a great many other programs and has contributed significantly to reducing the overall time and resources that need be devoted to this largely routine service.

The main office also houses a legal staff handling a limited number of cases that are selected because they raise major poverty issues in public housing, welfare, urban renewal and, more recently, in the consumer area. The cases are referred to the staff from community organization or neighborhood office lawyers. In time the main office attorneys have become specialists in the particular areas in which they work, in contrast with most attorneys in the neighborhood offices who, given the diversity of legal problems they have to deal with and the relatively little time they have to give any particular case, remain essentially general practitioners.

The foundation was largely the creation of Charles Baumbach, a politically astute young lawyer who put together a coalition of white militant lawyers (primarily Jewish) and minority professionals (mainly black) who held positions in the local poverty power structure. The founders had a common cause in their insistence on neighborhood control of legal services.

For the lawyer-founders, community control was in part a means of negating control by the organized bar which they felt would be opposed to a more aggressive form of advocacy, one that would seek to use the law as an instrument of social change. The lawyers were also committed to altering the conventional power relation between the poor and the agencies that purport to serve them. Community control would create new opportunities for the poor to participate in determining agency policy and decisions, and this principle should also apply to legal service programs for the poor, or so it was felt.

For their part, the neighborhood poverty leaders had just fought and won a battle with the mayor for majority control of the EOC by representatives from the "target" areas, and they wanted control of the legal services component as well. Their reasons were complex: in part they were simply extending the demand for self-determination; in part they had learned to resent the paternalism and insensitivity of traditional legal aid. But there was also a desire to expand a new power base by gaining control over jobs, services and other rewards for constituents.

Majority control of the board of directors by representatives of the poor was one expression of the neighborhood leaders' insistence on community control. Another was the very considerable autonomy given the neighborhood offices. The local leaders envisioned that each of the poverty areas would in effect have its own law firm. The chief counsel of the neighborhood office was to be selected by the board, rather than the coordinator, and it was assumed that the representatives on the board of a particular neighborhood would have primary say in choosing the attorney to head "their" office. Also, limiting the powers of coordinator would, it was hoped, minimize racial and ethnic jealousies —given the ethnic mix of San Francisco's poverty areas— and provide a hedge against a bad director.

Community control was the unifying issue for the lawyers

and neighborhood leaders who established the foundation. It was also the major issue in the foundation's sometimes bitter struggle with the legal establishment in San Francisco. After a year-long battle, the foundation won a stunning victory when it finally convinced OEO officials to fund it rather than the bar-supported Legal Aid Society of San Francisco. The foundation became the first OEO-funded legal service agency in the United States with majority control by representatives of the poverty community.

Although the neighborhood leaders expressed no particular views regarding the content of the legal program, the lawyer-founders had some very strong ideas about it. These ideas were derived from an analysis of traditional legal aid and some conceptions about law and social change. The lawyers wanted to create an agency that would not only provide remedial assistance to individual clients (albeit in a more sympathetic and aggressive fashion than legal aid), but would also work toward altering conditions that keep the poor powerless and victims of injustice. This aim was based in part upon a recognition of the impossibility, with limited resources, of handling more than a small fraction of the problems urgently calling for legal assistance, and the necessity, therefore, of a more "wholesale" approach. It rested also on the understanding that, as Jan Howard, Sheldon Messinger and I wrote in 1966,

> the legal problems of the poor . . . characteristically arise from systematic abuses embedded in the operation of various public and private agencies, affecting large numbers of similarly situated individuals. Effective solution of the problems may require the lawyer to direct his attention away from a particular claim or grievance to the broader interests and policies at stake, and away from the individual client to a class of clients, in order to challenge more directly and with greater impact certain structural sources of injustice.

Very generally speaking, we came in time to conceive of our mission in this way: to find leverage points in the system to bring about a redistribution of power and income more favorable to the poor. Two general approaches were developed: strategic advocacy and economic development. Under the first, we sought to enter into the variety of forums where the law is made and administered, to facilitate the development of new rights in areas where the law was vague or clearly biased against the poor, or to enforce existing law favorable to the poor which had remained unimplemented (e.g., enforcement of health and safety provisions of the housing code, prohibitions against fraud and misrepresentation in sale of consumer goods).

To a remarkable extent, it appeared that "the system"— be it welfare, urban renewal, private slum housing or the garment industry in Chinatown—could not operate successfully without breaking the law: the cost of compliance is generally greater than the operators of the system are willing to pay, especially since those most likely to be hurt have been least likely to complain. Consequently, we hoped that vigorous law enforcement might serve not only to redistribute income, but also to mount sufficient pressure to change the system.

The test for the efficacy of such activity was whether it would result in increasing the income or political bargaining power of a substantial number of poor persons. Litigation (with an emphasis on class suits) and administrative and legislative advocacy were the principal tools. In time, however, we learned that these measures, particularly court cases, by themselves were frequently ineffective unless combined with the mobilization of political support in the middle class as well as poverty communities.

By means of the second general approach we sought to promote entrepreneurial activity among ghetto residents. This came later and remained a subsidiary strategy.

Whatever else the foundation may have achieved, it gained a reputation in the community of being a tough advocate for the poor, of being willing to take on any and all opponents—police department, Housing Authority, United States Army, welfare department, used-car dealers, Redevelopment Agency, City Hall, board of education. In a skit presented at the Bar Association of San Francisco Annual Ball (December 1968), the following, written by an attorney member, was sung to the tune of "Glowworm":

We're from Neighborhood Legal Assistance
We encourage draft resistance
Nasty landlords are our nemesis
We keep tenants on the premises
We give deadbeats our protection
To frustrate any debt collection
The laws we use are not on your shelf
'Cause we make them up ourself

We soon recognized the importance of publicity in building a reputation: it has been said that we won more cases at press conferences than in the courts. We published our own newsletter which reached several thousand persons, mostly private attorneys in San Francisco, with reports of our more important and more interesting cases. We also made it a point to get our cases into the press. Some idea of the coverage, and the developing image, may be seen in the following:

In one of the most unusual cases handled by the Foundation in recent weeks, 20 year old Ted Townsend, who had been held for three months in the Presidio stockade as a suspected deserter, was freed after his Neighborhood Legal Assistance attorney pointed out . . . (*San Francisco Progress,* August 24, 1967).

A poverty program lawyer has filed a complaint with the Public Utilities Commission, seeking to end Pacific

Telephone's $25 deposit requirement for certain new customers (*Chronicle*, December 16, 1967).

The Neighborhood Legal Assistance Foundation filed a suit that seeks to prevent San Francisco policemen from carrying guns while off duty (*Chronicle*, November 9, 1968).

The San Francisco Neighborhood Legal Assistance Foundation has fired another salvo at the State Department of Social Welfare (*Examiner*, June 27, 1968).

The unit [the main office legal staff] is illustrative both of the length to which the young attorneys in Legal Assistance will go to attempt to help their clients and of the crusading idealism of the men who operate it (*Examiner*, October 9, 1968).

The Neighborhood Legal Assistance Foundation is seeking a breakthrough in labor practices to make unions more responsive to the needs of their members, especially minority group members with language and cultural problems (*Argonaut*, October 26, 1968).

The San Francisco Neighborhood Legal Assistance Foundation has joined the legal fight against Rudolph Ford, the Daley City car dealer (*Examiner*, January 14, 1969).

A San Francisco draftee who couldn't get anybody to listen to him finally was heard by a Federal judge who ordered the army to discharge the youth. . . . After a year Bibbs got his story to . . . an attorney with the Neighborhood Legal Assistance Foundation who filed a federal court suit and got Bibbs discharged (*Chronicle*, March 12, 1969).

A quiet little war has been going on between the San Francisco Neighborhood Legal Assistance Foundation and the state over welfare recipients' rights. . . (*Chronicle*, March 17, 1969).

Realtor Walter H. Shorenstein was accused yesterday [in a suit filed by the San Francisco Neighborhood Legal Assistance Foundation] of using his position as president of the Recreation and Park Commission to push the destruction of the International Hotel (*Chronicle*, March 28, 1969).

Our reputation gave us needed leverage in dealing with landlords, merchants, collection agencies, used-car dealers and public agency officials. Often a phone call was all that was necessary; people knew that we meant business and would follow through—indeed we enraged many slumlords' attorneys, who accused us (sometimes in letters to their congressmen) of using taxpayers' money to harass them.

In assessing the clout we developed it must be said that we have primarily benefited particular clients for whom we have been able to get a better deal in bargaining with merchants, landlords, welfare officials and others. Although often gratifying for the lawyer and his client, the benefits are generally remedial and short-lived—very little is basically changed. Housing is a good example. In three years we probably handled at least 4,000 individual cases involving some kind of landlord-tenant dispute. We undoubtedly brought some solace and relief to many individual tenants by delaying an eviction or forcing a landlord to make some repairs. Nevertheless, in those same three years the housing situation for poor people in San Francisco has become a great deal worse. The stock of low-income housing has been further reduced through public and private renewal programs. If plans for the latest renewal project in the Yerba Buena District are not changed, there will be approximately 4,000 fewer units in the city, which means more doubling up or worse, because there are virtually no vacancies among low-income units.

The bulk of the housing available to the poor is sub-standard (at least 60,000 units have been so labeled officially), and is deteriorating further. The waiting list for public housing went up to 5,000, at which point the Housing Authority stopped adding names. Rents have gone up with the decline in the housing stock and increasing taxes—in some areas they have doubled in the past few years. Against this background it might appear as though the foundation had made the process a little more humane without having any effect on the underlying machinery. But that is not quite the case.

There are two areas—redevelopment and welfare—in which we have made at least a small dent in the system, which may well mark the beginning of an even greater impact.

In surveying the general housing situation for the poor in San Francisco, it was clear that top priority had to be placed on preventing any further reduction in the stock of low-income housing. The principal offender in San Francisco, as in other parts of the United States, has been the federal urban renewal program administered through local redevelopment agencies. This program has proceeded on the understanding that there would be no enforcement of those provisions of the Federal Housing Act which require that persons displaced from a project area be relocated into safe, decent and sanitary housing at rents they can afford. If these provisions were to be enforced, then the renewal program would have to go into the business building low-income housing—and this it has never been willing or able to do. As a result, the program has produced a drastic net decline in housing for the poor and has substantially worsened slum conditions.

In 1966 redevelopment was on the move again in San Francisco after nearly a two-year lull caused by the voters'

approval of the anti-fair housing Proposition 14. The
Redevelopment Agency was eager to proceed with its plans
to demolish approximately 4,500 dwellings units of predominantly low-cost housing in the Western Addition,
thereby displacing close to 10,000 persons—mostly poor
and black. Failure of the agency to comply with the
relocation provisions of the Federal Housing Act would
provide, we hoped, the necessary leverage to challenge the
project. (Not only was the relocation plan patently de-
ficient—given San Francisco's unbelievably tight low-
income housing market and the absence of any provisions
for constructing new housing for displacees—but it turned
out that the Department of Housing and Urban Development [HUD] had been honoring agency requisitions for
financing the project without having first given its approval
of the agency's relocation plan—a clear and gross violation
of federal law.) The major obstacle that we faced was the
fact that the courts had, unfortunately, refused to monitor
federal urban renewal programs on behalf of project residents, on the theory that persons whose homes were being
destroyed did not have sufficient stake in the outcome
of litigation to give them standing to sue and that such
suits involved technical matters too complex for the courts
to get into. Even though public officials might be violating
the law to the grievous detriment of thousands of poor
residents forced out of their homes into even worse circumstances, the courts refused to open their doors to hear
these complaints. The principle hurdle, then, was the
court itself. Before anything else could be done we had to
establish for our clients a most basic right—the right to
be heard before a judicial tribunal.

A year and a day after the suit was filed in conjunction
with the NAACP Legal Defense Fund—and 16 months
after filing an administrative protest with HUD—the court

finally reached a decision on the jurisdictional question: it found that our clients had standing to challenge the legality of the agency's relocation plan and issued a preliminary injunction bringing the renewal project in the Western Addition to a grinding halt. This was clearly a landmark decision; it finally brought the federal renewal program under the scrutiny of judicial review, and for the first time in the United States a renewal project had been stopped in midstream.

The case had been brought on behalf of the Western Addition Community Organization (WACO), a federation of grass roots neighborhood organizations, put together a couple of years earlier by a Student Nonviolent Co-ordinating Committee organizer to fight the second round of redevelopment in the Western Addition. (The first round had been decisively lost—only a handful of families out of the many thousands previously residing in the area ever returned.) As a result of the court victory, WACO and the residents of the project area were at last given a voice in the decisions and plans so vitally affecting their lives—both in the sense of having gained entrée into the court and also by establishing a viable bargaining position with the Redevelopment Agency. Although the injunction was later dissolved by the court, the Redevelopment Agency had been significantly shaken—and a new and broader-based coalition emerged in the Western Addition which, under agreement with the agency, became an official participant in the renewal process.

Pressure on the Redevelopment Agency has been kept up as projects begin to move in other areas. The Yerba Buena project, which calls for the destruction of 4,000 housing units to make way for a new commercial complex, was also challenged by the foundation in a federal court suit. The clients, who are generally old as well as poor, have literally no place to go. The fight with the Redevelopment Agency, particularly in Yerba Buena, brought the foundation into a head-on confrontation with the San Francisco power structure, and the pressure began to mount, especially from City Hall. Nevertheless, the political alliances that had been forged in support of our clients' interests—including our allies among respectable middle-class groups and civic organizations—held firm. And once again, and far more rapidly than before, a federal court order was issued temporarily halting relocation of residents.

What then have we accomplished? We have at least slowed down the rate of destruction of low-income housing by public and private agencies. (By saving the International Hotel, which houses the remnant of the Filipino community in San Francisco, from demolition by private developers, we were able to extend some of the principles established in the WACO case into the private sector.) We have also helped fashion a legal-political force that the Redevelopment Agency and the city power structure will have to bargain with in determining housing policies for San Francisco. And we have provided hard evidence that in the area of redevelopment the arbitrary exercise of public power by local authorities and the federal government can be checked.

The other area in which the foundation has made some progress in its goal of institutional change is welfare. To begin with, we have enabled many more poor people to obtain public assistance: at least 60,000 people became eligible to receive welfare benefits as a result of our suit that invalidated California's residency requirement. We also prevented the cutoff of close to 2,000 needy persons from general assistance as an economy move by the San Francisco Department of Social Services. The foundation, moreover, has won several court decisions which, if and when they are implemented, will substantially increase dollar benefits to recipients. In the *Ivy* case the Superior Court ordered that rent allotments for AFDC recipients in San Francisco and Alameda counties be raised immediately to cover actual rentals (this will add about $19 million when extended statewide) and that a new list of rent allotments be issued reflecting the cost of safe and sanitary housing as required by state law (and this could add at least $30 million more). In the *Nesbitt* case (which we brought with the Alameda County Legal Aid Society), the court held that the state department of social welfare was violating recent state and federal regulations which, as an encouragement to seek employment, exempt a certain portion of the earnings of working recipients in calculating their welfare grant. As a result, it was estimated that working recipients were getting approximately $30 a month less than they were entitled to. Enforcement of this decision could increase payments to recipients by about $9 million. In the *Kaiser* case, also brought with the Alameda County Legal Aid Society, the federal court declared unconstitutional a California statute placing a ceiling on the amount of money that could be granted to AFDC recipients, a ceiling that was actually lower than the state's own determination of the minimum required for subsistence.

Insofar as we have sought to increase the amount of money going to welfare recipients, we appear to have been successful in adding somewhere between $50 and $100 million—this includes the $25 to $30 million a year estimated increase in welfare costs resulting from the residency decision. Not bad for a $3 million investment in legal services in San Francisco.

These figures, however, may turn out to be something

less than firm. The state has many options to limit, delay or in other ways frustrate the carrying out of the courts' decisions. The state department of social welfare can engage us in lengthy appellate proceedings; it can adopt new regulations to reduce the cost of particular decisions; it can simply refuse to comply with court orders (as it is now doing in the rent case); or the legislature may change the state law that was the basis for the court victory.

It became necessary, therefore, for us to attend to these other arenas. This required not only our presence at hearings and meetings of state and county welfare bodies and appearances before legislative committees, but the mobilizing of welfare recipients and others to bring pressure to bear on administrative and legislative decision-makers. Formation of an active citywide welfare rights organization was achieved in part through a series of welfare advocates' classes conducted in various neighborhoods by the foundation's welfare specialists.

Pressure from the poverty community has been fairly effective in San Francisco, but much less effective in Sacramento. Effectiveness in Sacramento requires not only statewide organization, but support from other than welfare recipients, and it is certainly questionable whether this support will be forthcoming when most middle-class voters feel that more money for welfare inevitably comes out of their pockets. Nevertheless, an important effect of the residency decision is that states like California, with relatively high benefits, will bring pressure on Congress for some kind of national income maintenance program.

Our aim has been not only to increase dollar benefits, but to enable recipients to gain some control over the welfare system—to render it less arbitrary and oppressive. We have been able to reform procedures within the welfare department to bring them more in line with constitutional, due process requirements. One of the cases, in which we have challenged the failure of the state to give recipients a hearing before their benefits are cut off, is now before the United States Supreme Court. In a sense, however, everything we've done in the welfare area has been calculated to maintain constant pressure on the system to maximize its responsiveness to the poor. We have in part succeeded. We have shaken up the system and even encouraged many on the inside to make changes they felt they could not make before.

The retiring director of the state department of social welfare acknowledged the impact of our efforts, and those of other poverty lawyers in California, in the statement he gave at his final news conference on November 28, 1969:

Here in California we have been challenged on dozens of issues, all of them coming back to the fact that for the first time, the poor have real and effective advocacy in our courts. This, again, is the significant point transcending all other considerations and consequences. An era of advocacy has begun out of which, I am sure, public assistance is never going to be the same. Not only is this happening through the courts, but also in the meetings and hearings of welfare boards, advisory commissions and administrators at every government level. The poor have come out of their apathy, and our accountability for what we do and why we do it is theirs to know—as it always has been under the law but never before so vocally sought.

As I indicated earlier, one of the strategies for institutional change was promotion of economic development in the poverty community. The foundation was one of the first legal service programs to launch a serious undertaking in this area. The initial project, a laundromat in the Mission District financed with the first Small Business Administration loan in the West to a business owned and operated by poor persons, was highly successful. This venture led to the establishment of the San Francisco Local Development Corporation (LDC) which was designed to serve as a catalyst in the development of other ghetto-owned enterprises, and eventually perhaps serve as a neighborhood development bank. This approach seemed to us to provide a more direct route to the redistributive goal than litigation. Although the LDC continues to function, and has assisted a number of ghetto residents in financing and managing new businesses, we have actually accomplished a great deal less over the past year or two in the economic area than we have in the courts. The slow pace of the LDC may be accounted for in part by staff problems and the time and energy that was consumed in obtaining initial funding. We also underestimated the difficulties in accumulating the capital and expertise necessary to move beyond the small retail or service business.

As we have seen, the foundation was initially conceived as a collection of largely autonomous neighborhood law firms with a central administrative staff to "keep the machinery running" and to provide liaison among the neighborhood offices and between them and the board and various outside agencies. This highly decentralized system was designed to insure maximum responsiveness to the particular needs of the various poverty communities.

I had become convinced from a brief study I had conducted for OEO in the summer of 1966 that a central research and planning staff was essential to implement the broader, strategic goals of the legal services program. Notwithstanding the greater dedication and competence of the attorneys in the OEO-funded agencies, I argued in my report that without structural changes that go beyond simply shifting the location of the office (into the neighborhood) there would be little difference in actual impact and operation between OEO legal programs and conventional legal aid. I suggested, therefore, a division of function between a central office and neighborhood offices. Lawyers in the central office would develop strategies for change and take the necessary steps to implement these strategies through test cases, class actions and the like. I contended that they should also maintain close relations with neighborhood organizations, "for the task of creative advocacy ought to reflect consultation with the slum community as well as feedback from the caseload of the neighborhood offices." The main task of the neighborhood office would be that "of serving a large volume clientele on something like a mass production basis," with some research and other assistance from the specialist attorneys.

Over the years, a strong central legal staff was built up in the main office of the foundation. The attorneys became specialists in housing and redevelopment, welfare and other areas, and they were responsible for the major cases of the foundation. The office was started with two attorneys. In the fall of 1969, there were approximately 15 attorneys (including most of the foundation's allotment of Reginald Heber Smith Fellows) and a total staff of about 25, not including the many law students working in the clinic program. The main office legal staff was now larger than any of the neighborhood offices. The main office attorneys were the "cosmopolitans" in the foundation: they were much more likely than the neighborhood attorneys to have contacts with other poverty lawyers across the United States—in OEO programs, the Legal Defense Fund—to attend regional and national conferences and training sessions and to keep up with the growing body of legal literature in their field.

From the very beginning, relations between the neighborhood offices and the main office were strained. In my report to OEO I had pointed out that one of the problems that might arise in setting up a separate structure for the strategic cases was

the tension between service to a mass clientele and creative advocacy. At any point the decision to allocate limited resources to a central planning staff may seem arbitrary, even heartless. For the decision will necessitate turning away desperate people who are, after all, entitled to the service. But unless this is done, little will be accomplished for the large majority of slum dwellers, and many of those who are served will receive only temporary relief.

Neighborhood attorneys felt that they were carrying the burden of providing legal services to the poverty community with little or no help from their main office colleagues. The latter were viewed as an expensive luxury—their case loads immorally small, the pace of their work annoyingly relaxed and the results highly dubious. Was the WACO case really worth all the time and effort that had gone into it, and what about the welfare cases that put a few more dollars in a recipient's pocket, if that? Is it fair to spend such a large share of the foundation's resources on these highly speculative cases when there are clear, tangible results obtained in eviction cases and divorce cases, where people really hurt? These questions bothered many neighborhood attorneys. Their growing resentment of main office attorneys was hardly diminished by the incidental benefits they seemed to enjoy—the many trips to conferences and meetings, the publicity in the newspapers and on television.

From the point of view of the main office attorneys, neighborhood lawyers were not only essentially engaged in a band-aid operation, but even on a remedial basis were frequently unable to give effective representation to their clients, given the unwillingness of the neighborhood offices either to limit caseloads or to accept more efficient, routinized procedures. Furthermore, several chief counsels were viewed as the prime perpetuators of a system in which the client community was often the loser.

Main office attorneys were also unhappy about what appeared to be the political restrictions on some neighborhood offices. The principal example was the unwillingness of the Western Addition office to represent WACO in its fight with the Redevelopment Agency. This decision, it was felt, was motivated in part by a reluctance to oppose the black establishment in the Western Addition (including the local EOC leaders) which supported redevelopment in exchange for more jobs for blacks in the agency and sponsorship of projects within the renewal area. Similarly, the Chinatown office was extremely reluctant to take an aggressive position against established interests in Chinatown. Thus it was fully two years before any action at all was taken against the sweatshops. It was no accident that these were the two offices in which the local establishment had most to do with the selection of the chief counsel.

Tensions were heightened by racial and ethnic differences. The main office legal staff has been predominantly white (it is interesting that a black lawyer who joined the staff has had little sympathy for the goals and methods of the office) and largely Jewish. Criticism of the main office has undoubtedly been affected by the feeling that it was inappropriate for white lawyers to be deciding what is best for poor blacks.

Although the neighborhood lawyers continued to be critical of the increase in staff at the main office and its failure to operate primarily as a back-up resource for them, an uneasy truce emerged between the neighborhood offices and the main office. The chief counsels agreed to leave the main office alone if it would not interfere in internal operations of the neighborhood offices. The sovereignty of the neighborhood offices was not to be trifled with. This was not a very happy solution. Indeed, it became increasingly difficult to effect even a modest degree of coordination. At stake was raising the quality of service in the neighborhood offices—and at the very least, preventing a deterioration in quality. This meant being able to do something about recruitment of attorneys, training of new attorneys and increasing office efficiency. Development of a rational recruitment program to take advantage of the foundation's nationwide reputation to attract top legal talent, particularly minority lawyers, simply was not possible with each office refusing to yield on its absolute power to hire and fire staff. A staff training program never really existed—some chief counsels resented the interference and one refused to permit his attorneys to attend training sessions. Development of standard legal forms and office procedures, sharing of information on cases, research memos and briefs to avoid duplication of effort and to insure the best thinking or approach to a case—all of these seemed unattainable despite repeated campaigns to bring them about. In response to a grant condition from OEO, the director of litigation (who is in effect the chief counsel for the main office legal staff) drew up a minimal plan to insure that information on more important or unusual cases would be made available to him and to the chief counsels in advance of filing, but leaving final control over the cases in the hands of the chief counsels. For a long period the chief counsels for one reason or another were unwilling to consider the plan on its merits.

We were caught in a bind. Our efforts to assist neighborhood offices in raising the quality of service to clients were generally opposed as undermining the autonomy of the neighborhood offices. As a result, the neighborhood job got tougher—with increasing resentment against the main office and a lowering of the quality of service to the clients in the neighborhoods. The offices continued operating essentially as independent law firms. Within the offices there was no real division of labor or specialization. Attorneys handled as best they could whatever cases and matters came their way on their interview days. Case loads were large and becoming more burdensome as the backlog of unfinished cases slowly but surely built up. Work with neighborhood groups was confined mostly to incorporation of essentially paper organizations. Moreover, the staff became less experienced, given the tendency to fill vacant slots with younger attorneys. And there was little effective supervision, since in most offices the chief counsel was playing primarily a political role in the community, having turned over the day-to-day administration of the office to his senior staff attorney or senior secretary. Consequently, in spite of the dedication and ability of most neighborhood attorneys, the quality of the work product in general declined.

The goal of community control had been institutionalized in the autonomous neighborhood offices, while the aim of institutional change was embodied in the main office legal staff. It was obvious that the growing antagonism between these two structures in large measure represented a conflict between the two goals. The lawyer-founders had been wrong in assuming that control by the client community was a necessary condition for, let alone compatible with, a program of institutional change. We were unfortunately burdened with some romantic notions of the poor.

The neighborhood leaders, particularly those identified with the poverty program, were following an old pattern fashioned by other ethnic groups as they fought their way up the power ladder. These leaders were, by and large, not out to change or seriously challenge the system; they simply wanted to be cut in. They were willing to have an understanding with the older, white establishment; in exchange for greater control of public programs aimed at helping the poor, and more control over jobs and other rewards for their constituents, they would keep the peace. The WACO suit was, of course, embarrassing: it was not until the Redevelopment Agency by its arrogance alienated its black allies in the Western Addition that the neighborhood leaders were able to openly support WACO's position.

It may well be the case that, with respect to their conception of legal services, the neighborhood leaders at this point are much closer to the conservative Republicans than to the militant white lawyers.

It is always possible, of course, that the neighborhood leaders may become radicalized—and the violent repression of the Panthers may be doing just that. And it is also possible that the young black lawyers coming out of the Reginald Heber Smith program may press for a more radical approach to legal services. Neither group, so far, however, seems to be prepared to move much beyond the issue of community control. The two principal demands of the black Reginald Heber Smith Fellows in a recent confrontation with OEO officials were higher salaries and control of the program.

By the spring of 1969 I was convinced that there would have to be some basic change in the structure of the foundation: although much of our work, particularly in housing and welfare, was beginning to pay off, the tensions within the foundation were becoming critical. The changes that would have to be brought about would necessarily mean limiting, if not doing away with, the autonomy of the neighborhood offices. In my view, this could only be accomplished by a black coordinator dedicated to institutional change, that is, by a militant black lawyer. I tried unsuccessfully for several months to find such a person. Finally, in October, having held the office for three years, and with a sense that we had accomplished in some ways a great deal more than I had ever expected, I resigned as coordinator of the foundation. It was now up to the board to find my successor, and hopefully a solution to our dilemma.

In December of 1969 my successor was chosen. The new coordinator is a black lawyer who had been a staff attorney in one of the neighborhood offices, and more recently held a top administrative post in the EOC. He is an able attorney, with a strong sense of professionalism and a flair for administrative efficiency. Although not unsympathetic to the aims and approach of the main office legal staff, he clearly represents the interests and perspective of the neighborhood offices. The tensions within the foundation should be significantly reduced, the divisions healed. I assume that the commitment to institutional change will gradually become weaker and that the main office legal staff will be reduced in size and given a different direction—to serve primarily as back-up resource for the neighborhood offices.

In retrospect, this probably represents the only solution that was realistically open to the foundation. Reorganization in the image of the main office legal staff would have brought the foundation into more direct and intolerable confrontations with the establishment and would have seriously jeopardized neighborhood support. Perhaps at this point the main objective should be the survival of the foundation as a major institution serving the ghetto under ghetto control.

If the militant white lawyers move on, this should not be interpreted simply as a reaction to a shift in leadership and possible direction of the foundation. Some have become disillusioned with the capacity of the legal system to respond; others may be following new fashions. In one way or another, however, the old coalition will very likely be dissolved. Looking back, I suppose we have each used the other—the black professionals and neighborhood leaders have gained an organization, and we had the chance to put our theories into practice. Still, it's sad the partnership couldn't last.

April 1970

Justice Stumbles over Science

DAVID L. BAZELON

Modern criminal law lives almost as much in the shadow of Freud as of Blackstone. For a generation now, law and other social institutions have been receiving revolutionary new information about human beings from the behavioral sciences. This information seldom solves our problems; in fact, it often seems to complicate them.

Some judges and lawyers say that the findings of behavioral science are too revolutionary to be allowed in the courtroom. But I cannot see that we have any choice but to allow them. To quote Havelock Ellis:

. . . However imperfect the microscope may be, would it be better to dispense with the microscope? Much less when we are dealing with criminals, whether in the court of justice or in the prison, or in society generally, can we afford to dispense with such science of human nature as we may succeed in attaining.

Science does not create complexities for the law—it reveals them.

201

Are the two systems—law and science—properly informed about and related to each other? We have problems about introducing new knowledge and understanding into the legal system and problems about the differences between the philosophies of science and of law. But as a judge I am primarily troubled by the man in the dock—about how the behavioral sciences are used in our criminal courts.

Over 100 years ago English law produced the M'Naghten rule to be used in deciding whether an accused person should be excused on the ground of insanity. That rule has come to symbolize one of the great debates between law and the behavioral sciences. M'Naghten provided:

> The party accused must be labouring under such a defect of reason, from disease of the mind, as not to know the nature and quality of the act he was doing, or, if he did know it, that he did not know he was doing what was wrong.

The United States adopted England's M'Naghten rule. In our time it has evoked swelling criticism from psychiatrists who say it places undue emphasis on man's reason and fails to recognize the emotional forces that drive him. A judge on my court put it this way:

> Psychiatry does not conceive that there is a separate little man in the top of one's head called reason whose function it is to guide another unruly little man called instinct, emotion, or impulse in the way he should go. The tendency of psychiatry is to regard what ordinary men call reasoning as a rationalization of behavior rather than the real cause of behavior.

Yet only if a defendant suffers from a defect of reason—of cognition—can he be excused from criminal responsibility under M'Naghten's rule. M'Naghten treats the insanity defense as a hole in the dike of responsibility, to be kept as small as possible lest the dike be weakened.

A story will illustrate how harshly this rule still operates and how this harshness is rationalized. Seven years ago a young man aged 22, Don White, beat an old woman to death and a few hours later stabbed to death a dockworker whom he had never met before. In neither case did the defendant flee from the scene of the crime. He waited to chat with passers-by and to watch the police come and go.

The court was told about his background. Don White had never lived with his mother. She was only 13 when he was born. When he was four months old, she left him at a railway depot. A porter turned him over to the woman who became his adoptive mother. Despite his superior intelligence—his IQ was about 130—White was expelled from every school he attended. He was in state institutions nine times, with a growing record of violence and delinquency. In 1951 a child psychiatrist said he was suffering from "a very malignant mental illness," that "institutionalization is absolutely necessary," and that "he will almost certainly wind up in prison or in a state mental hospital."

Between his chance meeting in the depot with his adoptive mother and his murderous chance meeting with the dockworker 20 years later, White was the subject of social service and of psychiatric studies time and time again.

What happened when—as we piously say—"he had his day in court?" Despite evidence of serious mental disorder, the defense of insanity was rejected because it was said that he was intelligent—that is, he had a high IQ and knew right from wrong. He was sentenced to die. The appellate court refused to alter the M'Naghten test:

The question before us is whether we, as the majority of jurisdictions, should refuse to extend absolute immunity from criminal responsibility to persons who, although capable of understanding the nature and quality of their acts (the ability to distinguish between right and wrong), are unable to control their own behavior as a result of mental disease or defect. . . . One argument for such change is that we must take advantage of new developments in psychiatry. [But] there is nothing new about the idea that some people who know what they are doing still cannot control their actions.

Recognizing that no new knowledge was necessary to see that White was grossly disordered, the court held that the insanity defense "is available only to those persons who have lost contact with reality so completely that they are beyond any of the influences of the criminal law." The court decided to retain the M'Naghten rule since it "better serves the basic purpose of the criminal law—to minimize crime in society. . . . When M'Naghten is used, all who might possibly be deterred from the commission of criminal acts are included within the sanctions of the criminal law."

Another horrible, but not atypical, example of the operation of M'Naghten is the New York case of an 18-year-old college freshman who killed his father. This boy was termed a schizophrenic by the examining psychiatrists. The murder was done several days before the young man was to take his final examinations in college, and apparently one of his psychotic reasons for committing the act was to avoid taking them. His disordered mind had made some connection between escape from taking the examinations, for which he was unprepared, and his hatred of his father and desire to reside again with his mother. On cross-examination, the prosecuting attorney attacked the doctor's diagnosis with a rather traditional line of questioning:

Q. . . . First, Doctor, psychiatry is not an exact science, is it?

A. Well, that's a matter of opinion.

Q. Well, let's put it this way, Doctor. Is it generally considered to be an exact science in the same sense that internal medicine or surgery is an exact science?

The prosecutor included an effort to show that the doctor was expressing a mere opinion, that the defendant did not suffer from an "organic" disease, that the doctor's perception of symptoms was "subjective"—and in general that the diagnosis had been made by a psychiatrist rather than an IBM machine.

But most strikingly in this case, the prosecuting attorney pursued a line of questioning based apparently on the assumption that if the boy knew that the knife in his hand when he killed his father was a knife and not a toothbrush, that if when he tried to hitch a ride to his home town on the night of the murder he knew he was headed for Elmira, New York, and not Timbuktu, and so on, *then* he knew what he was doing. Here is an excerpt from the testimony:

Q. ... He knew then on the Thursday before the murder when he went down and procured a knife that he was procuring a knife, didn't he?

A. He knew he had a knife. But he had a delusional motive when it came to the killing.

Q. Doctor, if you please, will you kindly just answer my question. ...

May I have the last part stricken?
The Court. Strike it out.

Q. Doctor, he knew the purpose for which he secured the knife, did he not?

A. He had a psychotic motivation at that time.
The Court. Answer the question.

More of the same follows, page after page of the transcript. The jury found the defendant guilty of murder in the first degree, and the New York Court of Appeals upheld the ruling and affirmed the death penalty.

I am reminded of the nineteenth century English judge, Lord Bramwell, who quaintly expressed his approval of the M'Naghten rule in these terms:

I think that, although the present law lays down such a definition of madness, that nobody is hardly ever really mad enough to be within it, yet it is a logical and good definition.

During my first three years on the bench I became increasingly troubled while passing on and reading cases like the ones I have just recounted. Many lawyers, judges, and jurors were troubled. Psychiatrists were protesting the resistance to use of their new understandings. Even when they were allowed to testify freely in court, the M'Naghten rule was, in effect, an invitation to disregard most of their testimony.

On the simple premise that fact-finders should be able to weigh any and all expert information about the accused's behavior, I wrote an opinion for my court which held that the M'Naghten rule was no longer adequate. That opinion, in the 1954 case of *Durham v. United States*, held that an accused is not criminally responsible "if his act was the product of mental disease or defect." We pointed out that:

The science of psychiatry now recognizes that a man is an integrated personality and that reason, which is only one element in that personality, is not the sole determinant of behavior.

All we sought to do was to give those who are charged with assessing the responsibility of a mentally disordered offender the data which modern understanding requires. Yet Durham raised a controversy in legal and behavioral circles similar to the controversy aroused in wider circles by the Supreme Court's decision of the same year which rejected the old notion that separate treatment of Negroes could really be equal. Opposition to the integration decisions is fast abating. Not so with the Durham decision.

The Durham rule has been adopted in very few of our states. Yet it has been considered, I believe, by the highest court of every state and by most federal courts as well. With such widespread "rejection," why does Durham command so much attention and so much opposition? Why is the controversy it aroused still such a live issue? I suggest that Durham touched an exposed nerve in the administration of criminal justice. We are all troubled by punishing people who suffer from mental and emotional disorders.

There was some amelioration of M'Naghten even before Durham, such as the "irresistible impulse" rule. There has been more since. Nonetheless, there remains a persistent reluctance to include information about sick people. At one level, this could be simple resistance to change. But in all fairness, it seems more complicated. It is a special aspect of the stress which has risen as we have tried to build a better bridge between two systems: our legal system, with its reluctance to assimilate knowledge from the behavioral sciences; and the behavioral sciences themselves, with their reluctance to clarify the state of the developing body of knowledge about human nature.

Why are professionals on each side failing to adapt? Why does the law find it so difficult to assimilate information which behavioral science has to offer? The principal reason, I believe, is uncertainty about where this information might lead.

We are in that terrible period known as "meanwhile." The behavioral sciences tell us enough to reveal the gross imperfections of present solutions, but not enough to provide perfect alternatives. Furthermore, what we are told is not limited to those recognizably mentally ill. Some light is also shed on those whom the law and society had always thought "bad" rather than "sick." The distinguished British sociologist Barbara Wootton points to the implications:

> The creation of the new category of psychopaths is the thin end of what may eventually prove to be an enormously thick wedge: so thick that it threatens to split wide open the fundamental principles upon which our whole penal system is based—undermining the simple propositions . . . as to the responsibility of every sane adult for his own actions, as to his freedom to choose between good and evil and as to his liability to be punished should he prefer evil.

She questions very seriously whether the criminal law, as we know it, can survive the onslaught of new information from psychiatry. My distinguished friend Chief Justice Weintraub of the New Jersey Supreme Court foresees the same problem. He argues that if we allow the psychiatrist to define mental illness for us—and not restrict its legal meaning to knowledge of right and wrong—then he will soon tell us about the factors which affect human behavior. Soon expert witnesses would be testifying about psychological, economic, social, and other matters which cause or contribute to anti-social behavior.

Information about a defendant's mental disorder may then prove most troubling to the court in seeking a "just" disposition of his case—and may trouble society, too, by revealing that societal disorders contributed to individual disorder. Scientists now generally agree that human behavior is caused rather than willed, that man is most vulnerable in early life, that compared with other species he is capable of learning for an inordinately long period of his life, that he usually responds more readily to reward than to punishment, and that he learns more readily from his peers than from his masters.

What implications does this information have for our notions of individual responsibility and for our correctional systems? If the information science can give is deeply troubling to our methods of coping with offenders, does this justify us in ignoring it?

Here is a concrete example of the kind of dilemma we face. A few years ago, I served on President Kennedy's Panel on Mental Retardation. I received quite an education since I was the only lawyer in a group that included biologists, geneticists, educators, and psychiatrists. I learned from them for the first time that a disability—retardation, for instance—may arise from wholly unrelated causes, yet produce the same effects. Specifically, my panel colleagues told me, a man may act one way because he has a brain lesion—and we could all understand and forgive the act. But given the same external circumstances, another man may act the same way because of a failure of learning. One who is without identifiable brain damage may become functionally retarded if as an infant or young child he was deprived of a certain minimum of attention, social education, and intellectual stimulation. He will act the same way as the man with the brain lesion.

If this new information is valid, what happens to our notions of morality? Can we call one man responsible because he is "just plain dumb" and the other man not responsible because of brain damage? Can we continue to condemn people for ignorance? And if not, where does this leave the criminal law?

There is a related and somewhat less philosophical cause for resistance to new knowledge. Each lawyer, judge, and juror conceives his goal to be a decision. All he needs for this is the evidence. The clearer the evidence, the easier the decision. But psychiatry has not yet advanced (perhaps it never will) to the point where it can unequivocally specify what responsibility means. Opinion evidence—especially the opinions of behavioral scientists—is rarely given in black and white. Opinion is, after all, a balance of probabilities. But the psychiatrist sometimes finds this difficult to explain in court. Excerpts from a case transcript will show how a psychiatrist may be berated for inability to give a categorical answer to the prosecutor's questions:

Defense counsel on direct examination: Would you state in your opinion whether there was a causal connection between the mental illness and the crime?

Doctor: In my opinion, there probably was.

Court: No, not probably. I want your expert opinion, not probability. Either you have an expert opinion or you do not.

Doctor: Well, my expert opinion is I do not know for sure.

Court: No, no. That doesn't answer the question.

Counsel: Just give us your opinion—was there a causal connection between the crime and the mental disease?

Doctor: I believe there was.

Court: No. Not what you believe. You must answer the question, Doctor. He is asking for your expert opinion.

Counsel: He said, "I believe there was." I think that is an honest answer.

Court: That is begging the question. I want a direct answer.

Doctor: Does your Honor mean Yes or No?

Court: No, I mean that you must state your opinion. . . . State your expert opinion, not "I believe," or "I guess." . . . Now, I don't want any guessing. If you have an expert opinion, I want it.

Doctor: Yes, my opinion is that the crime is probably

the product of illness.

Court: Not probably.

Counsel: We are not concerned with the word "probably." Can you give us your opinion?

Doctor: That is my opinion.

Court: That is not an opinion.

Doctor: I cannot answer Yes or No. I cannot answer it in terms of black and white.

Often the best kind of psychiatric evidence is "merely" opinion. It is an educated, knowledgeable, and often a logical and analytical judgment.

The decision-maker, whether judge or jury, is still left with the ancient and often agonizing tasks of evaluation, interpretation, and decision. In too many cases, the task of evaluation and interpretation are quickly abandoned, and the decision is reached by a much shorter route.

A short route to decision is to accept whichever expert gives the most clean-cut answers. It is the heart of my thesis that the M'Naghten rule encourages this spurious simplicity, while the facts of the sciences of behavior—at present— often lead toward uncertainty.

But if the law has not gone half-way to welcome behavioral science into the courtroom, neither have the psychiatrists faced up to their challenge.

What is usually required of the expert is a statement in simple terms of why the accused acted as he did—the psychodynamics of his behavior. In rare instances this is achieved. It occurs most often when the accused or his family has the money to employ a private expert to undertake the comprehensive study required. Then the psychiatrist will learn not only the factors that precipitated the behavior but how the accused became the sort of person he is, and how he must act. This, I repeat, is the exception. Where it occurs under the Durham rule, the accused may be seen as a sick person and confined to a hospital for treatment, not to a prison for punishment.

Of course it may not be possible for the psychiatrist—or any collection of witnesses—fully to explain *why* the accused acted as he did. The purpose of the Durham rule was to admit a wide range of complexity. But any point in that range, or any uncertainty, may be expressed with clarity.

The task of the expert witness is difficult. He must delve deep into the background of the accused. He must study, analyze, and co-ordinate physical, neurological, and psychological examinations. He must attempt to explain the whole man. He must provide the best explanation of the behavior. He cannot merely attach—or refuse to attach—a few labels or an IQ score. As our court emphasized in 1957:

Unexplained medical labels—schizophrenia, paranoia, psychosis, neurosis, psychopathy—are not enough. . . . The chief value of an expert's testimony in this field, as in all other fields, rests upon the material from which his opinion is fashioned and the reasoning by which he progresses from his material to his conclusion . . . ; it does not lie in his mere expression of conclusion.

In a more recent case, I had occasion to make the harsh comment that:

As far as the psychiatric testimony was concerned, [the defendants] might as well have been tried *in absentia.* They were not present in the conclusionary labels of the psychiatrists or in the perfunctory leading questions of counsel.

Why is the psychiatrist prone to give the court his diagnostic conclusion and little more? Basically, I often suspect, because he has little more to give. Our society will not divert enough of its resources to study those charged with crime. This goes to the root of our social system. Our psychiatrists may not be devoted entirely to the rich, but they certainly are seldom familiar with the poor. Most defendants charged with crimes of violence are poor, uneducated, deprived, and segregated. Socially and professionally, most psychiatrists are in the middle class. Psychotherapy has been called the therapy of communication. But many psychiatrists cannot communicate with those accused of crime—and too often they don't try.

Ignorance is compounded by the refusal to admit it. Doctors at one of our federal mental hospitals have often told me in private conversation that they do not have adequate staff and time to make thorough studies of the accused. But once in the courtroom they nevertheless try to live up to our expectations—they will not admit that they do not have all the answers. I sometimes feel that my psychiatrist friends who embrace Durham and then testify beyond their knowledge have done more to warp the Durham concept than the conservative lawyers who oppose it.

Enthusiastic psychiatrists often assume that *they* are being asked to make the moral and legal decision on guilt. They try to become lawyer, judge, jury, and society all rolled into one. They assume they "know" the law and what is good for society and for the accused. They give what we have begun to term "dispositional diagnoses."

Here is an example from a case which came before our court a few years ago. A man was indicted for arson. He gave such a complete written confession that even the police suggested he "was sick and needed psychiatric treatment." The confession revealed the classic symptoms of the sexual pyromaniac. He had been starting fires since he was 12 years old; he had set about 100 of them; the fire at which he had been apprehended was the second he had lit in that house that night.

A psychiatrist submitted the following written report—
this and nothing more:

As a result of this examination and a previous examination . . . it is my opinion that the [accused] is of sound
mind. Nothing is elicited which would lead me to the
opinion that the act . . . was committed as a result of
an irresistible impulse or otherwise as a result of mental
illness.

The trial court accepted this report as submitted.

Some time after the appeal to our court was concluded,
I met the psychiatrist—whom I knew quite well. I said
to him, "John, you examined the pyromaniac—didn't you
think he was sick?"

"Sure," he answered, "he was sick as hell."

"And dangerous," I pursued.

"Why, of course."

"Well, why did you tell the court he was of sound
mind?"

"Because he was—well, he was not psychotic—he had
no delusions or hallucinations—none of the symptoma-
tology of psychosis."

Plainly, this psychiatrist believed that by some absolute
legal fiat insanity means psychosis and nothing else. And
even after I told him that such was not the law and that his
report was therefore terribly misleading, he came forth with
this clincher:

I think I would still limit my report to whether or not
psychosis was present because it would be too difficult
and uncertain to draw the line anywhere else.

Wittingly or not, he was writing the law.

I have been concerned principally with the behavioral
scientists, the psychiatrists, and the psychologists who are
now generally accepted as expert witnesses. But other fields

are also contributing new knowledge about human behavior. The biologist, the geneticist, and the biochemist
are making fantastic strides in developing information about
human personality and the brain.

For a lawyer and a judge, I have had a unique opportunity to observe and participate in the discussions of some
of these scientists. The initial (albeit perhaps misguided)
enthusiasm for Durham either pulled or propelled me into
their midst. I have not yet extricated myself. So I sit by and
hear scientists explain the discovery of the genetic code. I
hear them expound on the factors that affect how a human
being will develop even before he is born. At the same
time I learn that identical cells will act differently depending
on the environment in which they are placed. These sciences
are now bringing in clues to even more revolutionary findings, as far as ethics and law are concerned. The use of
drugs to tranquilize or otherwise influence the mind will
have far-reaching implications for our concepts of responsibility and justice.

Full of such facts and speculation, I come back from
meetings with scientific groups at the Salk Institute for
Biological Studies and various other institutions, and I try
to concentrate on the cases which come before me for
decision. But I must forget most of what I learned from
the sciences of behavior when I judge the behavior of the
real human beings who come before our courts.

It seems to me that the criminal law will find it harder
and harder not to think about the science explosion. I sometimes wonder how long it will be before our orderly legal
processes are shaken by our expanding knowledge of the
human being and his behavior. And I wonder whether the
biochemist will fare any better in the courtroom than his co-
worker, the psychiatrist.

The relations between the individual and society cannot

be left to the scientists alone. The criminal law has a role to play. It enforces society's expectations. One might even say that the purpose of the criminal law has been to administer the effects of our disappointed expections. The law has traditionally sought to reduce the gap between society's expectations and the incapacity of some to fulfill them by minimizing recognition of that incapacity. M'Naghten seems designed to do precisely this. We put our expectations in one compartment and our learned sense of reality in another. There is little communication between the two. We are fearful that explanation may be taken as tolerance or absolution.

Yet my contention is the opposite. I contend that personal responsibility is linked—indeed locked—to understanding; and that as expectations are altered by growing knowledge, so a utilitarian morality will give way to a humane yet practical morality. A serious inquiry into the defendant's criminal responsibility can provide the catalyst for change.

That inquiry can be compared to a post mortem. The post mortem will not return the dead to life; the trial will not undo a heinous act. But in each case we can learn the causes of failure. And in the trial the entire community can learn—and thereby more clearly understand its responsibility for the act and for the redemption of the actor.

Admittedly the courtroom is not a scientific instrument. But our law libraries are actually man's greatest psychological archive of the natural history of human behavior. Psychological knowledge may reach mankind in many ways. To my mind, the courtroom can become one of the most incisive ways of explaining man and his failings to his fellow men. It can teach us yet again that "no man is an island"; that "though we are not all guilty, we are all responsible."

July/August 1967

FURTHER READING SUGGESTED BY THE AUTHOR:

Crime and the Criminal Law by Barbara Wootton (London: Stevens & Sons, 1963).

Psychoanalysis, Psychiatry and Law by Katz, Goldstein, Dershowitz (New York: The Free Press, 1967).

The Family and the Law by Goldstein and Katz (New York: The Free Press, 1965).

Insanity and the Criminal Law: From McNaghten to Durham, and Beyond by Simon E. Sobeloff (American Bar Association Journal—Vol. 41, September 1955).

President's Panel on Mental Retardation—Report of the Task Force on Law, January 1963, Library of Congress Catalogue Card No. 63-60030.

Juvenile Justice...
Quest and Realities

EDWIN M. LEMERT

The juvenile court is intended to succeed where parents have failed. But the family—even though disturbed by conflict, morally questionable, or broken by divorce or death—is the institution best suited for nurturing children into stable adults. Neither the Spartan *gymnasium,* nor the Russian *crèche,* nor the kibbutz nurseries, nor American orphanages, "homes," and reformatories can successfully duplicate the complex social and psychological construction of the family. Explicit recognition of this might well replace the pious injunction now in many laws that "care, custody, and discipline of children under the control of the juvenile court shall approximate that which they would receive from their parents."

In the majority opinion this May in *Gault v. Arizona,* which provided for some of the rights of criminal justice to be introduced into juvenile courts, Justice Abe Fortas pointedly wrote of the kind of care an incarcerated delinquent can expect from the state:

Instead of mother and father and sisters and brothers and friends and classmates, his world is peopled by guards, custodians, state employes, and "delinquents" confined with him for anything from waywardness to rape and homicide.

The harrassed juvenile court judge is not a father; a halfway house is not a home; a reformatory cell is not a teenager's bedroom; a hall counselor is not an uncle; and a cottage matron is not a mother. This does not mean that the system of children's justice should not seek kindly and dedicated people, but that it is a system with its own requirements. The judges, counselors, and matrons are permanent parts of the system; but their interests cannot be guaranteed to be the same as those of the children who are just passing through.

They do not pass through unmarked, however. An unwanted but unavoidable consequence to any child subjected to the system—including dependent and neglected children as well as delinquents—is the imposition of stigma. ("Dependent" refers to a residual category of nondelinquent children, such as orphans, for whom the state must take responsibility.) The necessary insight and social stamina to manage such stigma are not given to many people—least of all to the kind of children most likely to come into the juvenile court. Social rejections provoked by the stigma of wardship may convince the individual that he is "no good" or "can't make it on the outside." These beliefs may feed a brooding sense of injustice which leads to further delinquency.

An important rationale of state intervention is the faith that delinquency can be prevented and that the court can prevent it. The viability of this idea can be traced to a repressive Puritan psychology reinforced by the propaganda of the mental hygiene movement of the early twentieth century, which helped produce child guidance clinics, school social work, and juvenile courts. The metaphor is from medicine: High blood sugar warns of diabetes and a high cholesterol count is a warning of arteriosclerosis. In the early days of children's courts the comparable signs of juvenile delinquency were thought to be smoking and drinking, shining shoes, selling newspapers, or playing pool. The modern version is found in such ideas as pre-delinquent personality or delinquency proneness and in state laws which make truancy, running away from home, or incorrigibility bases for juvenile court control.

As yet, nothing has been isolated and shown to be a sure indicator of delinquency, nor is it likely that anything will be. Furthermore, things called "delinquent tendencies" often are found on close inspection to correspond not to any particular behavior, but rather to arbitrary definitions by school authorities, parents, and police. One investigation in New York found that, to a degree, truancy was simply a measure of the willingness or availability of parents to write excuses. Incorrigibility as found in juvenile court cases may mean anything from ignoring a mother's order not to see a boyfriend to assault with a deadly weapon—and often turns out to be parental neglect or unfitness.

The brave idea that the juvenile court can prevent delinquency is deflated or even reduced to absurdity by sociological studies of hidden delinquency which show that the majority of high school and college students at some time or another engage in delinquencies, not excluding serious law violations. The main difference between college students and youths who are made wards of juvenile courts is that the latter group contains more repeaters. While several interpretations are possible, these findings demand explanation. Why do youths who are made court wards commit more rather than fewer delinquencies? The conclusion that the court processing in some way helps to fix and perpetuate delinquency is hard to escape.

It must also be remembered that most youths pass through a time when they engage in delinquency. Children normally play hookey, help themselves to lumber from houses under construction, and snitch candy from dime stores; adolescent boys frequently swipe beer, get drunk, "borrow" cars, hell around, learn about sex from available females or prostitutes, or give the old man a taste of his own medicine. Transitional deviance not only is ubiquitous in our society but universal to all societies, especially among boys turning into men—Margaret Meade's droll observations on adolescence in the South Seas to the contrary notwithstanding.

Most youths outgrow their socalled predelinquency and their law flouting; they put away childish things as they become established in society by a job, marriage, further education, or by the slow growth of wisdom. Maturation out of the deviance of adolescence is facilitated when troublesome behavior, even petty crime, is dealt with by parents, neighbors, and policemen, and treated as a manifestation of the inevitable diversity, perversity, and shortcomings of human beings—in other words, as a problem of everyday living calling for tolerable solutions, not perfection. This means the avoidance whenever possible of specialized or categorical definitions which invidiously differentiate, degrade, or stigmatize persons involved in the problems. The cost of muddling through with children who become problems have multiplied with the rising plateau of mass conformities needed for a high-energy society, but they must be absorbed in large part where the alternatives are even more costly.

The ideology of delinquency prevention is much more urban than rural. Handling problems of youthful disorders and petty crime in rural areas and small towns—characteristically by sheriff's deputies, town police, the district attorney, and the probation officer—has been largely informal. Sharp distinctions are drawn between less consequential moral and legal infractions—"Mickey Mouse stuff"—and serious delinquencies, with no implication that one leads to the other. This is reflected in the reluctance of elective officials and those beholden to them to make records of their actions, but at the same time they want action in serious misdemeanors and felonies by youth to be swift and punitive. The juvenile court usually reserves formal action for "real problems" of families and the community; the functional context of youthful misconduct ordinarily can be realistically gauged and its consequences dealt with in a number of different situations.

A major difficulty in the bureaucratic urban juvenile court is that the functional context of child problems directed to it easily gets lost; it has to be reconstructed by bits and pieces of information obtained through investigations and inquiries conducted under highly artificial circumstances and communicated in series of stereotyped written reports. There is little or no direct community criticism or reaction that might put individual cases into a common-sense context. This plus the rapidity with which cases are heard in large courts (three minutes per case in Los Angeles in 1959) explains why the distinction between trivia and serious child problems breaks down. A notorious illustration came to light in Orange County, California, in 1957 when a private attorney put his own investigator to work on a case of an eight-year-old boy and a nine-year-old girl accused of a "sex crime" against a seven-year-old girl. He found that the case had been presented in court by a probation officer who was only repeating without investigation what he had been told. This private inquiry pared the charge down to an imputed incident witnessed by no one and reported two days after it supposedly occurred.

It would push facts too far to insist that the ideology of preventing delinquency is used by juvenile court workers and judges to justify slipshod operations. Nevertheless, it has allowed them to change the basis of jurisdiction from one "problem" to another. The practice is baldly indicated in the statement of a California judge arguing for retention under juvenile court jurisdiction of simple traffic violations by juveniles:

Moreover it seems to have been demonstrated that the broad powers of the juvenile court can be helpfully invoked on behalf of children whose maladjustment has been brought to light through juvenile traffic violations. A girl companion of a youthful speeder may be protected from further sexual [sic] experimentation. Boys whose only amusement seems to be joyriding in family cars can be directed to other more suitable forms of entertainment before they reach the stage of "borrowing" cars when the family car is unavailable.

The police generally are less concerned with the prevention of delinquency in individual cases than with prevention and control in the community as manifested in gang violence, disturbances of public order, a rise in crime rates, or mounting property losses. The utility of specious legal categories describing delinquent tendencies is most obvious when the police seek to break up youthful gang activity, quell public disturbances such as occur at drive-ins or public parks, or seek access to witnesses or informants to solve a crime or to recover stolen property. While the arrest and detention of youth to "clear up other crimes" may be efficient police tactics, abuses may arise at the expense of individual youths if such methods can be pursued under diffuse charges. Unfortunately there have been and are judges willing to allow juvenile detention to be used for these purposes. It was for these reasons that the Juvenile Justice Commission of California, following a statewide survey, recommended in 1960 the use of citations for minor offenses by juveniles, and the requirement that detention hearings be held within specified time limits to act as a check on overzealous police action.

It is true that, in a number of areas, the police have sought to aid juveniles to avoid clashes with the law through setting up recreation programs, "big brother" assignments, systems of referral to welfare agencies, informal probation, and even police social work. But such undertakings have declined in recent years and tend to be looked upon as divergent from essential police functions such as apprehension of criminals, recovery of property, and maintenance of public order. This may also point to growing police disillusionment with more generalized or community delinquency prevention programs. Police in some cities sharply disagree with community organizers of such projects over the issue of maintaining the autonomy of neighborhood gangs. They take a jaundiced view of attempts to divert such groups into more compliant pursuits, preferring rather to break them up.

Research assessments of community programs to prevent delinquency—such as the Chicago Area Project, the Harlem Project, and the Cambridge-Somerville Youth Study—have been disappointing; results either have been negative or inconclusive. Possible exceptions are community coordinating councils, especially in the Western United States where they originated. These councils bring police, probation officers, judges, and social workers together in face-to-face discussions of local youth problems. However, they seem to work best in towns between 2,000 and 15,000 population; it remains unclear whether they can be adapted successfully to large urban areas. Significantly, they work chiefly by exchanging agency information and referrals of cases to community agencies, with full support and cooperation of the police. In effect they represent concerted action to bypass the juvenile court, and it might be said that their purpose, if not function, is prevention of delinquency by preventing, wherever possible, the adjudication of cases in the court.

Much of what has already been said about preventing delinquency through the juvenile court is equally applicable to therapeutic treatment through the court. The ideal of treatment found its way into juvenile court philosophy from social work and psychiatry. Its pervasiveness is measurable by the extent to which persons educated and trained in social work have indirectly influenced the juvenile court or moved into probation and correction. A premise of therapeutic treatment of children is that scientific knowledge and techniques make possible specific solutions to problems.

Scientific social work has come to lean heavily on Freudian theories. Updated versions of socially applied psychoanalysis conceive of delinquency as an acting out of repressed conflicts in irrational, disguised forms. The accent is on internal emotional life rather than upon external acts: The social worker or the psychiatrist is a specialist who understands the problems while the client does not; the specialist "knows best," studies, analyzes, and treats— much in the manner of the authoritative medical practitioner.

A divergent, competing line of thought in social work repudiates scientific treatment in favor of a simpler task of helping, in which problems are confronted in whatever terms the child or youth presents them; responsible involvement of the client is a sine qua non of success in this process.

Generally speaking, social workers advocate assigning to other agencies many of the tasks the court has assumed. Some social workers seriously doubt whether the helping process can be carried on in an authoritarian setting, and to emphasize their stand refuse as clients children who have been wards of the court. Other social workers believe that judges should not go beyond their competence, but should use their power solely for adjudication, with determination of treatment left to social work agencies. A smaller number of social workers hold to a more sanguine view of reconciling personal help and authority within the role of the probation officer. Finally, there are some social workers who are not above using juvenile court power as a tool for getting access to clients or prolonging their contacts with them because they will "benefit from treatment." This pattern became aggravated in Utah when juvenile courts were under the administrative control of the state department of welfare.

Actually, comparatively few juvenile court cases are referred to social workers for treatment, and many juvenile court judges and probation officers are hostile to social workers. According to a U.S. Children's Bureau study, the most frequent disposition of juvenile court cases was dismissal; next was informal or formal supervision by a probation officer. Dismissals can scarcely be called treatment, even though the associated court appearance before an admonitory judge may have a chastening effect upon some youths. At most, such cases feature a brief exchange with an investigating officer who asks some questions, issues a stern warning, and says he hopes he will not see the boy again.

The consequences of supervision of delinquents by probation officers have been little studied and the outcome, even when successful, little understood. Probation practices with juveniles have little in common across the nation, and often they consist of a meager combination of office interviews and phone or mail reports. Probation officers frequently claim that they could give more help to their charges if they had more time, but this must be regarded as an occupational complaint rather than an accurate prediction. What little experimental research there is on the subject shows that mere reduction of the size of caseloads of probation and parole officers does not in itself lower rates of recidivism. More time to deal with their client's problems is a necessary, but not a sufficient, condition of success by court workers.

If the results of probation supervision of delinquents on the whole are disappointing or inconclusive, even less can be said in behalf of the treatment of juvenile offenders in institutions. Sociological analysis and evaluations of such correctional programs tend to be negative. Some writers even say that the goals of correctional programs in prisons and reformatories are inherently self-defeating. This follows from the very fact of incarceration, which by imposing personal deprivation on inmates generates hostility to formal programs of rehabilitation. Furthermore, the population of repeaters shapes inmate socialization.

The problems of juvenile correction and rehabilitation have been highlighted in the popular press and literature as poor physical plants, meager appropriations, and underpaid, undereducated personnel, but they lie far deeper. It remains doubtful whether even the generously funded and well-staffed California Youth Authority has neared its original purpose of providing individualized treatment for

youthful offenders. This cannot be traced to lack of dedication in the leadership, but to the task of administering
the institutions, where bureaucratic values and organizational inertia conspire daily to defeat the purpose of treatment. These dilemmas have led the CYA to begin
establishing community treatment projects on a large scale
and subsidizing probation programs with the hope of stim-
ulating local innovation of alternatives to incarceration.

I do not mean to exclude the possibility that clinically
trained and humanly wise people can help youth solve
problems which have brought them athwart the law.
Rather the intent is to leaven professional pretense with
humility, to place the notion of treatment in a more realistic perspective, and to point out the differences between
dealing with problems of human relationships and treatment as it has evolved in the practice of medicine. The
treatment of delinquency is best regarded as a kind of
guidance, special education, and training—much more akin
to midwifery than medicine—in which hopeful intervention into an ongoing process of maturation is undertaken.
The judge, probation officer, correctional counselor, or
institutional psychiatrist can be at most a small influence
among the many affecting development and emergence
into adulthood. Although the juvenile court can determine
that certain influences will take place in a prescribed order
in the process of socialization, it cannot control the meanings and values assigned to such occurrences.

If there is a defensible philosophy for the juvenile
court, it is one of judicious nonintervention. It is properly
an agency of last resort for children, holding to the anal-
ogy of appeal courts, where all other remedies must be
exhausted before a case will be considered. This means
that problems accepted for action by the juvenile court will
be demonstrably serious by testable evidence ordinarily dis-

tinguished by a history of repeated failures at solutions by parents, relatives, schools, and community agencies. The model should be the English and Canadian juvenile courts, which receive very few cases by American standards.

This statement of juvenile court philosophy rests upon the following propositions:

■ Since the powers of the juvenile court are extraordinary, properly it should deal with extraordinary cases.

■ Large numbers of cases defeat the purposes of the juvenile court by leading to bureaucratic procedures inimical to individual treatment.

■ The juvenile court is primarily a court of law and must accept limitations imposed by the inapplicability of rule and remedy to many important phases of human conduct and to some serious wrongs. Law operates by punishment, injunction against specific acts, specific redress, and substitutional redress. It cannot by such means make a father good, a mother moral, a child obedient, or a youth respectful of authority.

■ When the juvenile court goes beyond legal remedies, it must resort to administrative agents, or itself become such an agency. This produces conflicts and confusion of values and objectives. Furthermore, it remains problematic whether child and parental problems can be solved by administrative means.

It may be protested that here I am narrowing the conception of the juvenile court severely and that my model can hardly be recognized as a juvenile court at all by present standards.

However, organized nonintervention by the juvenile courts can become a definite protection for youth. Children need as much or more protection from the unanticipated consequences of organized movements, programs, and services in their behalf as they need from the formless "evils" which gave birth to the juvenile court. America no longer has a significant number of Fagins, exploiters of child labor, sweatshops, open saloons, houses of prostitution, street trades, immoral servants, cruel immigrant fathers, traveling carnivals and circuses, unregulated race tracks, much open gambling, or professional crime of the old style. The battles for compulsory education have long since been won, and technological change has eliminated child labor—perhaps too well. The forms of delinquency have changed as the nature of society has changed; social and personal problems of youth reflect the growth of affluence in one area of society and the growth of hostility and aggression in a nonaffluent sector. Current sociological theories of delinquency, stress as "causes" drift and risk-taking, on the one hand, and dilapidated opportunity structures, on the other.

The basic life process today is one of adaptation to exigencies and pressures; individual morality has become functional rather than sacred or ethical in the older sense. To recognize this at the level of legislative and judicial policy is difficult because social action in America always has been heavily laden with moral purpose. However, if the juvenile court is to become effective, its function must be reduced to enforcement of the "ethical minimum" of youth conduct necessary to maintain social life in a high-energy, consuming, pluralistic society. It can then proceed to its secondary task of arranging the richest possible variety of assistance to those specially disadvantaged children and youth who come under its jurisdiction.

A philosophy of judicious nonintervention demands more than verbal or written exhortation for implementation. Action is needed to reshape the juvenile court. Ideally it will be so structured that it will have built-in controls, feedback mechanisms, and social scanning devices which make it self-regulating and adaptive. This by no means signifies that the juvenile court should or will become "inner directed"; if anything, contacts and interaction with the community and its agencies will have more importance, if for no other reason than to protect its stance of non-intervention.

Relationships between juvenile courts and policing agencies probably will become more critical with a shrinkage in juvenile court functions. However, it can be hoped that this will be an irritant leading more police departments to develop juvenile bureaus and to upgrade their competence for screening and adjusting cases within the department. Even now it is common practice for police departments to dismiss large numbers of juvenile arrests or "adjust" them within the department. More and better juvenile officers and rational procedures can greatly decrease referrals to juvenile courts. This does not mean that police will undertake probation or social work, but rather will parsimoniously work with relatives and community agencies, or at most will engage in brief, policeman-like counseling with youths whom they believe they can help.

Since the police will never entirely forsake their habit of using the juvenile court for their own special purpose of keeping law and order, the second line of defense for judicious nonintervention must be the intake workers of the court or probation department. Ideally, the most competent workers would be organized into a fairly autonomous division of intake, referral, and adjustment, which would be oriented toward community agencies and given the prerogative of denying petitions for court jurisdiction.

As has been noted, referral of cases from juvenile courts to social work agencies is complicated because the agencies do not want to work with hostile or uncooperative clients.

Juvenile courts trying to treat children with small difficulties—often indistinguishable from those being handled in large numbers by welfare agencies—lose the chance to refer them to the agencies later. For this reason, referrals should be made immediately—no detention, no confrontation with child or parent, no detailed investigation. The court intake procedure should not be turned into a fishing expedition to uncover and record "problems" to justify further court action.

In general, juvenile courts are granted control over dependent and neglected, as well as delinquent, children. Despite the early aim of the juvenile court to take stigma away from these statuses, the pall of moral questionability settles over all court wards in spite of category.

It is virtually impossible to defend the court's jurisdiction over dependent children on any grounds but convenience. Just why, for example, a child whose mother has been committed to a mental institution should be made the ward of a latently criminal court is not readily explainable. The same is true for children whose parents are troubled by unemployment or illness, and likewise for orphaned or illegitimate children. Granted that they need protection with legal sanction, there is no proof that the civil courts cannot entrust this job to the welfare agencies, assuming full protection of the rights of parents and children. Some probation officers find justification for juvenile court jurisdiction where some children in a family are delinquent and others merely dependent. But there is as much justification in such cases for allowing civil agencies jurisdiction over all but the most seriously delinquent children.

The arguments for supervision of neglected children by juvenile courts are only slightly more forceful. If the child's problem is truly the fault of his parents, why should the child be branded? The suspicion is strong that juvenile courts are used to gain control over children where the proof of parental neglect is too flimsy to stand scrutiny in an adult criminal court. It is a knotty problem, admittedly, but children should not be paying the costs of official indirection. If the parents can be shown in a general court to be at fault, let the custody of the children go to a welfare agency if necessary. If the parents cannot be shown to be at fault, let the matter end.

At the root of this desire to keep dependent and neglected children under the eye of the court is the persistent belief that crime and delinquency are caused by dependency and neglect. This idea, descended from hoary biblical notions and Victorian moralism, still turns up, as in the description of the dependency and neglect unit in the recent annual report of an urban probation department:

> Implicit in the function of this unit is the concept that it is very probable that the basis for delinquent acting has been laid in the children and that delinquency prevention is, therefore, a primary concern.

Little durable evidence has been discovered to support the contention that poverty, broken homes, or parental failures—alcoholism, sexual immorality, or cruelty—are in themselves causes of delinquency. Most delinquents come from intact homes, and there is little unanimity on whether broken homes produce more than their proportional share of delinquents. Furthermore, every delinquent from a broken home averages two or more brothers and sisters who are not delinquent.

If we are to have judicious nonintervention, then we cannot continue to have statutory jurisdiction defined in such subjective fashion. Given the untoward consequences of labeling, we cannot continue to work under diffuse definitions which allow almost any child, given compromising circumstances, to be caught up in the net of the court.

When such specious legal grounds as incorrigibility, truancy, and running away from home are warrants for juvenile court action, they allow parents, neighbors, school officials, and police—even the youths themselves—to solve their problems by passing them on to the court. Note, for instance, the lengthy conflict between juvenile court workers and school officials, in which the school people are accused of foisting off their own failures on the court. The educators reply heatedly that the court is unreceptive or does nothing about "really mean kids." Probation officers ruefully discover in some counties that sheriff's deputies expect them to settle all neighborhood quarrels in which juveniles are involved. Parents or relatives many times make it clear in court that they desire their child to be punished for highly personal reasons. A depressing sidelight is that the court itself can be a cause for incorrigibility. Failure to obey an order of the court can be an official reason for severe punishment, even though the original excuse for taking jurisdiction may have been minor.

Runaways must be understood in the same context as incorrigibles, with the added difference that they are more frequently girls. Often running away is a dramatic demonstration—a little like suicide attempts by adult women. California girls sometimes demand to be placed in detention in order to expose the "hatefulness" of their homes or to embarrass their parents. While police action often is clearly indicated for runaways, action by the court is decidedly not. If drama is needed, it should be staged under some other auspices.

Incorrigibility, truancy, and running away should not be in themeselves causes for court jurisdiction. The social agencies are well equipped to handle such problems. In fact, an inquiry in the District of Columbia showed that agencies were handling 98 percent of the runaways, 95 percent of the truants, 76 percent of the juvenile sex offenses, and 46 percent of the incorrigibles.

Much has been said of the "philosophy" of the juvenile court and little can be added, other than to note that this very preoccupation with philosophy sets it apart from other courts. In general, American courts for children have been given broad legislative grants to help and protect children, to depart from strict rules of legal procedure, and to utilize what in other courts is excluded evidence. One result has been that, under the noble guise of humanitarian concern and scientific treatment, the courts have often simply deprived the children of justice and fair play. The juvenile court originated in humanitarian concern rather than the police powers of the state, and legislators are disposed to treat it as a child welfare agency. Thus, few procedures were specified in early statutes. Later accretions in statutes and common law have proved to be extremely divergent, and little in the way of case law developed, particularly since it took until the 1960's for the first juvenile court appeal to reach the Supreme Court of the United States.

Inattention to procedure has led to the absence of hard rules on hearings, with the result that in many courts hearings are attenuated, ambiguously accusatory, or even nonexistent. Thus, the least we can ask of judicious nonintervention is that a hearing be given any child whose freedom is likely to be abridged by the court. A further desirable change would be the introduction of split hearings: one devoted to factual findings rich enough to justify taking jurisdiction, and one to ascertain what should be done with the child. Both hearings should be rigorous, but the second should admit social data which might make clear the reasons for the delinquent act. This procedure will prevent the

court from taking jurisdiction on the basis of impression-
istic hearsay evidence, but will also allow such evidence to
help the judge make the punishment fit not the crime, but
the criminal. This division should be made most clear, for
studies of split hearings in New York and California have
showed that about two-thirds of the judges continued to
read social reports before asserting jurisdiction, thus de-
feating the purpose of the split hearings. Appellate courts
in California feel the social report is germane to adjudication; those in New York do not. Instead of more opinions,
we should set about finding out whether the minority judges
in these two states, as well as all English juvenile court
judges, are hampered by the absence of this information in
asserting jurisdiction.

Wherever the social report is admitted in the process, it
should be subject to scrutiny. This implies the presence of
lawyers for the prosecution and defense. In its decision in
the Gault case this May, the Supreme Court assured the
presence of defense lawyers, a practice which has been
followed for several years in California, New York, Minnesota, and the District of Columbia. The traditional argument against this practice, which was used by Justice
Potter Stewart in his dissent in Gault, is that the introduction of counsel may rob the juvenile court of its informal
ad hoc quality and turn it into little more than a miniature
criminal court. My own California studies indicate that
advising parents and children of the right to counsel, as
ordered by the legislature in 1961, has increased the statewide use of counsel from 3 percent of the cases to 15 percent. In some counties, the rise was from 0 to 1 or 2 percent; in others it was from 15 percent to 70 or even 90
percent. In assigning counsel, the courts have favored dependent or neglected children and those charged with
serious offenses. I have found no indication of racial or

social discrimination in assignments.

One problem that has emerged is that private attorneys tend to lack knowledge of the system and regularly assigned public defenders tend to get wired into it. In both instances, the client may be hurt. Mere introduction of counsel seems insufficient to guarantee judicious nonintervention if the intake of cases is not reduced.

Introduction of defense counsel has not automatically meant introduction of prosecutors. The presentation of the state's case has fallen in many instances to the probation officer, who lacks both the training and the temperament to prosecute. He knows that active prosecution will later make it difficult or impossible to help the child. Where a judge takes over the interrogation, defense attorneys may be left in the untenable position of objecting to his questions and then hearing him rule on the objections. The police are more enthusiastic about placing prosecutors in the courts than the prosecutors are, and judges are not yet disposed to permit hearings to become all-out adversary struggles. Their attitude is not ill considered. I have seen an attorney in such a situation attempt to attack the credibility of a witness—a 15-year-old girl—by bringing her juvenile record into court and referring to sexual experiences for which she received money.

My research has shown that cases with attorneys are more likely to be dismissed, less likely to result in wardship, and more likely to end in a suspended sentence than cases without an attorney. The dismissals were not evenly distributed among the delinquent, the dependent, and the neglected children, however; the cases of neglected children—that is, those actions alleging unfit homes—were the ones most frequently dismissed. Attorneys were often successful in attacking imprecise charges and having them reduced. Attorneys were also able to negotiate alternative dispositions of cases, such as finding relatives to take a child rather than sending him to a foster home, proposing psychiatric help rather than commitment to a ranch school, or sometimes convincing the client that cooperation with the probation officer is preferable to resistance and ending with loss of parental control. If these findings are indicative, the adversary function is likely to be marginal in relation to the attorney's function as a negotiator and interpreter between the judge and family. Of course, the very likelihood of an attorney entering cases has a monitory value in reinforcing the new consciousness of court workers regarding the rights of juveniles. The New York concept of the attorney as a law guardian seems most fitting.

The interest in the role of attorneys in the juvenile court has brought about a concern with the sort of evidence to be accepted and the levels of proof required. The judges I have studied in California deal with the problem of hearsay evidence by admitting everything, on the assumption that they can consider only the competent evidence. This view has some support in legal opinion, where it is argued that the hearsay rule was aimed at controlling gullible juries rather than judges. But in the juvenile court much evidence is in the form of reports which are little more than compilations of professional hearsay; whether the ordinary judge is always qualified to sift this sort of evidence is questionable. Many judges seem remarkably naive about evaluating psychiatric and social science reports.

In civil courts—where only property is at stake—a preponderance of evidence is sufficient to decide the case. Considering the nature of the evidence in juvenile court, however, this may be insufficient. I would suggest that clear and convincing proof, that which admits only one conclusion, be the standard for determining guilt. For the most grievous juvenile crimes, the standard of criminal proof, guilt beyond all reasonable doubt, should prevail, as it does, for example, in English juvenile courts.

Although the justices did not discuss standards of evidence and proof explicitly in the Gault case, they did apply standards of adult courts in the right to counsel, the protection against self-incrimination, the right of confrontation and cross-examination, and the right to timely and explicit notice of the charges. Altogether, this is a strong indication that the extensive use of hearsay will not be viewed lightly when and if the Supreme Court is called upon to rule on standards of evidence and proof.

The words of the court in *Kent v. United States,* the first juvenile court case it ever heard, characterize the present state of affairs:

There is evidence, in fact, that there may be grounds for concern that the child receives the worst of both worlds; that he gets neither the protections accorded to adults nor the solicitous care and regenerative treatment postulated for children.

The doctrine of judicious nonintervention is nothing more than a plea that the child in court be granted the best of both worlds. Welcome as the Gault decision is in granting some of the protections accorded to adults, until some attempt is made to stem the flow of cases into the juvenile courts, solicitous care and regenerative treatment may be impossible.

July/August 1967

FURTHER READING SUGGESTED BY THE AUTHOR:

Justice for the Child edited by Margaret K. Rosenheim (Glencoe, Illinois: Free Press, 1962) A collection of critical essays raising questions of the quality of justice in juvenile courts.

The Juvenile Courts by F. T. Gile (London: George Allen and Unwin Ltd., 1946). A highly readable discussion of the work and problems of English juvenile courts, with some tart things to say about their American counterparts.

Delinquents Without Crimes

PAUL LERMAN

About 100 years ago, the state of New Jersey built a special correctional facility to save wayward girls from a life of crime and immorality. Over the years the ethnic and racial backgrounds of the institutionalized girls changed; the educational level of their cottage parent-custodians shifted upward; and the program of correction grew more humane. But the types of offenses that constitute the legal justification for their incarceration in the State Home for Girls have not changed appreciably.

The vast majority of the girls in the Home today, as in past years, were accused of misbehavior that would not be considered crimes if committed by adults. They were formally adjudicated and institutionalized as delinquents, but most of them have not committed real criminal acts. Over

An earlier version of this chapter was commissioned by the Work Group on Self-Concept of the Social Science Research Council Subcommittee on Learning and the Educational Process, January 1970.

80 percent of them in 1969 were institutionalized for the following misdeeds: running away from home, being incorrigible, ungovernable and beyond the control of parents, being truant, engaging in sexual relations and becoming pregnant. Criminologists classify this mixture of noncriminal acts "juvenile status offenses," since only persons of a juvenile status can be accused, convicted and sentenced as delinquents for committing them. Juvenile status offenses apply to boys as well as girls, and they form the bases for juvenile court proceedings in all 50 states.

Historical Background

Most Americans are probably unaware that juveniles are subject to stricter laws than adults, and to more severe penalties for noncriminal acts than are many adults who commit misdemeanors and felonies. This practice, so apparently antithetical to our national image of child-centeredness, began well before the Revolution. The Puritans of the Plymouth Bay Colony initiated the practice of defining and treating as criminal children who were "rude, stubborn, and unruly," or who behaved "disobediently and disorderly towards their parents, masters, and governors." In 1824, when the House of Refuge established the first American juvenile correctional institution in New York City, the board of managers was granted explicit sanction by the state legislature to hold in custody and correct youths who were leading a "vicious or vagrant life," as well as those convicted of any crime. The first juvenile court statute, passed in Illinois in 1899, continued the tradition of treating juvenile status offenses as criminal by including this class of actions as part of the definition of "delinquency." Other states copied this legislative practice as they boarded the bandwagon of court reform.

The contention that juvenile status offenders are still handled through a *criminal* process will be disputed by many defenders of the current system who argue that the creation of the juvenile court marked a significant break with the past. They contend that juvenile courts were set up to deal with the child and his needs, rather than with his offense. In line with this benign aim, the offense was to be viewed as a symptom of a child's need for special assistance. The juvenile court was designed to save children—not punish them. Only "neglectful" parents were deemed appropriate targets of punishment.

Unfortunately, the laudable intentions of the founders of the court movement have yet to be translated into reality. The U.S. Supreme Court, in 1967, reached this conclusion; so, too, did the Task Force on Delinquency of the President's Commission on Law Enforcement and the Administration of Justice. Both governmental bodies ruled that juvenile court dispositions were, in effect, sentences that bore a remarkable resemblance to the outcomes of adult criminal proceedings. The Supreme Court was appalled at the idea that 15-year-old Gerald Gault could be deprived of his liberty for up to six years without the benefits of due process of law found in adult courts. The majority was persuaded that the consequences of judicial decisions should be considered, not just the ideals of the founders of the juvenile court.

From an historical perspective, the Supreme Court's ruling appears quite reasonable—although it was 70 years overdue. The juvenile court was grafted onto an existing schema for defining youthful misdeeds as illegal behavior. It was also grafted onto a correctional system that had begun separating youngsters from adults, and boys from girls, for many years before the first juvenile court was established. Long before there was a juvenile court, the

American predilection for utilizing legal coercion to control youthful behavior had been well established. The form of the jurisdictional mandate changed with the emergence of the juvenile court—but the substantive range and scope of youthful liability for noncriminal behavior has not really changed.

Since the Supreme Court ruling in *Gault v. Arizona,* there has been increased concern and debate over the introduction of legal counsel and minimal procedural rights in the operation of the juvenile court. The preoccupation with legal rights in the courtroom has, however, obscured the fact that the sociolegal boundaries of delinquency statutes were unaffected by *Gault.* Nevertheless, some revision of the laws has been undertaken by the states, at least since 1960 when the Second United Nations Congress on the Prevention of Crime and the Treatment of Offenders recommended that juveniles should not be prosecuted as delinquents for behavior which, if exhibited by adults, would not be a matter of legal concern.

One state, New York, even approached a technical compliance with the United Nations standard. In New York, juvenile status offenders are adjudicated with a separate petition alleging a "person in need of supervision" (PINS); traditional criminal offenses use a petition that alleges "delinquency." However, true to American tradition, both types of petitioned young people are locked up in the same detention facilities and reform schools. One of the most "progressive" juvenile court laws in the country was initially enacted with restrictions on mixing, but this was soon amended to permit the change to be merely semantic, not substantive. Besides New York, six other states have amended their juvenile codes to establish a distinctive labeling procedure to distinguish criminal and noncriminal acts. Each of these states (California, Illinois,

Kansas, Colorado, Oklahoma and Vermont) has banned *initial* commitment to juvenile reformatories of children within the noncriminal jurisdiction of the court. Whether this ban will be continued in practice (and in the statutes) is uncertain. Meanwhile, young people can still be mixed in detention facilities, transfers to reformatories are technically possible, and subsequent petitions permit commitments to delinquent institutions. In addition, it is doubtful whether the public (including teachers and prospective employers) distinguishes between those "in need of supervision" and delinquents.

Discretionary Decision-Making

If the letter and spirit of American juvenile statutes were rigorously enforced, our delinquency rates and facilities would be in even deeper trouble than they are today. For few American youths would reach adulthood without being liable to their stern proscriptions. However, mitigating devices are used to avoid further overcrowding court dockets and institutions, and to demonstrate that parents and enforcement officials can be humane and child-centered. Adult authorities are permitted to exercise discretionary behavior in processing actions by official petitions. The American system is notorious for its widespread use of unofficial police and judicial recording and supervision of juveniles, whether status offenders or real delinquents. As a matter of historical fact, the hallmark of the American system is the intriguing combination of limitless scope of our delinquency statutes and enormous discretion granted in their enforcement and administration. Our statutes appear to reflect the image of the stern Puritan father, but our officials are permitted to behave like Dutch uncles—if they are so inclined.

Discretionary decision-making by law enforcement officials has often been justified on the grounds that it permits an "individualization" of offenders, as well as for reasons of pragmatic efficiency. While this may be true in some cases, it is difficult to read the historical record and not conclude that many juvenile status actions could have been defined as cultural differences and childhood play fads, as well as childhood troubles with home, school and sex. Using the same broad definition of delinquency, reasonable adults have differed—and continue to differ—over the sociolegal meaning of profanity, smoking, drinking, sexual congress, exploring abandoned buildings, playing in forbidden places, idling, hitching rides on buses, trucks and cars, sneaking into shows and subways, and so forth. While many judgments about the seriousness of these offenses may appear to be based on the merits of the individual case, delinquency definitions, in practice, employ shifting cultural standards to distinguish between childhood troubles, play fads and neighborhood differences. Today, officials in many communities appear more tolerant of profanity and smoking than those of the 1920s, but there is continuing concern regarding female sexuality, male braggadocio and disrespect of adult authority. In brief, whether or not a youth is defined as delinquent may depend on the era, community and ethnic status of the official—as well as the moral guidelines of individual law enforcers.

Extent of the Problem Today

National studies of the prevalence of the problem are not readily available. However, we can piece together data that indicate that the problem is not inconsequential. A conservative estimate, based upon analysis of national juvenile court statistics compiled by the United States Children's Bureau, indicates that juvenile status crimes comprise about 25 percent of the children's cases initially appearing before juvenile courts on a formal petition. About one out of every five boys' delinquency petitions and over one-half of all girls' cases are based on charges for which an adult would not be legally liable even to appear in court.

The formal petitions have an impact on the composition of juvenile facilities, as indicated by the outcomes of legal processing. A federal review of state and local detention facilities disclosed that 40 to 50 percent of the cases in custody, pending dispositional hearings by judges, consisted of delinquents who had committed no crimes. A companion study of nearly 20 correctional institutions in various parts of the country revealed that between 25 and 30 percent of their resident delinquent population consisted of young people convicted of a juvenile status offense.

The figures cited do not, however, reveal the number of youths that are treated informally by the police and the courts. Many young people are released with their cases recorded as "station adjustments"; in a similar fashion, thousands of youths are informally dealt with at court intake or at an unofficial court hearing. Even though these cases are not formally adjudicated, unofficial records are maintained and can be used against the children if they have any future run-ins with the police or courts. The number of these official, but nonadjudicated, contacts is difficult to estimate, since our requirements for social bookkeeping are far less stringent than our demands for financial accountability.

One careful study of police contacts in a middle-sized city, cited approvingly by a task force of the President's Commission on Law Enforcement and the Administration of Justice, disclosed that the offense that ranked highest as a delinquent act was "incorrigible, runaway"; "disorderly conduct" was second; "contact suspicion, investigation, and information" ranked third; and "theft" was a poor fourth. In addition to revealing that the police spend a disproportionate amount of their time attending to noncriminal offenses, the study also provides evidence that the problem is most acute in low-income areas of the city. This kind of finding could probably be duplicated in any city—large, small or middle-sized—in the United States.

Legal Treatment of Delinquents without Crimes

A useful way of furthering our understanding of the American approach to dealing with delinquents without crimes is provided by comparing judicial decisions for different types of offenses. This can be done by reanalyzing recent data reported by the Children's Bureau, classifying offenses according to their degree of seriousness. If we use standard FBI terminology, the most serious crimes can be labeled "Part I" and are homicide, forcible rape, armed robbery, burglary, aggravated assault and theft of more than $50. All other offenses that would be crimes if committed by an adult, but are less serious, can be termed "all other adult types" and labeled "Part II." The third type of offenses, the least serious, are those acts that are "juvenile status offenses." By using these classifications, data reported to the Children's Bureau by the largest cities are reanalyzed to provide the information depicted in the table. Three types of decisions are compared in this analysis: (1) whether or not an official petition is drawn after a complaint has been made; (2) whether or not the juvenile is found guilty, if brought before the court on an official petition; and (3) whether or not the offender is placed or committed to an institution, if convicted. The rates for each decision level are computed for each of the offense classifications.

TABLE I: DISPOSITION OF JUVENILE CASES
AT THREE STAGES IN THE JUDICIAL PROCESS
19 OF THE 30 LARGEST CITIES, 1965

	Part I (Most Serious Adult Offenses)	Part II (All Other Adult Offenses)	Juvenile Status Offenses
% Court Petition	57%	33%	42%
after complaint	N=(37.420)	(52,862)	(33,046)
% Convicted—	92%	90%	94%
if brought into court	N=(21,386)	(17,319)	(13,857)
% Placed or Com-	23%	18%	26%
mitted—if convicted	N=(19,667)	(15,524)	(12,989)

The table discloses a wide difference between offense classifications at the stage of deciding whether to draw up an official petition (57 percent versus 33 percent and 42 percent). Part I youth are far more likely to be brought into court on a petition, but juvenile status offenders are processed at a higher rate than all other adult types. At the conviction stage the differences are small, but the juvenile status offenders are found guilty more often. At the critical decision point, commitment to an institution, the least serious offenders are more likely to be sent away than are the two other types.

It is apparent that juvenile justice in America's large cities can mete out harsher dispositions for youth who have committed no crimes than for those who violate criminal statutes. Once the petitions are drawn up, juvenile judges appear to function as if degree of seriousness is not an important criterion of judicial decision making. If different types of offenders were sent to different types of institutions, it might be argued that the types of sentences actually varied. In fact, however, all three offender types are generally sent to the same institutions in a particular state—according to their age and sex—for an indeterminate length of time.

Length of Institutionalization and Detention

If American juvenile courts do not follow one of the basic components of justice—matching the degree of punishment with the degree of social harm—perhaps the correctional institutions themselves function differently. This outcome is unlikely, however, since the criteria for leaving institutions are not based on the nature of the offense. Length of stay is more likely to be determined by the adjustment to institutional rules and routine, the receptivity of parents or guardians to receiving the children back home, available bed space in cottages and the current treatment ideology. Juvenile status offenders tend to have more family troubles and may actually have greater difficulty in meeting the criteria for release than their delinquent peers. The result is that the delinquents without crimes probably spend more time in institutions designed for delinquent youth than "real" delinquents. Empirical support for this conclusion emerges from a special study of one juvenile jurisdiction, the Manhattan borough of New York City. In a pilot study that focused on a random sample of officially adjudicated male cases appearing in Manhattan Court in 1963, I gathered data on the range, median and average length of stay for boys sent to institutions. In New York, as noted earlier, juvenile status youth are called "PINS" (persons in need of supervision), so I use this classification in comparing this length of institutionalization with that of "delinquents."

The range of institutional stay was two to 28 months for

delinquents and four to 48 months for PINS boys; the median was nine months for delinquents and 13 months for PINS; and the average length of stay was 10.7 months for delinquents and 16.3 months for PINS. Regardless of the mode of measurement, it is apparent that institutionalization was proportionately longer for boys convicted and sentenced for juvenile status offenses than for juveniles convicted for criminal-type offenses.

These results on length of stay do not include the detention period, the stage of correctional processing prior to placement in an institution. Analyses of recent detention figures for all five boroughs of New York City revealed the following patterns: (1) PINS boys and girls are more likely to be detained than are delinquents (54 to 31 percent); and (2) once PINS youth are detained they are twice as likely to be detained for more than 30 days than are regular delinquents (50 to 25 percent). It is apparent that juvenile status offenders who receive the special label of "persons in need of supervision" tend to spend more time in penal facilities at *all* stages of their correctional experience than do delinquents.

Social Characteristics of Offenses and Offenders

The offenses that delinquents without crimes are charged with do not involve a clear victim, as is the case in classical crimes of theft, robbery, burglary and assault. Rather, they involve young people who are themselves liable to be victimized for having childhood troubles or growing up differently. Three major categories appear to be of primary concern: behavior at home, behavior at school and sexual experimentation. "Running away," "incorrigibility," "ungovernability" and "beyond the control of parental supervision" refer to troubles with parents, guardians or relatives. "Growing up in idleness," "truanting" and creating "disturbances" in classrooms refer to troubles with teachers, principals, guidance counselors and school routines. Sexual relations as "minors" and out-of-wedlock pregnancy reflect adult concern with the act and consequences of precocious sexual experimentation. In brief, juvenile status offenses primarily encompass the problems of growing up.

Certain young people in American society are more likely to have these types of troubles with adults: girls, poor youth, rural migrants to the city, underachievers and the less sophisticated. Historically, as well as today, a community's more disadvantaged children are most likely to have their troubles defined as "delinquency." In the 1830s the sons and daughters of Irish immigrants were overrepresented in the House of Refuge, the nation's first juvenile correctional institution. In the 1970s the sons and daughters of black slum dwellers are disproportionately dealt with as delinquents for experiencing problems in growing up.

Unlike regular delinquents, juvenile status offenders often find a parent, guardian, relative or teacher as the chief complainant in court. Since juvenile courts have traditionally employed family functioning and stability as primary considerations in rendering dispositions, poor youth with troubles are at a distinct disadvantage compared to their delinquent peers. Mothers and fathers rarely bring their children to courts for robbing or assaulting nonfamily members; however, if their own authority is challenged, many parents are willing to use the power of the state to correct their offspring. In effect, many poor and powerless parents cooperate with the state to stigmatize and punish their children for having problems in growing up.

Recent Criticisms

At least since *Gault*, the system of juvenile justice has been undergoing sharp attacks by legal and social critics. Many of these have pertinence for the processing and handling of juvenile status offenders. The current system has been criticized for the following reasons:

1. The broad scope of delinquency statutes and juvenile court jurisdictions has permitted the coercive imposition of middle-class standards of child rearing.

2. A broad definition has enlarged the limits of discretionary authority so that virtually any child can be deemed a delinquent if officials are persuaded that he needs correction.

3. The presence of juvenile status offenses as part of the delinquency statutes provides an easier basis for convicting and incarcerating young people because it is difficult to defend against the vagueness of terms like "incorrigible" and "ungovernable."

4. The mixing together of delinquents without crimes and real delinquents in detention centers and reform schools helps to provide learning experiences for the nondelinquents on how to become real delinquents.

5. The public is generally unaware of the differences between "persons in need of supervision" and youths who rob, steal and assault, and thereby is not sensitized to the special needs of status offenders.

6. Statistics on delinquency can be misleading because we are usually unable to differentiate how much of the volume reflects greater public and official concern regarding home, school and sex problems, and how much is actual criminal conduct by juveniles.

7. Juvenile status offenses do not constitute examples

of social harm and, therefore, should not even be the subject of criminal-type sanctions.

8. Juvenile institutions that house noncriminal offenders constitute the state's human garbage dump for taking care of all kinds of problem children, especially the poor.

9. Most policemen and judges who make critical decisions about children's troubles are ill equipped to understand their problems or make sound judgments on their behalf.

10. The current correctional system does not rehabilitate these youths and is therefore a questionable approach.

Two Unintended Consequences

In addition to the reasons cited, there are two unintended consequences that have not been addressed, even by critics. Analysis of the data presented earlier provides evidence that the current system is an unjust one. Youngsters convicted of committing the least serious offenses are dealt with more severely by virtue of their greater length of detention and institutionalization. Any legal system that purports to accord "justice for all" must take into account the degree of punishment that is proportionate to the degree of social harm inflicted. The current system does not meet this minimal standard of justice.

The recent ruling by the U.S. Supreme Court (*Gault v. Arizona*) found that the juvenile court of Arizona—and by implication the great majority of courts—were procedurally unfair. The court explicitly ruled out any consideration of the substantive issues of detention and incarceration. It may have chosen to do so because it sincerely believed that the soundest approach to insuring substantive justice is by making certain that juveniles are granted the constitutional safeguards of due process: the right to confront accusers and cross-examine, the right to counsel, the right to written charges and prior notice, and the right against self-incrimination. While this line of reasoning may turn out to be useful in the long run of history, adherence to this approach would involve acceptance of an undesirable system until the time that substantive justice could catch up with procedural justice. The likelihood that the injustice accorded to youth is not intentional does not change the current or future reality of the court's disposition.

Nevertheless, the inclusion of juvenile status offenders as liable to arrest, prosecution, detention and incarceration probably promotes the criminalization of disadvantaged youth. Earlier critics have indicated that incorrigible boys and girls sent to reform schools learn how to behave as homosexuals, thieves, drug users and burglars. But what is the impact at the community level, where young people initially learn the operational meaning of delinquency? From the child's point of view, he learns that occurrences that may be part of his daily life—squabbles at home, truancy and sexual precocity—are just as delinquent as thieving, robbing and assaulting. It must appear that nearly anyone he or she hangs around with is not only a "bad" kid but a delinquent one as well. In fact, there are studies that yield evidence that three-quarters of a generation of slum youth, ages ten to 17, have been officially noted as "delinquent" in a police or court file. It seems reasonable to infer that many of these records contain official legal definitions of essentially noncriminal acts that are done in the family, at school and with peers of the opposite sex.

It would be strange indeed if youth did not define themselves as "bad cats"—just as the officials undoubtedly do. It would be strange, too, if both the officials and the young people (and a segment of their parents) did not build on these invidious definitions by expecting further acts of "delinquency." As children grow older, they engage in a more consistent portrayal of their projected identity—and the officials dutifully record further notations to an expected social history of delinquency. What the officials prophesy is fulfilled in a process that criminalizes the young and justifies the prior actions of the official gate-keepers of the traditional system. Our societal responses unwittingly compound the problem we ostensibly desire to prevent and control—real delinquent behavior.

In the arena of social affairs it appears that negative consequences are more likely to occur when there is a large gap in status, power and resources between the "savers" and those to be "saved." Evidently, colonial-type relationships, cultural misunderstandings and unrestrained coercion can often exacerbate problems, despite the best of intentions. Given this state of affairs, it appears likely that continual coercive intrusion by the state into the lives of youthful ghetto residents can continue to backfire on a large scale.

We have probably been compounding our juvenile problem ever since 1824 when the New York State Legislature granted the board of managers of the House of Refuge broad discretionary authority to intervene coercively in the lives of youth until they become 21 years of age—even if they had not committed any criminal acts. Generations of reformers, professionals and academics have been too eager to praise the philanthropic and rehabilitative intentions of our treatment centers toward poor kids in trouble—and insufficiently sensitive to the *actual* consequences of an unjust system that aids and abets the criminalization of youth.

New Policy Perspectives

Sophisticated defenders of the traditional system are aware of many traditional criticisms. They argue that the intent of all efforts in the juvenile field is to help, not to punish, the child. To extend this help they are prepared to use the authority of the state to coerce children who might otherwise be unwilling to make use of existing agencies. Not all acts of juvenile misbehavior that we currently label "status offenses" are attributable to cultural differences. Many youngsters do, in fact, experience troubles in growing up that should be of concern to a humane society. The fundamental issue revolves on how that concern can be expressed so as to yield the maximum social benefits and the minimum social costs. Thus, while the consequences of criminalizing the young and perpetuating an unjust system of juvenile justice should be accorded greater recognition than benign intentions, it would be a serious mistake to propose an alternative policy that did not incorporate a legitimate concern for the welfare of children.

The issue is worth posing in this fashion because of a recent policy proposal advanced by the President's Commission on Law Enforcement and the Administration of Justice. The commission suggested that "serious consideration should be given complete elimination from the court's jurisdiction of conduct illegal only for a child. Abandoning the possibility of coercive power over a child who is acting in a seriously self-destructive way would mean losing the opportunity of reclamation in a few cases."

Changing delinquency statutes and the jurisdictional scope of the juvenile court to exclude conduct illegal only for a child would certainly be a useful beginning. However, the evidence suggests that the cases of serious self-destructiveness are not "few" in number, and there is reason to believe that many adjudicated and institutionalized young people do require some assistance from a concerned society. By failing to suggest additional policy guidelines for providing the necessary services in a *civil* context, the commission advanced only half a policy and provided only a limited sense of historical perspective.

Traditional American practices toward children in trouble have not been amiss because of our humanitarian concern, but because we coupled this concern with the continuation of prior practices whereby disliked behavior was defined and treated as a criminal offense (that is, delinquent). Unfortunately, our concern has often been linked to the coercive authority of the police powers of the state. The problems of homeless and runaway youths, truants, sex experimenters and others with childhood troubles could have been more consistently defined as *child welfare* problems. Many private agencies did emerge to take care of such children, but they inevitably left the more difficult cases for the state to service as "delinquents." In addition, the private sector never provided the services to match the concern that underlay the excessive demand. The problem of the troublesome juvenile status offender has been inextricably linked to: (1) our failure to broaden governmental responsibility to take care of *all* child welfare problems that were not being cared for by private social agencies; and (2) our failure to hold private agencies accountable for those they did serve with public subsidies. We permitted the police, courts and correctional institutions to function as our residual agency for caring for children in trouble. Many state correctional agencies have become, unwittingly, modern versions of a poorhouse for juveniles. Our *systems* of child welfare and juvenile justice, not just our legal codes, are faulty.

The elimination of juvenile status offenses from the jurisdiction of the juvenile court would probably create an anomalous situation in juvenile jurisprudence if dependency and neglect cases were not also removed. It would be ironic if we left two categories that were clearly noncriminal within a delinquency adjudicatory structure. If they were removed, as they should be, then the juvenile court would be streamlined to deal with a primary function: the just adjudication and disposition of young people alleged to have committed acts that would be criminal if enacted by an adult. Adherence to this limited jurisdiction would aid the court in complying with recent Supreme Court rulings, for adversary proceedings are least suited to problems involving family and childhood troubles.

If these three categories were removed from the traditional system, we would have to evolve a way of thinking about a new public organization that would engage in a variety of functions: fact finding, hearing of complaints, regulatory dispositions and provision of general child care and family services. This new public agency could be empowered to combine many of the existing functions of the court and child welfare departments, with one major prohibition: transfers of temporary custody of children would have to be voluntary on the part of parents, and all contested cases would have to be adjudicated by a civil court. This prohibition would be in harmony with the modern child welfare view of keeping natural families intact, and acting otherwise only when all remedial efforts have clearly failed.

We have regulatory commissions in many areas of social concern in America, thereby sidestepping the usual judicial structure. If there is a legitimate concern in the area of child and family welfare, and society wants to ensure the maintenance of minimum services, then legally we can build on existing systems and traditions to evolve a new kind of regulatory service commission to carry out that end. To ensure that the critical legal rights of parents and children are protected, civil family courts—as in foster and adoption cases—would be available for contest and appeal. However, to ensure that the agencies did not become bureaucratic busybodies, additional thought would have to be given to their policy-making composition, staffing and location.

Citizen Involvement

A major deficiency of many regulatory agencies in this country is that special interests often dominate the administration and proceedings, while affected consumers are only sparsely represented. To ensure that the residents most affected by proposed family and child welfare boards have a major voice in the administration and proceedings, they could be set up with a majority of citizen representatives (including adolescents). In addition, they could be decentralized to function within the geographical boundaries of areas the size of local elementary or junior high school districts. These local boards would be granted the legal rights to hire lay and professional staff, as well as to supervise the administration of hearings and field services.

The setting up of these local boards would require an extensive examination of city, county and state child welfare services to ensure effective cooperation and integration of effort. It is certainly conceivable that many protective family and child welfare services, which are generally administered without citizen advice, could also be incorporated into the activities of the local boards. The problems to be ironed out would of course be substantial, but the effort could force a reconceptualization of local and state responsibilities for providing acceptable, humane and effective family and child welfare services on a broad scale.

Citizen Involvement

The employment of interested local citizens in the daily operation of family and child welfare services is not a totally new idea. Sweden has used local welfare boards to provide a range of services to families and children, including the handling of delinquency cases. While we do not have to copy their broad jurisdictional scope or under-representation of blue-collar citizens, a great deal can be learned from this operation. Other Scandinavian countries also use local citizen boards to deal with a range of delinquency offenses. Informed observers indicate that the nonlegal systems in Scandinavia are less primitive and coercive. However, it is difficult to ascertain whether this outcome is due to cultural differences or to the social invention that excludes juvenile courts.

There exist analogues in this country for the use of local citizens in providing services to children in trouble. In recent years there has been an upsurge in the use of citizen-volunteers who function as house parents for home detention facilities, probation officers and intake workers. Besides this use of citizens, New Jersey, for example, has permitted each juvenile court jurisdiction to appoint citizens to Judicial Conference Committees, for the purpose of informally hearing and handling delinquency cases. Some New Jersey counties process up to 50 percent of their court petitions through this alternative to adjudication. All these programs, however, operate under the direct supervision and jurisdiction of the county juvenile court judges, with the cooperation of the chief probation officers. It should be possible to adapt these local innovations to a system that would be independent of the coercive aspects of even the most benign juvenile court operation.

Opposition to Innovation

Quite often it is the powerful opposition of special interest groups, rather than an inability to formulate new and viable proposals for change, that can block beneficial social change. Many judges, probation workers, correction officers, as well as religious and secular child care agencies, would strenuously oppose new social policies and alternatives for handling delinquents without crimes. Their opposition would certainly be understandable, since the proposed changes could have a profound impact on their work. In the process of limiting jurisdiction and altering traditional practices, they could lose status, influence and control over the use of existing resources. Very few interest groups suffer these kinds of losses gladly. Proponents of change should try to understand their problem and act accordingly. However, the differential benefits that might accrue to children and their families should serve as a reminder that the problems of youth and their official and unofficial adult caretakers are not always identical.

Experts' Claims

One proposal in particular can be expected to call forth the ire of these groups, and that is the use of citizens in the administration and provision of services in local boards. Many professional groups—psychiatrists, social workers, psychologists, group therapists and school guidance counselors—have staked out a claim of expertise for the treatment of any "acting out" behavior. The suggestion that citizens should play a significant role in offering assistance undermines that claim. In reply, the professionals might argue that experts—not laymen—should control, administer and staff any programs involving the remediation of childhood troubles. On what grounds might this kind of claim be reasonably questioned?

First, there is nothing about local citizens' control of child and family welfare activities that precludes the hiring of professionals for key tasks, and entrusting them with the operation of the board's program. Many private and public boards in the fields of correction and child welfare have functioned this way in the past.

Second, any claims about an expertise that can be termed a scientific approach to correction are quite premature. There does not now exist a clear-cut body of knowledge that can be ordered in a text or verbally transmitted that will direct any trained practitioner to diagnose and treat effectively such classic problems as truancy, running away and precocious sex experimentation. Unlike the field of medicine, there are no clear-cut prescriptions for professional behavior that can provide an intellectual rationale for expecting a remission of symptoms. There exist bits and pieces of knowledge and practical wisdom, but there is no correctional technology in any acceptable scientific sense.

Third, a reasonable appraisal of evaluations of current approaches to delinquents indicates that there are, in fact, no programs that can claim superiority. The studies do indicate that we can institutionalize far fewer children in treatment centers or reform schools without increasing the risks for individuals or communities; or, if we continue to use institutional programs, young people can be held for shorter periods of time without increasing the risk. The outcome of these appraisals provides a case for an expansion of humane child care activities—not for or against any specific repertoire of intervention techniques.

Fourth, many existing correctional programs are not now

controlled by professionals. Untrained juvenile court judges are administratively responsible for detention programs and probation services in more than a majority of the 50 states. Many correctional programs have been headed by political appointees or nonprofessionals. And state legislatures, often dominated by rural legislators, have exercised a very strong influence in the permissible range of program alternatives.

Fifth, the professionalization of officials dealing with delinquent youth does not always lead to happy results. There are studies that indicate that many trained policemen and judges officially process and detain more young people than untrained officials, indicating that their definition of delinquency has been broadened by psychiatric knowledge. At this point in time, there is a distinct danger that excessive professionalization can lead to overintervention in the lives of children and their families.

Sixth, there is no assurance that professionals are any more responsive to the interests and desires of local residents than are untrained judges and probation officers. Citizens, sharing a similar life style and knowledgeable about the problems of growing up in a given community, may be in a better position to enact a *parens patrie* doctrine than are professionals or judges.

Seventh, in ghetto communities, reliance on professional expertise can mean continued dependence on white authority systems. Identification of family and child welfare boards as "our own" may compensate for any lack of expertise by removing the suspicion that any change of behavior by children and parents is for the benefit of the white establishment. The additional community benefits to be gained from caring for "our own" may also outweigh any loss of professional skills. The benefits accruing from indigenous control over local child welfare services would hold for other minority groups living in a discriminatory environment: Indians, Puerto Ricans, Mexicans, hillbillies and French Canadians.

Alternative Policy Proposals in Decriminalization

The proposal to create family and child welfare boards to deal with juvenile status offenses may be appealing to many people. However, gaining political acceptance may be quite difficult, since the juvenile justice system would be giving up coercive power in an area that it has controlled for a long period of time. The proposal may appear reasonable, but it may constitute too radical a break with the past for a majority of state legislators. In addition, the interest groups that might push for it are not readily visible. Perhaps participants in the Women's Lib movement, student activists and black power groups might get interested in the issue of injustice against youth, but this is a hope more than a possibility. In the event of overwhelming opposition, there exist two policy proposals that might be more acceptable and could aid in the decriminalization of juvenile status offenses.

The two alternatives function at different ends of the traditional juvenile justice system. One proposal, suggested by the President's Task Force on Delinquency, would set up a youth service bureau that would offer local field services and be operated by civil authorities as an alternative to formal adjudication; the second proposal, suggested by William Sheridan of the Department of Health, Education, and Welfare, would prohibit the mixing of juvenile status offenders and classic delinquents in the same institutions. The youth service bureau would function between the police and the court, while the prohibition would function after judicial disposition. Both proposals, separate or in concert, could aid in the decriminalization of our current practices.

However, both proposals would still leave open the possibility of stigmatization of youth who had committed no crimes. The youth service bureau would provide an array of services at the community level, but the court and police would still have ultimate jurisdiction over its case load, and any competition over jurisdiction would probably be won by the traditional justice system. The prohibition of mixing in institutions would, of course, not change the fact that young people were still being adjudicated in the same court as delinquents, even though they had committed no crimes. In addition, the proposal, as currently conceived, does not affect mixing in detention facilities. These limitations are evident in the statutes of states that have recently changed their definitions of "delinquency" (New York, California, Illinois, Colorado, Kansas, Oklahoma and Vermont).

Both proposals deserve support, but they clearly leave the traditional system intact. It is possible that youth service bureaus could be organized with a significant role for citizen participation, thus paving the way for an eventual take-over of legal jurisdiction from the juvenile court for juvenile status offenses (and dependency and neglect cases, too). It is conceivable, too, that any prohibitions of mixing could lead to the increased placement of children in trouble in foster homes and group homes, instead of reform schools, and to the provision of homemaker services and educational programs for harried parents unable to cope with the problems of children. Both short-range proposals could, in practice, evolve a different mode of handling delinquents without crimes.

The adaptation of these two reasonable proposals into an evolutionary strategy is conceivable. But it is also likely they will just be added to the system, without altering its jurisdiction and its stigmatic practices. In the event this occurs, new reformers might entertain the radical strategy that some European countries achieved many years ago—removal of juvenile status offenders from the jurisdiction of the judicial-correctional system and their inclusion into the family and child welfare system.

New Definitions and New Responses

What is the guarantee that young people will be serviced any more effectively by their removal from the traditional correctional system? The question is valid, but perhaps it underestimates the potency of social definitions. Children, as well as adults, are liable to be treated according to the social category to which they have been assigned. Any shift in the categorization of youth that yields a more positive image can influence such authorities as teachers, employers, military recruiters and housing authority managers. For there is abundant evidence that the stigma of delinquency can have negative consequences for an individual as an adult, as well as during childhood.

It is evident, too, that our old social definitions of what constitutes delinquency have led us to construct a system of juvenile justice that is quite unjust. By failing to make reasonable distinctions and define them precisely, we not only treat juvenile status offenders more harshly but undermine any semblance of ordered justice for *all* illegal behavior committed by juveniles. Maintenance of existing jurisdictional and definitional boundaries helps to perpetuate an unjust system for treating children. That this unjust system may also be a self-defeating one that compounds the original problem should also be taken into account before prematurely concluding that a shift in social labeling procedures is but a minor reform.

We would agree, however, with the conclusion that a mere semantic shift in the social definition of children in trouble is not sufficient. The experience of New York in providing a social label of "person in need of supervision" (PINS)—without providing alternative civil modes for responding to this new distinction—indicates that reform can sometimes take the guise of "word magic." Children are often accused of believing in the intrinsic power of words and oaths; adults can play the game on an even larger scale.

We need alternative social resources for responding to our change in social definitions, if we are at all serious about dealing with the problem. Whether we are willing to pay the financial costs for these alternatives is, of course, problematic.

One approach to this issue might be to identify funds currently spent for noncriminal youth in the traditional police, court, and correctional subsystems, and then re-allocate the identified dollars into a new child welfare service. This reallocation strategy would not require new funding, but merely a financial shift to follow our new social definitions and intended responses. The choices would be primarily legal, political, and moral ones and not new economic decisions.

A second strategy for funding a new policy might be based on a more rational approach to the problem. We could attempt to assess the societal "need" for such services and then compute the amount of financial resources required to meet this newly assumed public responsibility. This approach could prove more costly than the reallocation strategy. Conceivably, the strategies of assessed need and reallocation could be combined at the same time or over the years. However, whether we might be willing to tax ourselves to support a more reasonable and moral social policy may turn out to be a critical issue. Perceived in this manner, the problem of defining and responding to children in trouble is as much financial as it is poltical, legal, and moral. But this, too, is an integral part of the American approach to delinquents without crimes.

July/August 1971

FURTHER READINGS SUGGESTED BY THE AUTHOR:

Children and Youth in America: A Documentary History, edited by Robert H. Bremner (Cambridge, Mass.: Harvard University Press, 1970, 2 vols.).

Juvenile Defenders for a Thousand Years: Selected Readings from Anglo-Saxon Times to 1900 edited by Wiley B. Sanders (Chapel Hill: The University of North Carolina Press, 1970).

The Child Savers: The Invention of Delinquency by Anthony M. Platt (Chicago: University of Chicago Press, 1969).

Children in Urban Society: Juvenile Delinquency in Nineteenth-Century America by Joseph M. Hawes (N.Y.: Oxford University Press, 1971).

Borderland of Criminal Justice: Essays in Law and Criminology by Frances A. Allen (Chicago: University of Chicago Press, 1964).

Delinquency and Social Policy, edited by Paul Lerman (New York: Praeger, 1970).

President's Commission on Law Enforcement and the Administration of Justice, (a) *Task Force Report: Juvenile Delinquency and Youth Crime* (Washington, D.C.: U.S. G.P.O., 1967), (b) *Task Force Report: Corrections.*

Crime and Punishment in Early Massachusetts by Edwin Powers (Boston, Mass.: Beacon Press, 1966).

Varieties of Police Behavior by James Q. Wilson (Cambridge, Mass.: Harvard University Press, 1968).

Dilemmas of Social Reform: Poverty and Community Action in the United States by Peter Marris and Martin Rein (New York: Atherton Press, 1967).

Pornography-
Raging Menace or Paper Tiger?

WILLIAM SIMON / JOHN H. GAGNON

Since the task of defining pornography has fallen more and more on the Supreme Court—and since not much research exists on what effect pornography has on the social actions of individuals—what standard is the court using?

The Supreme Court seems to be erecting a more complex standard for judging pornography to replace the old concern with individual morality. Some interesting insights into the confusion surrounding the topic can be drawn from three court decisions of March 21, 1966: *Ginzburg* v. *United States, Mishkin* v. *New York,* and *Memoirs of a Woman of Pleasure* v. *Massachusetts.* Although this set of decisions was almost immediately accorded distinction as a landmark by the public, the Nine Old Men themselves did not seem quite so sure of the meaning of the affair. The justices produced among them 14 separate opinions in the three cases. Only three judges were in the majority in all cases. The decisions were divided, respectively, 5-4, 6-3, and 6-3.

Ginzburg is the key decision. The court reversed the suppression of *Memoirs,* better known as *Fanny Hill,* under the Roth test of 1957—that is, "whether to the average person, applying contemporary standards, the dominant theme of the material taken as a whole appeals to a prurient interest." The conviction of Edward Mishkin, owner of the Main Stem and Midget book stores in New York City, was upheld. In the words of the court, Mishkin "was not prosecuted for anything he said or believed, but for what he did." What he did was commission, publish, and sell such illustrated books as *Mistress of Leather, Cult of Spankers,* and *Fearful Ordeal in Restraintland* for an audience interested in sadomasochism, transvestitism, fetishism.

Ralph Ginzburg was being tried on postal charges of obscenity for three publications: *The Housewife's Handbook of Selective Promiscuity,* an issue of the biweekly newsletter *Liaison,* and a volume of the hardbound magazine *Eros.* In this case the court departed from earlier rulings by considering not the obscenity of the specific items, but rather the appeal to prurient interest made in the advertising campaigns. The court remarked, "Where the purveyor's sole emphasis is on the sexually provocative aspects of his publications, that fact may be decisive in the determination of 'obscenity.' "

To the court, one of the proofs of Ginzburg's motives was his request for second-class mailing privileges at Intercourse or Blue Ball, Pennsylvania, before obtaining them at Middlesex, New Jersey. One of the indicators of the social worth of *Fanny Hill,* conversely, was the translation of the book into braille by the Library of Congress.

Three of the justices voting for reversal filed written dissents in which they argued that the court was creating a

new crime—that of pandering, exploitation, or titillation—
which Ginzburg could not have known existed when he
committed it. Furthermore, the dissenters said, if a statute
creating such a crime had come before the court, it would
be found unconstitutional.

It is the Ginzburg decision that gives us the primary
thread to follow in seeking to understand "obscenity" as it
is now seen by the Supreme Court and the sexual
arousal caused by what is conventionally termed
pornography. With this decision the court has moved—in a
way that may be inimical to the conception of law as abstract principle—toward a more realistic determination of
the factors relevant to triggering a sexual response. The
court's sociological discovery—whether intentional or not—
is that in sex the context of the representation is significant.
That is, sex as a physical object or symbolic representation
has no power outside a context in which the erotic elements
are reinforced or made legitimate.

In doing this, the court did not change the rules under
which any work will be considered outside its context. If
a book is charged—as *Fanny Hill* was—with being obscene
under the Roth decision, it will be treated in exactly the
same way as it would have been in the past. When aspects
of the context of advertising or sale—the acts of labeling—
are included in the original charges, then the Ginzburg rules
will be applied. This was demonstrated in the court's decision this May on a number of girlie magazines. Obscenity
convictions against the magazines were overturned because,
as the court stated, "In none was there evidence of the sort
of pandering which the court found significant in *Ginzburg
v. United States.*"

Whether the majority of the court was aware of the significance of the change it made in the definition of obscenity is not clear. From the tone of the opinions, it is obvious

the court felt it was dealing with a problem of nuisance behavior—not only to the public, but to the court itself—quite analogous to keeping a goat in a residential area, or urinating in public. By making the promotion of the work a factor in determining its obscenity, the court was reinforcing the right of the person to keep his mailbox clean and private, not to mention the likelihood that it was cutting down the amount of misleading advertising.

The court apparently considers pornography to have two major dimensions. The first can be defined as dealing with sexual representations that are offensive to public morality or taste, which concerned the court most importantly in the Ginzburg case. The second centers on the effect of pornography on specific individuals or classes, which is the focus of most public discussions and prior court decisions on pornography. This dimension was mentioned only twice in the array of decisions of 1966, but much of the confusion in discussions of pornography reflects a difficulty in distinguishing between these dimensions or a tendency to slip from one to the other without noting the change.

The first dimension—offenses to a public morality—not only appears more objective, but also has a cooler emotional tone. The problem becomes one of tolerating a public nuisance, or defining what constitutes a public nuisance. This issue becomes complex because the heterogeneity of an urban society makes it difficult to arrive at a consensus on what the limits of public morality might be. We might also add the complicating factor of our society's somewhat uneven libertarian tradition that affirms the theoretical existence of the right to subscribe to minority versions of morality. These obviously touch upon important issues of constitutional freedoms. As important as the implicit issues may be, however, the explicit issue is public nuisance, a misdemeanor, usually bringing only a fine or, at most, up to a year in the county jail. Talk of offense to public morality or public taste is relatively remote from the old fears of serious damage to the community or its members.

The second dimension—effects upon persons exposed to pornographic productions—generates more intense emotions. Claims are made that exposure to pornography results in infantile and regressive approaches to sexuality that can feed an individual's neuroses or, at the other extreme, that exposure tends to fundamentally and irreversibly corrupt and deprave. The latter argument asserts that exposure to pornography either awakens or creates sexual appetites that can only be satisfied through conduct that is dangerous to society. More simply stated: Pornography is a trigger mechanism that has a high probability of initiating dangerous, antisocial behavior. There also exists what can be called a major counterargument to these, but one that shares with them a belief in the effectiveness of pornography. This argument is that pornography serves as an alternative sexual outlet, one that releases sexual tensions that might otherwise find expression in dangerous, antisocial behavior. For the proponents of this view, pornography is seen as a safety valve or a psychological lightning rod.

The very act of labeling some item as pornographic or obscene creates a social response very close to that brought on by pornography itself. The act of labeling often generates sexual anticipation centered on fantasies about the business of pornography and the erotic character of those who produce it. How else could such benign and hardly erotic productions as family-planning pamphlets and pictures of human birth have come under the shadow of the pornography laws? As with other unconventional sexual expressions, in public consideration of pornography even the dreary details of production, distribution, and sale are matters for erotic speculation. This simplification—defining as totally sexual that which is only marginally connected with sexuality—is perhaps one of the major sources of the public concern over pornography.

Labeling can also be done by individuals, who can thus make pornographic the widest range of materials—*Studs Lonigan, Fanny Hill, Playboy,* the Sears Roebuck catalog. This ability leads to the assumption that sexual fantasy and its agent, pornography, have a magical capacity to commit men to overt sexual action. In this view the sexual impulse lies like the beast in every man, restrained only by the slight fetters of social repression. This assumption, founded on the Enlightenment's notion of a social contract, underpins most of our discussions of sex and its sideshow, pornography.

These serious views of pornography can lead directly to the formulation of an empirically testable question. Unfortunately, no one has provided an answer acceptable as the outcome of reliable and systematic research procedures.

Of the data that are available on the effects of pornography, the best remain those provided by the investigations of the Institute for Sex Research. Kinsey and his associates indicate that the majority of males in our society are exposed, at one time or another, to "portrayals of sexual action." So are a smaller proportion of females. Further, 77 percent of males who had exposure to "portrayals of sexual action" reported being erotically aroused, while only 32 percent of women reported feelings of arousal. What is significant is that, arousal notwithstanding, no dramatic changes of behavior appeared to follow for those reporting both exposure and arousal. Perhaps even more significant is the fact that Paul H. Gebhard and his colleagues in their book *Sex Offenders* report:

> It would appear that the possession of pornography does not differentiate sex offenders from nonsex offenders. Even the combination of ownership plus strong sexual

arousal from the material does not segregate the sex offender from other men of a comparable social level. Summing up their feeling that pornography is far from being a strong determinant of sexual behavior and that the use of pornography tends to be a derivative of already existing sexual commitments, the authors observe: "Men make the collections, collections do not make the men."

However, given the intensity and frequency with which the argument of pornography's corrupting powers is raised, one might wonder whether thinking about pornography has not itself given rise to sexual fantasies, developing an image of men and women as being more essentially sexual than they may in fact be.

The two major dimensions—public offense versus public corruption—result in two different images of the pornographer. Projected through the rhetoric of public corruption we see him as someone self-consciously evil, a representative of the antichrist, the Communist conspiracy, or at the very least, the Mafia. We also tend to see him in terms of the obscenity of ill-gotten wealth as he deals in commodities that are assumed to generate high prices.

Thought of as a public nuisance, he appears in somewhat more realistic hues. Here we find not a sinister villain but a grubby businessman producing a minor commodity for which there is a limited market and a marginal profit and which requires that he live in a marginal world. Here our collective displeasure may be derived from his association with a still greater obscenity—economic failure. However, whether the pornographer is Mephistopheles or a Willie Loman, he is one of the few in our society whose public role is overtly sexual, and that is perhaps reason enough to abandon any expectations of rationality in public discussions of the role.

We tend to ignore the social context within which pornography is used and from which a large part of its significance for the individual consumer derives. The stag film is an excellent case in point. Out of context it is rarely more than a simple catalogue of the limited sexual resources of the human body. Stag films are rarely seen by females and most commonly by two kinds of male groups: those living in group housing in colleges or universities and those belonging to upper-lower class and lower-middle class voluntary social groups. The stag film serves both similar and different functions for the two major categories of persons who see them.

For the college male they are a collective representation of mutual heterosexual concerns and—to a lesser degree— they instruct in sexual technique. For this group the exposure is either concurrent with, or prior to, extensive sociosexual experience. Exposure comes later in life for the second group: after marriage or, at the very least, after the development of sociosexual patterns. For this audience the group experience itself provides validation of sexual appetites in social milieus where other forms of validation, such as extramarital activity, are severely sanctioned. The films primarily reinforce masculinity and only indirectly reinforce heterosexuality. This reinforcement of heterosexuality is reflected in the way the films portray the obsessive myths of masculine sexual fantasy. They emphasize, for example, that sexual encounters can happen at any moment, to anyone, around almost any corner—a belief that is a close parallel to the romantic love fantasy so very characteristic of female arousal. In the case of the male, however, sex replaces love as the central element. These films also reaffirm the myth of a breed of women who are lusty and free in both surrender and enjoyment. Last, given the kind of social context within which the films are shown, there is little reason to assume that their sexual arousal is not expressed through appropriate sexual or social actions.

Pictorial representations of sexual activity lend themselves to the same approach. Unlike films and more like written materials, their use is essentially private. Nonetheless, patterns of use remain congruent with other patterns of social life and process; they represent anything but the triggering mechanisms through which the social contract is nullified and raging, unsocial lust (whatever that might be) is unleashed. The major users of pictorial erotica are adolescent males. If these materials have any use, it is as an aid to masturbation. There is no evidence, however, that the availability of dirty pictures increases masturbatory rates among adolescents. This is a period in life when masturbatory rates are already extremely high, particularly for middle class adolescents. Indeed, in the absence of hard-core pornography, the boys create their own stimulation from mail-order catalogues, magazine ads, and so on. In middle class circles, many young men and the majority of females may grow up without ever having seen hard-core pornography.

If exposure to this kind of pornography, while facilitating masturbation, does not substantially affect masturbatory rates, it is still possible that such materials may shape the content of the masturbatory fantasy in ways that create or reinforce commitments to sexual practices that are harmful to the individual or to others. In this area little is known. It may be observed that most pornographic materials share with the masturbatory fantasy a sense of omnipotence, but the acts represented are rarely homosexual, nor are they sadistic beyond the general levels of violence common in contemporary kitsch. Once again, one suspects a reinforcing or facilitating function rather than one of initiation or creation.

The pornographic book, in contrast to photographs and films, represents a very different social situation. Few books are read aloud in our society, and it is very unlikely that this would occur with a book of descriptions of overt sexual activity. In fact, prosecutors take advantage of this by reading allegedly obscene books aloud in court with the aim of embarrassing the jury into a guilty verdict. The privately consumed erotic book merely provides fantasy content or reinforcement of fantasy that is already established. Few books lead to overt action of any kind, and the erotic book is unlikely to be an exception.

The most difficult problem in considering pornography is the fringeland found on newsstands: the pulp books, national tabloids, men's magazines, and pinup collections which line the racks in drugstores, bus stations, and rail and air terminals. The girlie magazines are often under attack for nude pictures. The current magic line of censorship is pubic hair, though recently it was the bare breast or exposed nipple. Not so very long ago, navels were ruthlessly airbrushed away and Jane Russell's cleavage was an issue in gaining the censor's approval of the movie "Outlaw." The Gay Nineties were made gayer with pinups of strapping beauties clad in tights revealing only the bare flesh of face and hands.

In our era the pulp book freely describes most sexual activity with some degree of accuracy, although less explicitly and more metaphorically than hard-core pornographic pulp books. Such books are clearly published for their capacity to elicit sexual arousal, and they are purchased by an audience that knows what it is buying.

To view these examples of fringe pornography exclusively in terms of a sexual function might well be misleading. Since we tend to overestimate the significance of sexual activity, we see the trends of representation in these works

as indicators of sexual behavior in the community. An increase in works about homosexual love is taken as an indication of an incipient homosexual revolution or even as the
cause of a homosexual revolution. If we find more books
about adultery, sadomasochism, or fast-living teenagers,
we believe that there must be more adulterers, sado-
masochists, and fast-living teenagers in our midst. With a
dubious logic reminiscent of primitive magic, many believe
that if the number of such representations increases, so will
the frequency of such acts, and conversely that the way to
cut down on this antisocial behavior is to suppress the
pornographic representations.

In the fringeland there is a greater attempt to place
sexual activity in the context of a social script, with a
greater concern for nonsexual social relations and social
roles, and a more direct treatment of appropriate social
norms. Some part of this, particularly its common trait of
compulsive moralizing, is an attempt to establish a spurious
—but defensible under the Roth decision—"redeeming
context." This may also represent the producer's awareness
that more than simple lust is involved, that the reader may
bring to the work a complex of motives, many of which
are nonsexual.

For example, the psychiatrist Lionel Ovesey links some
of the fantasies of his homosexual patients not to their
sexual commitments, but to their problems of managing
other personal relations, particularly in their jobs. The
management of dominance or aggression in nonsexual
spheres of life or the management of ideologies and moral-
ities of social mobility may be the organizing mechanisms
of such fantasies while sexuality provides an accessible and
powerful imagery through which these other social tensions
may be vicariously acted upon. Possibly it is overly simplistic to view this marginal pornography merely as something

exclusively sexual.

These items at the fringeland are of most concern in the formulation of community standards. The girlie magazine and the pulp book are visible and priced within the range of the mass market. The hardcover book available at a high price in a bookstore may well cause no comment until it goes on the drugstore racks in paperback. Because such items are sold at breaks in transportation or in locations that tap neighborhood markets, they are the most visible portion of the problem and are the source of the discontent among those who are committed to censorship.

The dilemma, then, becomes the formulation of community standards, and this has been the dilemma of the courts themselves. One interesting attempt to strengthen enforcement of conservative standards is the interpretation of federal law to allow prosecution of a seller in the jurisdiction in which materials are received rather than in the ones from which they are mailed. Thus in the rather liberal jurisdiction of New York, where the sale of obscene materials must be compared in the mind of the judge with all the other kinds of crimes that come before him, the seller may well be seen as a small-timer, his crime a misdemeanor. However, in a rural jurisdiction where religious standards are more conservative and a pornography offense is viewed more seriously—especially when compared with the strayed cows and traffic violations that make up the most of the court docket—the seller is a heinous criminal.

The Supreme Court may wish to establish a national standard, allowing some jurisdictions to be more liberal but none to be more conservative. Thus the Supreme Court may build a floor under the right of materials to be protected under the First Amendment, at the same time constraining, through the use of the Ginzburg decision, the importation of materials through wide mailing campaigns into conservative communities. In its more recent decision, the court indicated—somewhat Delphically—that its concern in the future would be with three areas, none of them directly concerned with the content of any works charged as pornographic. These were sales of smut to minors, obtrusive presentation, and "pandering" *a la* Ginzburg. The court's decisions, however, may well be too conservative in a period when a national society is being created through penetration by the mass media of larger and larger elements of the society. Indeed, it is likely that most legal revolutions have been imposed from above and that communities will fall back to the set floor, if allowed to do so.

Pornography is as elusive as mercury. That of the past often no longer fills the bill. The use and users of contemporary pornography vary. Indeed, it might be said that sex itself would not change if there were no more pornography. Pornography is only a minor symptom of sexuality and of very little prominence in people's minds most of the time. Even among those who might think about it most, it results either in masturbation or in the "collector" instinct.

What is most important about pornography is not that it is particularly relevant to sexuality, but that it elicits very special treatment when it confronts the law. In this confrontation the agencies of criminal justice, and especially the courts, behave in a very curious manner that is quite dangerous for the freedom of ideas as they might be expressed in other zones of activity such as politics, religion, or the family. Our best protection in this regard has been the very contradictory character of the courts which carefully excludes the consideration of sexual ideas from the general test of the expression of ideas: Do they give rise to a clear and present danger? Our problem is not that pornography represents such a danger—it is far too minor a phenomenon for that—but that the kind of thinking prevalent in dealing

with pornography will come to be prevalent in controlling
the advocacy of other ideas as well.

July/August 1967

FURTHER READING SUGGESTED BY THE AUTHORS:

The Other Victorians by Steven Marcus (New York City:
Basic Books, Inc., 1964). The social, literary, and psychoanalytic
study of Victorian pornography by a distinguished critic.

Hustlers, Beats, and Others by Ned Polsky (Chicago: Aldine
Publishing Co., 1967). The most explicit treatment of
pornography from a sociological perspective.

*Language and Silence: Essays in Language, Literature and the
Inhuman* edited by G. Steiner (New York City: Atheneum
Publishers, 1967). See "Night Words" by George Steiner,
a consideration of the impact of pornography on
public language and private fantasy.

Eros Denied, Part III by Wayland Young (New York City: Grove
Press, Inc., 1964). A defense of the role of pornography
in society.

"Viva La Policia"

DAVID DURK

I'm here because I'm a policeman and it's just very hard to say it, but these have been a very lonely five years for Frank Serpico, Paul Delise and me. I've had a lot of time to think about what being a cop means. So that's why I'd like to take a few minutes and tell you what being a cop means to me. Then maybe you can understand better some of the things I have said.

At the very beginning, the most important fact to understand is that I had and have *no special knowledge* of police corruption. We knew nothing about the PEP Squad that Waverly Logan didn't know. We knew nothing about the divisions that wasn't known and testified to by Officer Philips, that wasn't known to every man and officer in those divisions. We knew nothing about the police traffic in narcotics that wasn't known and testified to here by

---

This is the concluding statement of Sergeant David Durk at the Knapp Commission Hearing in New York City, December 17, 1971.

Paul Curran of the State Investigations Commission. We knew these things because we were involved in law enforcement in New York City. And anyone else who says he didn't know, had to be blind either by choice or by incompetence.

The facts have been there waiting to be exposed. This commission, to its enormous credit, has exposed them in a period of six months. We simply could not believe, as we do not believe today, that those with authority and responsibility in the area—whether the district attorneys, the police commanders, or those in power in City Hall—couldn't also have exposed them in six months, or at least six years: that is, if they wanted to do it.

Let me be explicit. I am not saying that all those who ignored the corruption were themselves corrupt. Whether or not they were is almost immaterial in any case. The fact is that the corruption was ignored. The fact is that when we reported the corruption to Commissioner Fraiman, he refused to act upon his responsibility. The fact is that almost wherever we turned in the police department, wherever we turned in the city administration, and almost wherever we went in the rest of the city, we were met not with cooperation, not with appreciation, not with an eagerness to seek out the truth, but with suspicion and hostility, and laziness and inattention, and with our fear that any moment our efforts might be betrayed.

There has been testimony that Frank Serpico didn't want to testify. Some of it has been critical in tone. Frank Serpico was willing to help. He was begging. All he wanted was support, and what did he get? Commissioner Walsh said yesterday that his plan was to "leave Frank on his own." Walsh was telling Frank, "You do it alone."

These are very tough things to believe if you're a cop. Because to me being a cop means believing in the rule of law. It means believing in a system of government that makes fair and just rules, and then enforces them.

Being a cop also means serving, helping others. If it's not too corny, to be a cop is to help an old lady walk the streets safely; to help a 12-year-old girl reach her next birthday without being gang-raped; to help a storekeeper make a living without keeping a shotgun under his cash register; to help a boy grow up without needles in his arm.

And therefore to me being a cop is not a job but a way to live a life. Some people say that cops live with the worst side of humanity—in the middle of all the lying and cheating, the violence and hate—and I suppose that in some sense is true. But being a cop also means being engaged with life. It means that our concern for others is not abstract, that we don't just write a letter to the *Times* or give ten dollars to the United Fund once a year; It means that we put something on the line from the moment we hit the street every morning of every day of our lives. In this sense police corruption is not about money at all, because there is no amount of money that can pay a cop to risk his life 365 days a year. Being a cop is a vocation, or it is nothing at all.

And that is what I saw being destroyed by the corruption of the New York City Police Department—destroyed for me, and for thousands of others like me. We wanted to believe in the rule of law; we wanted to believe in a system of responsibility; but those in high places everywhere—in the department, in the DA's offices, and in City Hall—were determined not to enforce the law but to turn their heads away when law and justice were being sold on every street corner.

We wanted to serve others, but the department was a home for the drug dealers and thieves; the force that was supposed to be protecting people was selling poison to their children. . . .

And there could be no life, no real life for me or anyone

else on that force, when everyday we had to face the facts of our own terrible corruption. I saw that happening to men all around me—men who could have been good officers, men of decent impulse and even of ideals; but men who were without decent leadership, men who were told in a hundred ways every day: go along. Forget about the law. Don't make waves. Shut up. So they did shut up, they did go along, they did learn the unwritten code of the department. They went along, and they lost something very precious. They weren't cops any more. They were a long way toward not being men any more.

And all the time I saw the other victims too—especially the children. Children of 14 and 15 and 16, wasted by heroin, turned into street corner thugs and whores, ready to mug their own mother for the price of a fix. That was the price of going along, the real price of police corruption; not free meals or broken regulations, but broken dreams and dying neighborhoods and a whole generation of children being lost. That was what I had joined the department to stop.

So that was why I went to the *New York Times*. Because attention had to be paid. And in a last desperate hope that if the facts were known someone must respond.

And now it is up to you. I speak to you now as nothing more and nothing less than a cop: a cop who has lived on this force, and who is *staying* on this force, and therefore as a cop who needs your help. My fellow policemen and I: we didn't appoint you; you don't report to us; but all the same there are some things that, as policemen, we must have from you.

First, we need you to fix responsibility for the rottenness that was allowed to fester. It must be fixed both inside and outside the department.

Inside the department, responsibility has to be fixed

against those top commanders who allowed or helped the situation to develop. Responsibility has to be fixed because no patrolman will believe that he should care about corruption if his superiors can get away with not caring. Responsibility also has to be fixed because commanders themselves have to be told, again and again, and not only by the police commissioner, that the entire state of the department is up to them. And most of all, responsibility has to be fixed because it is the first step toward recovering our simple but necessary conviction that right will be rewarded and wrongdoing punished.

Responsibility must also be fixed outside the department —on all the men and agencies that have helped bring us to our present pass, against all those who could have exposed this corruption, but never did. Like it or not, the policeman is convinced that he lives and works in the middle of a corrupt society; that everyone else is getting theirs, and why shouldn't he; and that if anyone really cared about corruption, something would have been done about it a long time ago. We are not animals. We are not stupid, and we know very well, we policemen, that corruption does not begin with a few patrolmen, and that responsibility for corruption does not end with one aide to the mayor or one investigations commissioner. The issue, for all of today's testimony, is not just Jay Kriegel or Arnold Fraiman. We know that there are many people beyond the police department who share in the corruption and its rewards. So your report has to tell us about the district attorneys and the courts and the bar, and the mayor and the governor—about what they have failed to do, and how great a measure of responsibility they also bear. Otherwise, if you suggest, or allow others to suggest, that the responsibility belongs only to the police—then for the patrolman on the beat and in the radio car, this commission will be just another part of the swindle. That is a harsh statement, and an impolite and a brutal statement. It also is a statement of the truth.

Second, you have to speak as the conscience of this city—speak for all those without a voice, all those who are not here to be heard today, although they know the price of police corruption more intimately than anyone here: the people of the ghetto, and all the other victims, those broken in mind and spirit and hope. Perhaps more than any other people in this city, they depend on the police and the law, to protect not just their pocketbooks but their very lives, and the lives and welfare of their children. Tow truck operators can write off bribes on their income tax; the expense account executive can afford a prostitute; but no one can pay a mother for the pain of seeing her children hooked on heroin.

This commission, for what I am sure are good reasons, has not invited testimony from the communities of suffering in New York City. But this commission must remind the force, as it must tell the rest of the city, that there are human lives at stake, that when police protect the narcotics traffic, then we are participatiing in the destruction of a generation of children. It is this terrible crime for which you are fixing the responsibility, and it is this terrible crime against which you must speak with the full outrage of the community's conscience.

Third, as a corollary, you must help to give us a sense of priorities, to remind us that corruption, like sin, has its gradations and classifications. Of course, all corruption is bad. But we cannot fall into the trap of pretending that all corruption is *equally* bad. There is a difference between accepting free meals and selling narcotics. If we are unable to make that distinction, then we are saying to the police that the life of a child in the South Bronx is of the same moral value as a cup of coffee. That cannot be true, for this society or for its police force. So you must show us the difference.

Finally, in your deliberations, you must speak for the policemen of this city—for the best that is in them, for what most of them wanted to be, for what most of them will be if we try.

Once I arrested a landlord's agent who offered to pay me if I would lock up a tenant who was organizing other tenants, and as I put the cuffs on the agent and led him away, a crowd of people assembled and started yelling, "Viva la policia!"

Of course, it was not just me, or even the police, that they were cheering. They were cheering because they had glimpsed, in that one arrest, the possibility of a system of justice that could work to protect them too. They were cheering because if that agent could get arrested, then that meant they had rights, they were citizens, and maybe one day life would really be different for their children.

For me, that moment was what police work is all about. But there have been far too few moments like it, and far too many times when I looked into the faces of the city and saw not hope and trust, but resentment and hate and fear. Far too many of my fellow officers have seen only hate; far too many of them have seen their dreams of service and justice frustrated and abandoned by a corrupt system, and superiors and politicians who just didn't care enough.

It took five years of Frank Serpico's life, and five years of mine, to help bring this commission about. It has taken the lives and dedication of thousands of others to preserve as much of a police force as we have. It has taken months of effort by all of you to help show this city the truth. What I ask of you now is to help make us clean

292/DAVID DURK

again; to help give us some leadership we can look to; to make it possible for all the men on the force to walk at ease with their better nature and with their fellow citizens —and perhaps one day, on a warm summer night, to hear again the shout of "Viva la policia."

December 1971

SELECTED BIBLIOGRAPHY

Abernathy, M. Glenn, *Civil Liberties and the Constitution*. New York: Dodd, Mead, 1968.

Abraham, Henry J., *The Judicial Process: An Introductory Analysis of the Courts of the United States, England, and France* (2nd ed.). New York: Oxford University Press, 1968.

Alex, Nicholas, *Black in Blue*. New York: Appleton-Century-Crofts, 1969.

Alexander, Franz G., and Selesnick, Sheldon T., *The History of Psychiatry*. New York: Harper and Row, 1966.

Allen, Francis A., *The Borderland of Criminal Justice: Essays on Law and Criminology*. Chicago: University of Chicago Press, 1964.

Allen, Richard C., Ferster, Elyce Zenoff, and Rubin, Jesse G. (eds.), *Readings in Law and Psychiatry*. Baltimore, Md.: Johns Hopkins Press, 1968.

Arendt, Hannah, *Eichmann in Jerusalem*. New York: The Viking Press, 1963.

Arens, Richard and Lasswell, Harold D., *In Defense of Public Order: The Emerging Field of Sanction Law*. New York: Columbia University Press, 1961.

Asbury, Herbert, *The Gangs of New York*. New York: Alfred A. Knopf, 1928.

Aubert, Vilhelm, *The Hidden Society*. Totowa, N. J.: The Bedminster Press, 1965.

Bacon, Selden D., *The Early Development of American Municipal Police: A Study of the Evolution of Formal Control in a Changing Society*. Unpublished Ph.D. dissertation. Yale University, New Haven, 1939.

Baker, Joseph, *The Law of Political Uniforms, Public Meetings and Private Armies*. London: H. J. Just, 1937.

Banton, Michael, *The Policeman in the Community*. New York: Basic Books Inc., 1965.

Barnet, Richard J., *Roots of War*. New York: Atheneum, 1972.

Barth, Alan, *Law Enforcement Versus the Law*. New York: Collier Books, 1963.

293

Bayley, David H. and Mendelsohn, Harold, *Minorities and the Police*. New York: The Free Press, 1969.

Becker, Harold K., *Law Enforcement: A Selected Bibliography*. Metuchen, N. J.: Scarecrow Press Inc., 1968.

Becker, Howard S., *Outsiders: Studies in the Sociology of Deviance*. New York: The Free Press, 1963.

Bedford, Sybille, *The Trial of Dr. Adams*. New York: Simon and Schuster, 1958.

Bell, Daniel, *The End of Ideology*. New York: Macmillan, 1958.

Belli, Melvin, *Dallas Justice*. New York: David McKay Co., 1964

Benjamin, Harry and Masters, R.E.L., *Prostitution and Morality*. New York: Julian Press, 1964.

Berger, Morroe, *Equality by Statute: The Revolution in Civil Rights* (revised ed.). Garden City, N. Y.: Doubleday, 1967.

Berman, Harold J., *Justice in the U.S.S.R.* (revised ed.). New York: Vintage Books, 1963.

Bedau, Hugo A. (ed.), *The Death Penalty in America*. Chicago: Aldine Publishing Co., 1964.

Berry, Mary Frances, *Black Resistance—White Law*. New York: Appleton-Century-Crofts, 1971.

Bird, Otto A., *The Idea of Justice*. New York: Frederick A. Praeger, 1967.

Black, Algernon D., *The People and the Police*. New York: McGraw-Hill, 1968.

Blau, Peter M., *The Dynamics of Bureaucracy*. Chicago: University of Chicago Press, 1966.

Blaustein, Albert P., *The American Lawyer*. Chicago: University of Chicago Press, 1954.

Blum, Richard H. (ed.). *Police Selection*. Springfield, Ill.: Charles C. Thomas, 1964.

Blumberg, Abraham S., *The Criminal Court: An Organizational Analysis,* Uupublished Ph.D. dissertation. New School for Social Research, New York, 1965.

——— *Criminal Justice*. Chicago: Quadrangle Books, 1967.

Bordua, David J., *The Police: Six Sociological Essays.* New York: John Wiley and Sons, 1967.

Bornecque-Winancy, E., *Histoire de la Police.* Paris: Les Editiones Int., 1950.

Boskin, Joseph, *Urban Racial Violence in the Twentieth Century.* Beverly Hills, Calif.: Glencoe Press, 1969.

Bramsted, Ernest J., *Dictatorship and Political Police.* London: Routledge and Kegan Paul, 1945.

Brant, Irving, *The Bill of Rights.* New York: New American Library, 1967.

Bromberg, Walter, *Crime and the Mind.* New York: Funk & Wagnalls, 1968.

Brown, Wenzell, *Women Who Died in the Chair.* New York: Collier Books, 1963.

Buisson, Henry, *La Police, Son Histoire.* Paris: Nouvelles Editiones Latines, 1958.

Cairns, Hunting, *Law and the Social Sciences.* New York: Harcourt, Brace and World, 1935.

Cameron, Mary Owens, *The Booster and the Snitch.* New York: The Free Press, 1964.

Camus, Albert, *The Stranger.* New York: Vintage Books, 1964.

Caplovitz, David, *The Poor Pay More.* New York: The Free Press, 1963.

Caplow, Theodore, *Principles of Organization.* New York: Harcourt, Brace and World, 1964.

Cardoza, Benjamin, *The Nature of the Judicial Process.* New Haven, Conn.: Yale University Press, 1931.

Carlin, Jerome E., Howard, Jan and Messinger, Sheldon L., *Civil Justice and the Poor: Issues for Sociological Research.* New York: Russell Sage Foundation, 1967.

——— *Lawyer's Ethics.* New York: Russell Sage Foundation, 1966.

——— *Lawyers on Their Own.* New Brunswick, N. J.: Rutgers University Press, 1962.

Carmichael, Stokely and Hamilton, Charles, *Black Power: The Politics of Liberation in America*. New York: Vintage Books, 1967.

Chambliss, William, *Crime and the Legal Process*. New York: McGraw-Hill, 1969.

Chambliss, William J. and Seidman, Robert B., *Law, Order and Power*. Reading, Mass.: Addison-Wesley Publishing Co., 1971.

Chapman, Brian, *Police State*. New York: Praeger Publishers, 1970.

Chapman, Samuel G., *The Police Heritage in England and America*. East Lansing, Mich.: Michigan State University Press, 1962.

Chevigny, Paul, *Police Power: Police Abuses in New York City*. New York: Pantheon, 1969.

———— *Cops and Rebels*. New York: Pantheon Books, 1972.

Cicourel, Aaron V., *The Social Organization of Juvenile Justice*. New York: John Wiley and Sons, 1968.

Cipes, Robert M., *The Crime War*. New York: New American Library, 1968.

Clark, Kenneth B., *Dark Ghetto*. New York: Harper and Row, 1965.

Clark, Ramsey, *Crime in America*. New York: Simon & Schuster, 1970.

Cleaver, Eldridge, *Soul on Ice*. New York: Delta Books, 1968.

Clegg, Reed K., *Probation and Parole*. Springfield, Ill.: Charles C. Thomas, 1964.

Cloward, Richard A. and Ohlin, Lloyd E., *Delinquency and Opportunity*. New York: The Free Press, 1960.

Conklin, John E., *Robbery and the Criminal Justice System*. New York: J. B. Lippincott Co., 1972.

Conot, Robert, *Rivers of Blood, Years of Darkness*. New York: Bantam Books, 1967.

Cook, Fred J., *The Corrupted Land*. New York: Macmillan, 1966.

———— *The F.B.I. Nobody Knows*. New York: Macmillan, 1964.

———— *The Secret Rulers*. New York: Duell, Sloan and Pearce, 1966.

Cramer, James, *The World's Police*. London: Cassell and Co., Ltd., 1964.

Cray, Ed, *The Big Blue Line*. New York: Coward-McCann, Inc., 1967.

Cressey, Donald R. and Ward, David A., *Delinquency, Crime and Social Process*. New York: Harper and Row, 1969.

———— *Theft of the Nation*. New York: Harper and Row, 1969.

Curran, William J., *Law and Medicine*. Boston: Little, Brown and Co., 1960.

Dahl, Robert A., *Pluralist Democracy in the United States: Conflict and Consent*. Chicago: Rand McNally, 1967.

Darrow, Clarence, *The Story of My Life*. New York: Scribner's, 1934.

Dash, Samuel, Knowlton, Robert and Schwartz, Richard, *The Eavesdroppers*. New Brunswick, N. J.: Rutgers University Press, 1959.

Deutsch, Albert *The Trouble with Cops*. New York: Crown Publishers Inc., 1955.

Dickens, Charles, *Bleak House*. London: J. M. Dent and Sons, Ltd., 1907.

Domhoff, G. William, *The Higher Circles: The Governing Class in America*. New York: Random House, 1970.

Donnelly, Richard, Goldstein, J. and Schwartz, Richard D., *Criminal Law*. New York: The Free Press, 1962.

Dorsen, Norman, ed., *The Rights of Americans*. New York: Vintage Books, 1972.

Douglas, Jack D., ed., *Observations of Deviance*. New York: Random House, 1970.

———— *Crime and Justice in American Society*. New York: The Bobbs-Merrill Co., Inc., 1971.

Dressler, David, *Practice and Theory of Probation and Parole*. New York: Columbia University Press, 1959.

Durkheim, Emile, *The Division of Labor in Society*. New York: Macmillan, 1933.

———— *The Rules of Sociological Method*. New York: The Free Press, 1964.

Eidelberg, Paul, *The Philosophy of the American Constitution: A Reinterpretation of the Intentions of the Founding Fathers*. New York: The Free Press, 1968.

Eisner, Victor, *The Delinquency Label*. New York: Random House, 1968.

Emerson, Robert M., *Judging Delinquents: Context and Process in Juvenile Court*. Chicago: Aldine Publishing Co., 1969.

Erikson, Kai T., *Wayward Puritans*. New York: John Wiley and Sons, 1966.

Etzioni, Amitai, *A Comparative Analysis of Complex Organizations*. New York: The Free Press, 1964.

Evan, William M., ed., *Law and Sociology: Exploratory Essays*. New York: The Free Press, 1962.

Eysenck, H. J., *Crime and Personality*. Boston: Houghton Mifflin Co., 1964.

Falk, Richard A., *Legal Order in a Violent World*. Princeton, N. J.: Princeton University Press, 1968.

Falk, Richard A., Kolko, Gabriel, and Lifton, Robert Jay, *Crimes of War*. New York: Vintage Books, 1971.

Faralicq, Rene, *The French Police from Within*. London: Cassell and Co., 1933.

Feifer, George, *Justice in Moscow*. New York: Simon and Schuster, 1964.

Ferri, Enrico, *Criminal Sociology*. New York: Appleton, 1896.

Fontana, Vincent J., *The Maltreated Child*. Springfield, Ill.: Charles C. Thomas, 1964.

Ford, Gerald R. and Stiles, John R., *Portrait of the Assassin*. New York: Simon and Schuster, 1965.

Fosdick, Raymond, *European Police Systems*. New York: Century Company, 1915.

Frank, Jerome, *Courts on Trial*. Princeton, N. J.: Princeton University Press, 1949.

———— *Law and the Modern Mind*. New York: Tudor Publishing Co., 1935.

Frankfurter, Felix, *The Case of Sacco and Vanzetti*. Boston: Little, Brown and Co., 1927.

Freund, Paul A., *On Law and Justice*. Cambridge, Mass.: Harvard University Press, 1968.

Friendly, Alfred and Goldfarb, Ronald, *Crime and Publicity*. New York: Twentieth Century Fund, 1967.

Fuller, Lon L., *The Morality of Law*. New Haven, Conn.: Yale University Press, 1964.

Gage, Nicholas, *The Mafia is Not an Equal Opportunity Employer*. New York: McGraw-Hill, 1971.

Gagnon, John H. and Simon, William, *Sexual Deviance*. New York: Harper and Row, 1967.

Gebhard, Paul H., Gagnon, John H., Pomeroy, Wardell B. and Christenson, Cornelia V., *Sex Offenders: An Analysis of Types*. New York: Harper and Row, 1965.

Gellhorn, Walter, *Ombudsmen and Others: Citizen Protectors in Nine Countries*. Cambridge, Mass.: Harvard University Press, 1966.

Germann, A. C., Day, Frank D. and Gallati, Robert R. J., *Introduction to Law Enforcement*. Springfield, Ill.: Charles C. Thomas, 1962.

Giallombardo, Rose, *Society of Women*. New York: John Wiley and Sons, 1966.

Glaser, Daniel, *Adult Crime and Social Policy*. Englewood Cliffs, N. J.: Prentice-Hall, 1972.

Goffman, Erving, *Asylums*. Garden City, N. Y.: Doubleday-Anchor Books, 1961.

Goldfarb, Ronald, *Ransom*. New York: Harper and Row, 1965.

Goldman, Nathan, *The Differential Selection of Juvenile Offenders for Court Appearance*. New York: National Council on Crime and Delinquency, 1963.

Goldstein, Abraham S., *The Insanity Defense*. New Haven, Conn.: Yale University Press, 1967.

Goulden, Joseph C., *The Superlawyers*. New York: Weybright and Talley, 1972.

Graham, James, *The Enemies of the Poor*. New York: Random House, 1970.

Graham, Hugh D. and Gurr, Ted R., *Violence in America*. New York: Signet Books, 1969.

Green, Edward, *Judicial Attitudes in Sentencing*. New York: St. Martin's Press, 1961.

Griswold, H. Jack, et al., *An Eye For an Eye*. New York: Holt, Rinehart and Winston, 1971.

Guttmacher, Manfred S. and Weihofen, Henry, *Psychiatry and the Law*. New York: W. W. Norton and Co., 1952.

Hall, Jerome, *Theft, Law and Society* (2nd ed.). Indianapolis: Bobbs-Merrill Co., 1952.

Halleck, Seymour L., *Psychiatry and the Dilemmas of Crime*. New York: Harper and Row, 1967.

Harris, Richard, *The Fear of Crime*. New York: Frederick A. Praeger, 1969.

———— *Decision*. New York: Ballantine Books, 1972.

Hart, H. L. A., *The Concept of Law*. London: Oxford University Press, 1961.

———— *Law, Liberty and Morality*. Stanford, Calif.: Stanford University Press, 1963.

———— *Punishment and Responsibility: Essays in the Philosophy of Law*. New York: Oxford University Press, 1967.

Hart, J. M., *The British Police*. London: Allen and Unwin, 1951.

Heilbroner, Robert L., et. al., *In the Name of Profit: Profiles in Corporate Irresponsibility*. New York: Doubleday and Co., 1972.

Heller, Joseph. *Catch-22*. New York: Dell Publishing Co., 1961.

Henry, Andrew F. and Short, James F., Jr., *Suicide and Homicide*. New York: The Free Press, 1964.

Hersey, John, *The Algiers Motel Incident.* New York:
Alfred A. Knopf, 1968.

Hewitt, Wiliam H., *A Bibliography of Police Administration,
Public Safety and Criminology,* Springfield, Ill.: Charles
C Thomas, 1967.

—————— *British Police Administration.* Springfield, Ill.,
Charles C Thomas, 1965.

Hilberg, Raul, *The Destruction of the European Jews.* Chicago:
Quadrangle Books, Inc., 1961.

Hills, Stuart L., *Crime, Power, and Morality.* Scranton, Pa.:
Chandler Publishing Co., 1971.

Hobbes, Thomas, *Leviathan.* New York: E. P. Dutton and
Co., Inc., 1950.

Hoebel, E. Adamson and Llewellyn, Karl N., *The Cheyenne
Way.* Norman, Okla.: University of Oklahoma Press, 1941.

—————— *The Law of Primitive Man.* Cambridge, Mass.:
Harvard University Press, 1954.

Hoffman, Abbie, *Steal This Book.* New York: Pirate
Editions, Inc., 1971.

Hofstadter, Richard, *The Paranoid Style in American Politics.*
New York: Alfred A. Knopf, 1965.

Holmes, Oliver Wendell, *The Common Law* (edited by
Mark DeWolfe Howe). Cambridge, Mass.: Belknap Press of
Harvard University Press, 1963.

Honnold, John, *The Life of the Law.* New York: The
Free Press, 1964.

Hunt, Morton, *The Mugging.* New York: Atheneum, 1972.

Hurst, James W., *The Growth of American Law: The Law
Makers.* Boston: Little, Brown and Co., 1950.

Inbau, Fred E. and Reid, John E., *Criminal Interrogation and
Confessions.* Baltimore, Md.: Williams and Wilkins, 1962.

Inbau, Fred E. and Sowie, Claude R., *Cases and Comments on
Criminal Justice.* Brooklyn, N. Y.: The Foundation Press, 1964.

Irwin, John, *The Felon.* Englewood Cliffs, N. J.: Spectrum
Books, 1970.

Jackson, Bruce, *Outside the Law: A Thief's Primer*. New Brunswick, N. J.: Transaction Books, 1972.

Jacobs, Paul, *Prelude to Riot*. New York: Random House, 1968.

Janowitz, Morris, *Social Control of Escalated Riots*. Chicago: University of Chicago Center for Policy Study, 1968.

Jaspan, Norman with Black, Hillel, *The Thief in the White Collar*. New York: J. B. Lippincott Co., 1960.

Jeffrey, Sir Charles, *The Colonial Police*. London: M. Parrish, 1952.

Johnson, Richard M., *The Dynamics of Compliance: Supreme Court Decision-Making From a New Perspective*. Evanston, Ill.: Northwestern University Press, 1968.

Jones, Alfred W., *Life, Liberty, and Property*. New York: Octagon Books, 1964.

Jones, Harry W. (ed.), *The Courts, the Public, and the Law Explosion*. Englewood Cliffs, N. J.: Prentice-Hall, 1965.

———— *Law and the Social Role of Science*. New York: Rockefeller University Press, 1967.

Jordan, Winthrop D., *White Over Black*. Baltimore, Md.: Pelican Books, 1969.

Josephson, Matthew, *The Robber Barons*. New York: Harcourt, Brace and World, 1962.

Kafka, Franz, *The Trial*. New York: Vintage Books, 1969.

Kalven, Harry, Jr. and Zeisel, Hans, *The American Jury*. Boston: Little, Brown and Co., 1966.

Kamisar, Yale, Inbau, Fred and Arnold, Thurman, *Criminal Justice in Our Time*. Charlottesville, Va.: The University Press of Virginia, 1965.

Karlen, Delmar, *Anglo-American Criminal Justice*. New York: Oxford University Press, 1967.

———— *The Supreme Court and Political Freedom*. New York: The Free Press, 1968.

Karpman, Benjamin, *The Sexual Offender and His Offenses*. New York: Julian Press, 1954.

Kefauver, Estes, *Crime in America*. New York: Doubleday, 1951.

Keller, Suzanne, *Beyond the Ruling Class*. New York: Random House, 1963.

Kennedy, Robert F., *The Pursuit of Justice*. New York: Harper and Row, 1964.

Kenny, John P. and Pursuit, Dan G., *Police Work with Juveniles* (3rd ed.). Springfield, Ill.: Charles C Thomas, 1965.

Kephart, William M., *Racial Factors and Urban Law Enforcement*. Philadelphia: University of Pennsylvania, 1957.

Kirchheimer, Otto, *Political Justice*. Princeton, N. J.: Princeton University Press, 1961.

Kittrie, Nicholas N., *The Right to Be Different*. Baltimore: The Johns Hopkins Press, 1971.

Krislov, Samuel, *The Supreme Court and Political Freedom*. New York: The Free Press, 1968.

Kronhausen, Eberhard and Kronhausen, Phyllis, *Pornography and the Law*. New York: Ballantine Books, 1959.

LaFave, Wayne R., *Arrest: The Decision to Take a Suspect into Custody*. Boston: Little, Brown and Co., 1965.

Lane, Roger, *Policing the City: Boston 1822-1882*. Cambridge, Mass.: Harvard University Press, 1967.

———— *Policing the City: Boston 1822-1885*. New York: Atheneum, 1971.

Lefcourt, Robert (ed.)., *Law Against the People*. New York: Vintage Books, 1971.

Lemert, Edwin M., *Human Deviance, Social Problems and Social Control*. Englewood Cliffs, N. J.: Prentice-Hall, Inc., 1967.

Leopold, Nathan F., *Life Plus 99 Years*. New York: Doubleday, 1958.

Levi, Primo, *Survival in Auschwitz*. New York: Collier Books, 1961.

Liebow, Elliot, *Tally's Corner*. Boston: Little, Brown and Co., 1967.

Lindesmith, Alfred R., *The Addict and the Law*. Bloomington, Ind.: Indiana University Press, 1965.

Lipset, Seymour M., *Political Man*. Garden City, N. Y.: Doubleday and Co., 1960.

Lofton, John, *Justice and the Press*. Boston: Beacon Press, 1966.

Lorenz, Konrad, *On Aggression*. Marjorie Wilson, tr., New York: Harcourt, Brace and World, 1966.

Lowenthal, Max, *The Federal Bureau of Investigation*. New York: Sloane Associates, 1950.

Maine, Sir Henry J., *Ancient Law*. London and Toronto: J. M. Dent and Sons; New York: E. P. Dutton and Co., 1931.

Mannheim, Hermann, *Comparative Criminology*. Boston: Houghton-Mifflin Co., 1965.

———— (ed.), *Pioneers in Criminology*. Chicago: Quadrangle Books, 1960.

Marshall, Geoffrey, *Police and Government*. London: Mathuen and Co., 1965.

Marshall, James, *Intention in Law and Society*. New York: Funk and Wagnalls, 1968.

———— *Law and Psychology in Conflict*. Garden City, N. Y.: Doubleday-Anchor, 1969.

Marx, Gary T., *Protest and Prejudice*. New York: Harper and Row, 1969.

Matza, David, *Becoming Deviant*. Englewood Cliffs, N. J.: Prentice-Hall, Inc., 1969.

Mayers, Lewis, *The American Legal System*. New York: Harper and Row, 1964.

McCague, James, *The Second Rebellion: The Story of the New York City Draft Riots of 1863*. New York: Dial Press, 1968.

Medalie, Richard J., *From Escobedo to Miranda*. Washington, D. C.: Lerner Law Book Co., 1966.

Medvedev, Zhores A. and Medvedev, Roy A., *A Question of Madness*. New York: Alfred A. Knopf, 1971.

Menninger, Karl, *The Crime of Punishment*. New York: The Viking Press, 1968.

———— *The Vital Balance*. New York: The Viking Press, 1964.

Michael, Jerome and Adler, Mortimer, *Crime, Law and Social Science*. New York: Harcourt, Brace and Co., 1933.

Minton, Robert J., Jr. (ed.), *Inside: Prison American Style*. New York: Random House, 1971.

Mintz, Morton and Cohen, Jerry S., *America, Inc.: Who Owns and Operates the United States*. New York: Dial Press, 1971.

Mitford, Jessica, *The Trial of Dr. Spock*. New York: Alfred A. Knopf, 1969.

Mollenhoff, Clark, *Tentacles of Power: The Story of Jimmy Hoffa*. Cleveland: The World Publishing Co., 1965.

Murphy, Walter F. and Pritchett, C. Herman, *Courts, Judges and Politics*. New York: Random House, 1961.

Myers, Gustavus, *History of the Great American Fortunes*. New York: Modern Library, 1936.

Nash, Jay Robert, *Citizen Hoover: A Critical Study of the Life and Times of J. Edgar Hoover and His FBI*. Chicago: Nelson-Hall, 1972.

Navasky, Victor S., *Kennedy Justice*. New York: Atheneum, 1971.

Neumann, Franz, *Behemoth*. London: V. Gollancz, 1942.

Newman, Donald J., *Conviction: The Determination of Guilt or Innocence Without Trial*. Boston: Little, Brown and Co., 1966.

Newton, George D. and Zimring, Franklin E., *Firearms and Violence in American Life*. Washington, D. C.: U.S. Government Printing Office, 1969.

Niederhoffer, Arthur, *Behind the Shield*. Garden City, N. Y.: Doubleday and Co., 1967.

———— *A Study of Police Cynicism*. Unpublished doctoral dissertation. New York University, N. Y., 1964.

Niederhoffer, Arthur and Blumberg, Abraham S., *The Ambivalent Force: Perspectives on the Police*. Waltham, Mass.: Ginn and Co., 1970.

Norman, Charles, *The Genteel Murderer*. New York: Collier Books, 1962.

Nye, F. Ivan, *Family Relationships and Delinquent Behavior*. New York: John Wiley and Sons, 1958.

Oaks, Dallin H. and Lehman, Warren, *A Criminal Justice System and the Indigent: A Study of Chicago and Cook County*. Chicago: University of Chicago Press, 1968.

O'Gorman, Hubert J., *Lawyers and Matrimonial Cases*. New York: The Free Press, 1963.

Packer, Herbert L., *The Limits of the Criminal Sanction*. Stanford, Calif.: Stanford University Press, 1968.

Pearlstein, Stanley, *Psychiatry, the Law and Mental Health*. Dobbs Ferry, N. Y.: Oceana Publications, 1967.

Peltason, Jack W., *Federal Courts in the Political Process*. Garden City, N. Y. Doubleday, 1955.

Piven, Frances Fox and Cloward, Richard A., *Regulating the Poor*. New York: Random House, 1971.

Platt, Anthony, *The Child Savers: The Invention of Delinquency*. Chicago: University of Chicago Press, 1969.

Ploscowe, Morris, *Sex and the Law*. New York: Ace Books, 1962.

Polier, Justine W., *The Rule of Law and the Role of Psychiatry*. Baltimore, Md.: Johns Hopkins Press, 1968.

Polsky, Ned, *Hustlers, Beats, and Others*. Chicago: Aldine Publishing Co., 1967.

Porterfield, Austin L., *Youth in Trouble*. Fort Worth: Leo Potishman Foundation, 1946.

Poston, Richard W., *The Gang and the Establishment*. New York: Harper and Row, 1971.

Pound, Roscoe, *Social Control Through Law*. New Haven, Conn.: Yale University Press, 1942.

President's Commission on Law Enforcement and Administration of Justice. Task Force Reports: The Police; the Courts; Corrections; Juvenile Delinquency and Youth Crime; Organized Crime; Science and Technology; Assessment of Crime; Narcotics and Drugs; Drunkenness. Washington, D. C.: U.S. Government Printing Office, 1967.

Pritchett, C. Herman, *The American Constitution* (2nd ed.). New York: McGraw-Hill, 1968.

Puttkammer, Ernest W., *Administration of Criminal Law*. Chicago: University of Chicago Press, 1963.

Quinney, Richard (ed.), *Crime and Justice in Society*. Boston: Little, Brown and Co., 1969

Raab, Selwyn, *Justice in the Back Room*. Cleveland: The World Publishing Co., 1967.

Radzinowicz, Leon, *A History of English Criminal Law and Its Administration from 1750,* Vols. 1-4. New York: Barnes and Noble, 1968.

Radzinowicz, Leon and Wolfgang, Marvin E. (eds.), *Crime and Justice,* 3 vols. New York: Basic Books, 1971.

Ray, Isaac, *A Treatise on the Medical Jurisprudence of Insanity,* Winfred Overholser (ed.). Cambridge, Mass.: Harvard University Press, 1962.

Reed, John P. and Baali, Fuad, *Faces of Delinquency*. Englewood Cliffs, N. J.: Prentice-Hall, Inc., 1972.

Reiss, Albert J., Jr., *The Police and the Public*. New Haven: Yale University Press, 1971.

Reith, Charles, *The Blind Eye of History*. London: Faber and Faber, 1952.

———— *A New Study of Police History*. London: Oliver and Boyd, 1956.

Rheinstein, Max (ed.), *Max Weber on Law in Economy and Society* (trans. by E. Shils and M. Rheinstein). Cambridge, Mass.: Harvard University Press, 1954.

Richardson, James, *A History of Police Protection in New York City, 1800-1870*. Unpublished Ph.D. dissertation. New York City: New York University, 1967.

Rolph, C. H., (ed.), *The Police and the Public*. London: Heinemann, 1962.

Rose, Arnold M., *Libel and Academic Freedom: A Lawsuit Against Political Extremists*. Minneapolis: University of Minnesota Press, 1968.

Rosenberg, Charles E., *The Trial of Assassin Guiteau: Psychiatry and Law in the Guilded Age*. Chicago: University of Chicago Press, 1968.

Royal Commission on the Police, 1962, *Final Report*. Cmnd. 1728. London: Her Majesty's Stationery Office, 1962.

Saunders, Charles B., Jr., *Upgrading the American Police*. Washington, D. C.: The Brookings Institution, 1970.

Scheff, Thomas J. (ed.), *Mental Illness and Social Processes*. New York: Harper and Row, 1967.

Schneir, Walter and Schneir, Marian, *Invitation to an Inquest*. New York: Doubleday, 1965.

Schrag, Philip G., *Counsel for the Deceived: Case Studies in Consumer Fraud*. New York: Pantheon Books, 1972.

Schubert, Glendon (ed.), *Judicial Behavior*. Chicago: Rand McNally, 1964.

———— *Judicial Decision-Making*. New York: The Free Press, 1963.

Schur, Edwin M., *Crimes Without Victims*. Englewood Cliffs, N. J. Prentice-Hall, 1965.

———— *Drug Addiction in America and England*. Bloomington, Ind.: Indiana University Press, 1962.

———— *Law and Society: A Sociological View*. New York: Random House, 1968.

———— *Our Criminal Society*. Englewood Cliffs, N. J.: Prentice-Hall, Inc., 1969.

———— *Labeling Deviant Behavior*. New York: Harper and Row, 1972.

Scigliano, Robert G., *The Courts: A Reader in the Judicial Process*. Boston: Little, Brown and Co., 1962.

Seligman, Ben B., *Permanent Poverty: An American Syndrome*. Chicago: Quadrangle Books, 1968.

Shaw, George Bernard, *The Crime of Imprisonment*. New York: The Citadel Press, 1961.

Shoolbred, Claude F., *The Administration of Criminal Justice in England and Wales*. New York: Pergamon Press, 1966.

Simon, Rita James, *The Jury and the Plea of Insanity*. Boston: Little, Brown and Co., 1966.

———— (ed.), *The Sociology of Law: Interdisciplinary Readings*. San Francisco, Calif.: Chandler, 1968.

Skolnick, Jerome H., *Justice Without Trial: Law Enforcement in Democratic Society*. New York: John Wiley and Sons, 1966.

———— *The Politics of Protest*. New York: Ballantine Books, 1969.

Slater, Philip, *The Pursuit of Loneliness*. Boston: Beacon Press, 1970.

Smigel, Erwin O., *The Wall Street Lawyer*. New York: The Free Press.

Smith, Alexander B. and Neiderhoffer, Arthur, *Police-Community Relations Programs: A Study in Depth*. Washington, D. C.: U.S. Government Printing Office, 1969.

Smith, Alexander B. and Pollack, Harriet, *Crime and Justice in a Mass Society*. Waltham, Mass.: Xerox Corp., 1972.

Smith Bruce, *The New York Police Survey*. New York: Institute of Public Administration, 1952.

———— *Police Systems in the United States* (2nd rev. ed.). New York: Harper and Row, 1960.

Smith, Ralph L., *The Tarnished Badge*. New York: Thomas Y. Crowell Co., 1965.

Solmes, Alwyn, *The English Policeman, 1871-1935*. London: George Allen and Unwin, 1935.

Sowle, Claude R. (ed.), *Police Power and Individual Freedom*. Chicago: Aldine Publishing Co., 1962.

Starkey, Marion L., *The Devil in Massachusetts*. New York: Alfred A. Knopf, 1950.

Steffens, Lincoln, *Autobiography*. New York: Harcourt, Brace and World, 1936.

———— *The Shame of the Cities*. New York: McClure Phillips and Co., 1904.

Struggle For Justice: A Report on Crime and Punishment in America. American Friends Service Committee. (New York: Hill and Wang, 1971.

Sutherland, Arthur E., *Constitutionalism in America*. Boston: Blaisdell Publishing Co., 1965.

Sutherland, Edwin H., *White Collar Crime*. New York: Holt, Rinehart and Winston, 1949.

Sykes, Gresham, *Society of Captives*. Princeton, N. J.: Princeton University Press, 1958.

———— and Drobek, Thomas E., *Law and the Lawless*. New York: Random House, 1969.

Szasz, Thomas, *Law, Liberty and Psychiatry*. New York: Macmillan, 1963.
———— *Psychiatric Justice*. New York: Macmillan, 1965.

———— *The Manufacture of Madness*. New York: Harper and Row, 1970.

Talese, Gay, *Honor Thy Father*. Chicago: World Publishing Co., 1971.

Tannenbaum, Frank, *Crime and the Community*. New York: Columbia University Press, 1938.

Taylor, Telford, *Nuremberg and Vietnam: An American Tragedy*. Chicago: Quadrangle Books, Inc., 1970.

Thompson, Craig, *The Police State*. New York: E. P. Dutton and Co., 1950.

Thompson, Hunter S., *Hell's Angels*. New York: Random House, 1966.

Tiffany, Lawrence P., McIntyre, Donald M. Jr. and Rotenberg, David L., *Detection of Crime: Stopping and Questioning, Search and Seizure, Encouragement and Entrapment*. Boston: Little, Brown and Co., 1967.

Tobias, John J., *Urban Crime in Victorian England*. New York: Schocken Books, 1972.

Toch, Hans, *Violent Men: An Inquiry into the Psychology of Violence*. Chicago: Aldine Publishing Co., 1969.

Train, Arthur, *Courts, Criminals and the Camorra*. New York: C. Scribner's Sons, 1911.

Trebach, Arnold S., *The Rationing of Justice*. New Brunswick, N. J.: Rutgers University Press, 1964.

Turner, William, *The Police Establishment.* New York:
G. P. Putnam and Sons, 1968.

Turk, Austin T., *Criminality and the Legal Order.* Chicago:
Rand McNally and Co., 1969.

Tyler, Gus, *Organized Crime in America.* Ann Arbor, Mich.:
University of Michigan Press, 1962.

Virtue, Maxine, *Survey of Metropolitan Courts: Final Report.*
Ann Arbor, Mich.: The University of Michigan Press, 1962.

Vollmer, August, *The Police and Modern Society.* Berkeley,
Calif.: University of California Press, 1936.

Vollmer, Howard M. and Mills, Donald L. (eds.),
Professionalization. Englewood Cliffs, N. J.: Prentice-Hall
Inc., 1966.

Walker, Nigel, *Crime and Insanity in England: Vol. 1: The
Historical Perspective.* Edinburgh, Scotland: Edinburgh
University Press, 1968.

Wallace, Samuel E., *Skid Row As a Way of Life.* Ottowa:
The Bedminster Press, 1965.

Weber, Max, *The Theory of Social and Economic Organization.*
New York: The Free Press, 1964.

Wertham, Frederick, *A Sign for Cain.* New York:
Macmillan, 1966.

Westley, William A., *The Police: A Sociological Study of
Law, Custom and Mortality.* Unpublished Ph.D. dissertation.
Department of Sociology, University of Chicago, Chicago, 1951.

Weyrauch, Walter O., *The Personality of Lawyers.* New
Haven, Conn.: Yale University Press, 1964.

Whitaker, Ben, *The Police.* Middlesex, England:
Penguin Books, 1964.

Whittmore, L. H., *Cop: A Closeup of Violence and Tragedy.*
New York: Holt, Rinehart and Winston, 1969.

Wilkins, Leslie T., *Social Deviance.* Englewood Cliffs, N. J.:
Prentice-Hall, Inc., 1965.

Whyte, William F., *Street Corner Society.* Chicago:
University of Chicago Press, 1943.

Williams, Edward Bennett, *One Man's Freedom*. New York: Atheneum, 1962.

Wilson, James Q., *Varieties of Police Behavior*. Cambridge, Mass.: Harvard University Press, 1968.

Wilson, O. W., *Police Administration* (2nd ed.). New York: McGraw-Hill, 1963.

Wolfenden, Sir John and others, *Report of the Departmental Committee on Homosexual Offences and Prostitution*. London: Her Majesty's Stationery Office, 1956.

Wolfgang, Marvin E., *Patterns in Criminal Homicide*. Philadelphia: University of Pennsylvania Press, 1958.

Wolfgang, Marvin E. and Ferracuti, Franco, *The Subculture of Violence*. London: Tavistock Publications, 1967.

Wood, Arthur L., *Criminal Lawyer*. New Haven, Conn.: College and University Press, 1967.

Zeisel, Hans, Kalven, Harry, Jr., and Buckholz, Bernard, *Delay in the Court*. Boston: Little, Brown and Co., 1959.

David L. Bazelon ("Justice Stumbles Over Science") is chief judge of the United States Court of Appeals for the District of Columbia. He is also on the faculty of psychiatry at the Johns Hopkins School of Medicine and clinical professor of psychology at George Washington University.

Abraham Blumberg ("Law and Order: The Counterfeit Crusade," "Lawyers with Convictions") is a professor of sociology and law and chairman of the Division of Social Sciences, John Jay College of the City University of New York. For further information, see the cover.

Jerome E. Carlin ("Store Front Lawyers in San Francisco") is a lawyer, sociologist and teacher. He served as consultant for legal projects and coordinator of the San Francisco Neighborhood Legal Assistance Foundation, 1966-1969. He has recently taken up the art of painting.

David Durk ("Viva La Policia") is a sergeant in the New York City Police Department.

John H. Gagnon ("Pornography—Raging Menace or Paper Tiger?") is an associate professor in the Department of Sociology at the State University of New York, Stony Brook. With William Simon, he has worked in the areas of criminology, deviant behavior, youth, the community, and marriage and the family. He is a co-author of *Sex Offenders: An Analysis of Types* and, with William Simon, has edited *Sexual Deviance: A Reader* and co-edited *The Sexual Scene,* a Transaction Book.

Herbert Jacob ("Winners and Losers: Garnishment and Bankruptcy in Wisconsin") is a professor of political science at Northwestern University. He is the author of *Debtors in Court.*

Warren Lehman ("Lawyers for the Poor") has served as a housing specialist for the Chicago Commission on Human Relations and the Chicago Urban League and has written widely on urban renewals and race relations. Author of *Practical Law* and *Parlia-*

mentary Procedure, he is assistant professor and assistant dean of the Washington University School of Law. He is interested in the problem of achieving social change through legislation.

Edwin M. Lemert ("Juvenile Justice—Quest and Realities") is an associate of the Center for the Study of Law and Society at the University of California, Berkeley, where he does research on California's juvenile court system. He is former chairman of the department of sociology at the University of California at Davis. He served as a consultant on juvenile delinquency for the President's Commission on Law Enforcement and the Administration of Justice.

Paul Lerman ("Delinquents Without Crimes") is associate professor of social work at the Graduate School of Social Work, Rutgers University. He teaches courses on delinquency and social policy, social welfare policy and research. His major interest is in understanding societal responses to youthful deviance.

Stuart S. Nagel ("The Tipped Scales of American Justice," "Double Standard of American Justice") is professor of political science at the University of Illinois and practices law in Illinois. He has written many articles on inequality in the American legal system.

Dallin H. Oaks ("Lawyers for the Poor") is professor of law at the University of Chicago. He has written *The Wall Between Church and State* and is co-author of *Cases on the Law of Trusts.* He has worked as a prosecutor, defense attorney for indigent criminals and in general practice.

William Simon ("Pornography—Raging Menace ' or Paper Tiger?") is program supervisor in sociology and anthropology at the Institute for Juvenile Research in Chicago. At the Institute for Sex Research at Indiana University he collaborated with John H. Gagnon in the preparation of many articles on sexual behavior, deviance, youth, the community and marriage and the family. He is co-editor of *The Sexual Scene,* published by Transaction Books, and co-author of *The End of Adolescence: the College Experience,* and *The Social Sources of Sexual Conduct.*

James P. Spradley ("The Moral Career of a Bum") is associate professor of anthropology at Macalester College, St. Paul, Minnesota. He has written *Guests Never Leave Hungry: The Auto-*

biography of a Kwakiutl Indian and *You Owe Yourself a Drunk: An Ethnography of Urban Nomads.*

Lenore J. Weitzman ("Double Standard of American Justice") is assistant professor of sociology at the University of California at Davis and also on the faculty of the law school where she teaches a course on the legal status of women. Her research interests include socialization, missing persons and identity change, and the sociology of law.